Feeling Queer Jurisprudence is a powerful and original contribution to queer legal theory, reminding us of the affective resonances and political effects of LGBT engagements with law and rights. This beautifully written text engages with rich literatures on affect, emotion and feeling to enliven our understanding of the meaning and consequences of cases, litigation strategies and LGBT legal engagements.

Emily Grabham, Professor of Law,
University of Kent, UK

The most insightful critiques of law are those that engage with the idea of liberal 'progress,' with those moments when the royal 'no' is suspended. *Feeling Queer Jurisprudence* considers a range of contested emotions that find expression in and through law and highlights how, in opposition to its own self-image, law is full of emotion. That is, while law produces problematic *effects* in moments of reform, it is also fundamentally a place of *affect*. Senthorun Sunil Raj is to be congratulated for this groundbreaking book that extends legal analysis along this vector. For reform produces not only exclusions, both instrumental and discursive. It is also animated by emotions of disgust, hate, anger, fear and love. This book foregrounds emotional attachments in pro-LGBT cases in the areas of criminal, marriage, equality and asylum law, in order to identify the kinds of injury, intimacy and identity that law recognises, and demonstrates why accounting for emotion helps us to understand those attachments and thereby challenge their limits.

Alex Sharpe, Professor of Law,
Keele University, UK

One of the more challenging developments in legal scholarship over the past couple of decades has been the deployment of queer theory to illuminate, unsettle and challenge our assumptions about what law does and of what it can, and cannot, achieve in delivering progressive political and social change. In this thoughtful and important book, Senthorun Sunil Raj explores the vital, if often occluded, role emotion and affect have in cases concerning sexuality and helps us understand the jurisprudential dynamics in this exciting and challenging area of law.

Matthew Weait, Professor of Law,
University of Portsmouth, UK

Feeling Queer Jurisprudence

This book draws on the analytic and political dimensions of queer, alongside the analytic and political usefulness of emotion, to navigate legal interventions aimed at progressing the rights of LGBT people.

Scholars, activists, lawyers, and judges concerned with eliminating violence and discrimination against LGBT people have generated passionate conversations about pursuing law reform to make LGBT injuries, intimacies, and identities visible, while some challenge the ways legal systems marginalise queer minorities. Senthorun Sunil Raj powerfully contributes to these ongoing conversations by using emotion as an analytic frame to reflect on the ways case law seeks to "progress" the intimacies and identities of LGBT people from positions of injury. This book catalogues a range of cases from Australia, the United States, and the United Kingdom to unpack how emotion shapes the decriminalisation of homosexuality, hate crime interventions, anti-discrimination measures, refugee protection, and marriage equality. While emotional enactments in pro-LGBT jurisprudence enable new forms of recognition and visibility, they can also work, paradoxically, to cover over queer intimacies and identities. Raj innovatively shows that reading jurisprudence through emotions can make space in law to affirm, rather than disavow, intimacies and identities that queer conventional ideas about "LGBT progress", without having to abandon legal pursuits to protect LGBT people.

This book will be of interest to students and scholars of human rights law, gender and sexuality studies, and socio-legal theory.

Senthorun Sunil Raj is a Lecturer in Law at Keele University.

Part of the SOCIAL JUSTICE series
series editors
Sarah Keenan, Birkbeck College, University of London, UK
Davina Cooper, Kings College, University of London, UK
Sarah Lamble, Birkbeck College, University of London, UK

For information about the series and details of previous and forthcoming titles, see https://www.routledge.com/Social-Justice/book-series/RCSOCJ

Feeling Queer Jurisprudence

Injury, Intimacy, Identity

Senthorun Sunil Raj

First published 2020
by Routledge
2 Park Square, Milton Park, Abingdon, Oxon OX14 4RN

and by Routledge
52 Vanderbilt Avenue, New York, NY 10017

Routledge is an imprint of the Taylor & Francis Group, an informa business

© 2020 Senthorun Sunil Raj

The right of Senthorun Sunil Raj to be identified as author of this work has been asserted by him in accordance with sections 77 and 78 of the Copyright, Designs and Patents Act 1988.

All rights reserved. No part of this book may be reprinted or reproduced or utilised in any form or by any electronic, mechanical, or other means, now known or hereafter invented, including photocopying and recording, or in any information storage or retrieval system, without permission in writing from the publishers.

Trademark notice: Product or corporate names may be trademarks or registered trademarks, and are used only for identification and explanation without intent to infringe.

British Library Cataloguing-in-Publication Data
A catalogue record for this book is available from the British Library

Library of Congress Cataloging-in-Publication Data
Names: Raj, Senthorun Sunil, author.
Title: Feeling queer jurisprudence : injury, intimacy, identity / Senthorun Sunil Raj.
Identifiers: LCCN 2019055713 (print) | LCCN 2019055714 (ebook) | ISBN 9780815356509 (hardback) | ISBN 9781351128063 (ebook)
Subjects: LCSH: Sexual minorities—Legal status, laws, etc.—Australia. | Sexual minorities—Legal status, laws, etc.—Great Britain. | Sexual minorities—Legal status, laws, etc.—United States.
Classification: LCC K3242.3 .R35 2020 (print) | LCC K3242.3 (ebook) | DDC 342.08/7—dc23
LC record available at https://lccn.loc.gov/2019055713
LC ebook record available at https://lccn.loc.gov/2019055714

ISBN: 978-0-8153-5650-9 (hbk)
ISBN: 978-1-351-12806-3 (ebk)

Typeset in Galliard
by codeMantra

For Ammamah

Contents

	Acknowledgements	xi
1	Feeling progress: queer scholarship, emotional jurisprudence	1
2	Directing disgust: queerness and criminality	23
3	Healing hate: queer violence and punishment	50
4	Animating anger: queer discrimination and accommodation	73
5	Fighting fear: queer claims and asylum	94
6	Loosening love: queer kinship and marriage equality	116
	Conclusion: towards queer reparative futures	140
	Index	151

Acknowledgements

My expression of thanks cannot do justice to everyone who has supported the production of this book (and myself) over the past few years. The generous support of family, friends, mentors, and colleagues made this book possible.

This book was conceived as a PhD dissertation at Sydney Law School, University of Sydney. I am very grateful for the outstanding supervision provided by Arlie Loughnan and Fleur Johns during my doctoral studies. They have engaged comprehensively, compassionately, and critically with this project from its inception. They have encouraged me to be more adventurous with my thinking and writing in order to push my arguments in directions I was hesitant to go. I could not ask for more generous and kind supervisors. I am grateful to Kane Race, Ely Aharonson, Andrew Edgar, and Terry Carney for providing critical feedback on various aspects of my dissertation during my time at Sydney Law School. I am also grateful for the good humour and camaraderie of fellow postgraduate students, which made my PhD such an enjoyable experience. I completed a first draft of the PhD during a residency at New York University's School of Law and the Center for Human Rights and Global Justice. I would like to thank them for providing me with space, time, and freedom to refine my thinking in the final stages of writing my dissertation. I especially want to acknowledge Karin Loevy, Michael Kavey, and Kendall Thomas for providing helpful feedback on my chapter about marriage equality.

My PhD examiners, Emily Grabham, Leslie Moran, and Nan Seuffert, provided helpful recommendations on how to refine the thesis and then turn it into a book. I completed this book as a Lecturer in Law at Keele University. I want to thank my colleagues, especially Tsachi Keren-Paz and Alex Sharpe, for mentorship during this time.

I was fortunate to publish this manuscript in Routledge's Series in Social Justice, among a collection of outstanding texts that adorn my bookshelf. I want to thank Colin Perrin, commissioning editor and the two anonymous reviewers, for their enthusiasm for this project. Series editors Davina Cooper, Sarah Lamble, and Sarah Keenan read the manuscript with a critical eye and provided generous advice on how to strengthen my ambitious arguments. Nicola Sharpe and Nazrine Azeez carefully processed the manuscript for publication. Leo

Hermitt, a fabulous artist in Manchester, also has my gratitude for designing the frontispiece.

Finally, I must express my love to family and friends for, quite simply, being part of my life. They have provided me with food, shelter, shoulders, and sounding boards as I navigated (and still navigate) being queer in my personal and professional life. I especially must thank my parents, Ramani and Sunil, who made my life possible – including the queerness that constitutes it.

This book is dedicated to my Ammamah, Sivapackium Rajendram, who died last year. She read to me my first books and taught me from a young age that I could sparkle fabulously in my own fairy tale. It is only fitting that my first book is dedicated to her.

Earlier versions of some chapters in this book are published elsewhere. I would like to thank Palgrave Macmillan for providing permission to reproduce material (for Chapter 2) published as "Disturbing Disgust: Gesturing to the Abject in Queer Cases" in *Queering Criminology* (edited by Matt Ball, Angela Dwyer, and Thomas Crofts, Palgrave, 2015) and Cambridge Scholars Press for allowing me to reproduce material (for Chapter 5) published as "Queering Fears: Pro-LGBTI Refugee Cases" in *Consent and Control* (edited by Chris Ashford, Alan Reed, and Nicola Wake, Cambridge Scholars Press, 2016). Small sections from Chapters 1, 3, and 6 also appear in "Once More With Feeling: Queer Activist Legal Scholarship and Jurisprudence" (2018), *International Journal of Human Rights*.

Chapter 1

Feeling progress
Queer scholarship, emotional jurisprudence

Making a queer project

This book emerges from feeling queer about law. When I began to draft this book, Australia had announced it was conducting a postal survey on whether the law should be changed to let same-sex couples marry. At this point, Australia had spent over a decade "debating" what was largely a matter of formal legal equality (that is, the sex or gender of one's partner should not bar access to formal relationship recognition). When the survey announcement was made, I was furious. The government's decision to subject the lives of lesbian, gay, bisexual, and transgender (LGBT) people to hostile public scrutiny repulsed me. I also lamented the fact that this would channel significant community energies into campaigning for marriage equality when there was a range of other pressing human rights concerns (Australia, for example, continued to incarcerate Indigenous peoples at grossly disproportionate rates and warehouse asylum seekers in neighbouring island nations). Finally, I was also wary of how the forthcoming campaign for marriage equality would, out of political necessity, hold out access to marriage as a love-infused (legislative) antidote to a range of homo/transphobic problems like discrimination, bullying, stigma, and mental illness.

On November 15, 2017, the Australian Bureau of Statistics announced the result of the Marriage Law Postal Survey: 61.6 per cent of respondents (about 7.8 million) had endorsed same-sex marriage. As I sat awake late at night live-streaming the results coming in from Australia, like a student awaiting their final degree results, I felt an enormous wave of relief wash over me as the result was announced. Rainbow icons immediately began to circulate on Twitter and I, in my excitement, shared a meme of RuPaul hosing the air with glitter. The hashtag #lovewins saturated my social media feed. I received numerous emoji-filled text messages from friends and family congratulating me on the result, as if I had won some sort of prize or passed an exam. In many ways, the joy that I and others felt in that moment was tied to a sense of achievement; it reflected the difficult (and sometimes impossible) conversations LGBT people were forced to have with family, friends, colleagues, and even strangers to convince them to support their right to legal equality. Yet, this joy was also marred by frustration: how could the Australian government force LGBT people into a situation where they had to plead for such basic recognition? This then mutated into rage as soon as I saw that one form of legislation to allow same-sex marriage would actually enable people to use their "conscience" to discriminate against LGBT people on a whim in areas of public and commercial life, if they disapproved of same-sex couples.

This reflection is helpful as a window to observe that what activists or scholars cast as "legal progress", within the parameters of state recognition, can generate a range of contested emotions. Following emotion in my encounter with marriage equality reform in Australia exposes the disgust I had at the non-binding reform process, the fear the LGBT community had about the consequences of a vilifying public debate (particularly on young people), the love and hope that underpinned a public campaign to affirm same-sex relationship equality, and the persistent worry that some activists had about whether an intense focus to progress this issue would eclipse more urgent interventions to secure the well-being of LGBT people. Navigating this fraught emotional space requires more than identifying and evaluating my (or others') individual emotions. Activists and scholars interested in unpacking claims of "progress" must recognise how specific emotions manifest in broader structures that shape the terrain of progress. In other words, emotions shape political claims that orient us (as individuals, activists, or communities) to institutions capable of delivering progress and cohere norms that define the terms of what we understand as progress (see Hunter 2015). This raises some particularly difficult questions when dealing with law. How do legal interventions recognise emotions when addressing the emotional experiences of LGBT people? What are the consequences of crystallising emotions in jurisprudence that recognises the injury, intimacy, and identity of LGBT people? Why is it important to account for these emotions and map what they do? This book responds to these questions by theorising how emotion functions politically in legal interventions to recognise the injury, intimacy, and identity of LGBT people and uses emotion analytically to unpack how such injuries, intimacies, and identities are legally arranged in ways that eclipse queer possibilities of intimacy and identity.

Like emotion, this book uses "queer" in both its analytic and political registers. Queer, as a historically derisory term, carries histories of social stigma (Love 2007: 2). Queer theory derives analytic force by drawing from scenes of social stigma and offers a method of analysis to follow mo(ve)ments of discomfort, resistance, failure, and trouble in relation to privileged social norms while exposing what such mo(ve)ments produce and undo (see Edelman 2004; Halberstam 2011; Munoz 2009). By foregrounding how social norms cohere into social arrangements and the anti-normative mo(ve)ments that trouble them, queer theory offers us a framework to critique privileged social relations and render them less secure (Wiegman 2017: 237).[1] This framing around antinormativity and deconstruction provides a method for scholars to map how individuals or objects "turn" away from norms and generate new possibilities or paths through such deviations (Ahmed 2014: 8). These "new possibilities" speak to the political value of queer analysis. Making space for individuals who occupy marginal positions because of their disruptive sexual and gendered orientations is an act of political affirmation (Berlant and Warner 2000: 322; Valdes 2009: 107; Zanghellini 2008: 2). This approach draws from a rich tradition in critical race studies (see Harris 1993; Matsuda 1989; Williams 1988) and critical feminism (see Case 1995; Kapur 2005; MacKinnon 1987). As explained below, I position queer analysis alongside critical legal scholars who not only analyse legal doctrines that impact minorities, but are also concerned with exploring how such doctrines can politically serve the interests of those impacted minorities. As Aleardo Zanghellini insists, the appeal of using queer theory to analyse jurisprudence lies in the normative, political commitments for justice that this approach can affirm (Zanghellini 2008: 4).

Feeling Queer Jurisprudence: Injury, Intimacy, Identity draws on the aforementioned analytic and political dimensions of queer to explore the analytic and political usefulness of reading emotion in pro-LGBT cases that deal with LGBT people. Specifically, this book uses queer theory as a framework to map how progressive case law enacts emotion to address homo/transphobic injuries that limit the expression of nonconforming intimacies and identities and shows how these emotional enactments arrange injury, intimacy, and identity in ways that foreclose queer possibilities of intimacy and identity (see Eng 2010; Halberstam 2011; Povinelli 2011). Homo/transphobic violence (injury) works to police plural forms of sexual/gendered association (intimacy) and undermine sexual/gendered self-determination (identity) (see LaFont 2009: 106–8; Spade 2011: 89). This book considers how injury is emotionally rendered in acts that stigmatise, shame, or disavow non-heterosexual intimacies and identities because they disturb a social order that values matrimonial coupling and reproductive sexuality (Tomsen 2009: 13). As Dean Spade notes, injury is broader than the hurt of physical violence – it manifests legally and bureaucratically. Such "administrative violence" causes emotional injuries to people who are queer[2]: secures humiliation by disallowing a change of gender marker to affirm a person's self-identification, generates anxiety by deporting people to places where they have to conceal their sexual relationships, cultivates anger by limiting access to gender affirming healthcare, and prolongs pain by incarcerating marginalised communities (Spade 2011: 208). This book compiles cases that address the injuries, intimacies, and identities of LGBT people by looking at the affective relationship between social and legal exclusion alongside social and legal claims for inclusion. Of this compilation, I use emotion analytically to register the enactment of emotion in case law (by identifying how the emotions of individual litigants or defendants are channelled and crystallised through their jurisprudential recognition) and unpack how cases use emotion to progress the rights of LGBT people (by mapping how emotions arrange injury, intimacy, and identity through their jurisprudential articulation). This analytic lens has a political usefulness for LGBT people: it provides a framework for legal scholars, activists, lawyers, and judges to think about how "legal emotions" function politically in the pursuit of LGBT legal progress. The queer registering of jurisprudential emotions can create space in law to affirm, rather than disavow, intimacies and identities that queer the socio-legal articulation of LGBT progress without having to abandon legal projects to protect LGBT people.

It is important to caveat that the cases that structure this book speak to a range of wider institutional, cultural, and geographic specificities. By making visible affective conditions in pro-LGBT cases, and queering the ideas they present, I am interested in developing a queer method of emotionally organising, and evaluating, jurisprudence that will be of use to scholars, activists, lawyers, and judges wishing to advance the rights of LGBT people without being faithful to any one jurisdiction or area of law. As Mariana Valverde suggests, we need to expand the inventory of tools we use for socio-legal analysis that may come at the expense of disciplinary or doctrinal purity (Valverde 2015: 179). This book frames emotional enactments in pro-LGBT cases to identify the kinds of injury, intimacy, and identity law recognises and demonstrates why accounting for emotion is analytically useful to understand the attachments to, in order to challenge the limits of, progress these (legal) emotions generate.

Mapping queer legal scholarship

LGBT activist law reform projects reflect an emotional push by queers to be "seen". Over the last 60 years, feelings such as disgust, despair, anger, hope, and happiness (to name just a few) have animated activist, academic, and advocacy debates over the capacity of law to "see" injuries experienced by queer people, nonconforming intimacies, and sexual/gender identities. This section brings together critical legal scholarship with queer theory to sketch some of the disparate discursive terrain of what I term "activist-scholar-advocate" conversations about LGBT law reform.

In demands for equality, some legal scholars and practitioners have regarded progressive variants of law reform as "positive" outcomes, given the enormous purchase they have in society. For example, Yvonne Zylan argues that progressive legal reforms directed at sexual or gender minorities not only confer legal recognition but also symbolise increased (public) acceptance of LGBT visibility (Zylan 2011: 5). Reflecting an instrumentalist idea of the relationship between law and social change, Chris Ashford suggests that statutes and case law provide an easily discernible benchmark for measuring the progress made towards recognising sexual minorities and exposing what remains to be done (Ashford 2011: 265). These and other scholars have cast legal reforms as markers on a metaphorical ruler of social justice – markers that we still use to measure, and ultimately feel, the changes that have taken place in society.

Law can also function as an instrument that can free LGBT people from homo/transphobic marginalisation. As Lisa Bower suggests, we do (and should) put some investment in courts to further queer democratic politics (Bower 1994: 1009–10). Case law operates as a paradox: a source of empowerment for the disempowered that is affected by a necessary limit in representation. Rather than make a claim to abstract rights, Bower advocates a "direct address" to the courts – one that refuses static representations or legal language to shape new modes of recognition (Bower 1994: 1014). Queers subscribed to legal rhetoric may constrain their claims for sexual justice, but the invocation of "sexual justice" through litigation itself can transform law through advocacy registers that make visible new ideas of freedom or equality in court contexts (Robson 2007: 46; Rosenblum 2009: 49).

However, as queer sex remains the subject of policing, queer scholars have been sceptical of the law's capacity to remedy the injury it has been instrumental in causing. Queer legal scholars specifically have drawn attention to how legal violence (and the subsequent pain it causes) has become justified in the pursuit of progressive legal projects (see Adler 2018; Moran 2009). They are cautious of using a homophobic legal system to remedy homophobic harms (Spindelman 2013: 92). Law reform privileges assimilation into an existing system with limited visions of sexuality, justice, and citizenship, rather than contesting the marginalisation that such a system produces (Stychin 2000: 282). These critiques foreground a fundamental contradiction in liberal politics: the demand for gay and lesbian legal recognition rests on the discursive conditions that have historically been responsible for policing sexual minorities in the first place (Duggan 1994: 1; Zalnieriute 2017: 70). For scholars like Carl Stychin and Lisa Duggan, there is little point in seeking inclusion in a system that asserts itself through exclusion or marginalisation (of figures such as sexual minorities, the poor, the disabled, and so on). Duggan's argument explicitly critiques the ongoing desire for state-sanctioned intimacy because such desire acts covertly to benefit some (white, monogamous, male, middle-class) people at the expense of (sadomasochist, single, immigrant) others. Instead, she urges activists and scholars to engage in creative productions and political strategies that seek to "queer" the demands for state subordination of intimacy (Duggan 1994: 3, 10). In outlining an approach to "queer critical legal studies", Libby Adler reflects on how the persistence of LGBT equality discourse has not only focussed legal advocacy attention on state recognition but also functioned to pacify "professional anxieties" to maintain the purported neutrality of judicial recognition (Adler 2018: 6). She suggests that in order to address these limits of law reform, scholars, activists, lawyers, and judges need to recognise how legal conditions are implicated in socio-economic relations and how this impacts upon queer populations on a local level (Adler 2018: 170).

The queer analysis of legal interventions outlined above poses a shared question for scholars, activists, lawyers, and judges (many of whom have multiple professional identities): how can we pursue the passionate demands of LGBT people seeking legal recognition alongside queer critiques of parochial norms that enable legal recognition? This is why a queer turn to emotion in law is analytically and politically useful. In cases designed to progress the human rights of LGBT people, judicial decisions do not only have to engage with the emotions that animate LGBT individuals seeking progress, but they also legally distil these emotions through the text of judgments that shape the terms of LGBT progress. The scholarly activist-advocate conversations outlined above point to how law recognises, and sometimes embraces, LGBT people's emotions in the pursuit of progress. This book takes these conversations further analytically by following the jurisprudential crystallisation and refraction of those emotions in pro-LGBT cases. This makes visible modes of injury, intimacy, and identity while illuminating what these emotional forms of legal visibility obscure. This critical intervention is politically valuable for scholars, activists, lawyers, and judges who use law to make space for individuals who remain on the periphery of life, visibility, and protection (see Haritaworn, Kuntsman, and Posocco 2014: 2). *Feeling Queer Jurisprudence* develops a queer reading of emotion in jurisprudence to analyse how emotions arrange LGBT injury, intimacy, and identity and sustain socio-legal norms that inhibit recognition of queer intimacies and identities. Combining queer and emotion to generate an analytic framework to deconstruct legal progress allows us as scholars, activists, lawyers, and judges invested in LGBT rights to think politically about how to progress queer intimacies and identities by confronting, and loosening, emotional attachments in law through their jurisprudential articulation.

Categorising "Pro-LGBT Cases"

Feeling Queer Jurisprudence intervenes in debates about the limits of legal progress by drawing together widely celebrated and critically reviewed cases that seek to recognise the injury, intimacy, and identity of LGBT people. I choose to focus on judgments because they are data that evince the ways law reform goals, statutes, precedents, and parties come into contact. They evince the embodiment of law in both specific terms (the remedies for particular parties) and general terms (the precedents they establish and the social norms they express). I collate these cases on the basis of activists and scholars having celebrated them as progressive in the pursuit of visibility and equality. My use of case law spans jurisdictions, doctrines, and historical periods because I am trying to bring together the ways emotions shape progressive ideas of injury, intimacy, and identity across various sub-disciplines of law rather than trying to exhaustively account for their jurisdictional or cultural or stylistic particularity. My collation, therefore, is not systematic. I do not look at emotions in case law, as others have, in terms of how they are produced through judicial conversations and conventions (see Bellau, Johnson, and Bouchard 2007). Instead, I follow the queer call to move against what Judith Butler calls "proper objects" (Butler 1994: 4). Rather than "properly" focus on judgments as a collection of dispassionate doctrines or as an objective style of legal writing that crystallises neutral rules or norms within a specific jurisdiction, I look queerly at the crystallisation of emotion in law.

Contributing to a scholarly and activist community motivated by desires for individual and social justice involves moving against legal scholarship that diagnoses doctrines or makes prescriptions about "better" laws. In a provocative article titled "On Writing Dangerously", Fleur Johns articulates the need to engage in forms of legal research that interrupt the demand for "real-world" solutions. In a changing world, law is often invoked at moments of crisis that generate impulses for regulation. Legal scholars often arrive at such crises with a "problem-solving" mentality that imagines the "problem" as something external to the legal academic (Johns 2003: 475). Framing legal research in this way, however, discourages more reflexive and adaptive legal analysis that addresses the orientations, attachments, and complicities that researchers have within legal institutions (Johns 2003: 477). Rather than subscribe to reactive demands to "solve" a legal issue, Johns urges us to examine what it means to "linger" over a problem (Johns 2003: 479). This "lingering" invites us to reflect on what scholars use as their basis for analysis.

Navigating legal attempts to solve problems of LGBT inequality alongside an activist-scholarly curiosity to linger with how such problems have been jurisprudentially rendered has encouraged me to think politically about what emotions do in progressive jurisprudence to advance LGBT intimacies and identities from positions of injury. Sara Ahmed argues that analytically turning more closely towards emotion, rather than repudiating it in scholarly analysis, can shape new avenues for movement in critical politics and law (Ahmed 2004: 187). In order to acknowledge the intimate a/effects of homo/transphobia, for example, scholars cannot obscure negativity and shame. Moving away from injury is not a task of disavowal (of either law or emotion). Rather, scholars need to queer the intimacies and identities generated by injuries if activists, lawyers, and judges are to use law to pursue horizons where queer intimacies and identities (and their attendant negative emotions) are recognised. In doing so, this book does not offer normative or detailed prescriptions for activists, lawyers, and judges in their specific contexts of work. Instead, I argue that scholars must take the time to feel – and to feel reflective and critical about – what is all-too-readily regarded as law's LGBT progress. This analytic pursuit is crucial if those engaged with progress are to address or loosen emotional binds that pro-LGBT jurisprudence makes possible.

I use "pro-LGBT cases" in this book as a dynamic interpretive frame. It is not meant to be exhaustive or doctrinally self-contained (see Carbado 2009). Indeed, "LGBT" is an activist label that is culturally contingent (and certainly not universal). I adopt the more inclusive label of "pro-LGBT" rather than "pro-gay" here because the cases discussed in the following chapters have doctrinal implications for bisexual, lesbian, trans, and gender nonconforming people.[3] Yet, it is also important to note that many queers eschew identity labels altogether (see Bower 1994). Recognising these limitations, I adopt pro-LGBT cases as a descriptive (rather than normative) term to help characterise a catalogue of cases that have been used as barometers in activist and liberal academic circles to measure LGBT justice progress. These cases are held out to progress sexual and gender minorities from positions of injury to a place where their intimacies and identities can flourish under the law. I call the jurisprudence that I weave together "pro-LGBT cases" precisely because such a moniker also draws attention to how my reading of emotion in them does not fit neatly into predetermined doctrinal conversations about jurisdiction or discipline. Pro-LGBT cases – like the emotions that are apparent within them – circulate across jurisdictions as illuminating signs of progress towards equality. My construction of pro-LGBT cases should not be taken to suggest that the ideas generated in these cases are static. These cases not only generate public emotions of celebration or critique, but they can also be understood as emotional texts themselves with value beyond their precedential reach.

Reading emotion

Scholarly interest in emotion – what is loosely described as "the affective turn" – is not new. Feminist and queer scholarship has foregrounded the analytic and political usefulness of engaging with emotion. Emotion is a means of historical analysis and archival research (see Cvetkovich 2003; Scott 1991), a form of politics and activism (see Berlant 1997; Crimp 2002; Cvetkovich 2012; Halperin and Traub 2009; Lorde 1984), a subject of moral philosophy (see Gatens 1996; Nussbaum 2016), and a tactic of sociology (see Bondi 2005; Hochschild 1983). Law and emotion scholarship has emerged alongside analyses in these overlapping disciplines to identify how emotions relate to constitutional and political imaginations (see Gewirtzman 2008; Nussbaum 2013), psychological processes of judging (see Arkush 2008; Wiener, Bornstein, and Voss 2006), and dynamics of legal regulation (see Acorn 2004; Lange 2002). I build a queer theory of legal emotions on this existing scholarly terrain by recasting judicial texts in terms of their emotional enactments. This theory does not seek to claim sense (as if such sense was authoritatively knowable) of the feelings of litigants, lawyers, and judges, nor does it try to diagnose the feelings of legal actors or institutions. Rather, reading emotion in law is a queer analytic strategy that exposes the reach of socio-legal norms in recognising LGBT injury, intimacy, and identity and queer intimacies and identities that deviate from view (Ahmed 2006: 3).

Before I can begin to read how emotion manifests in pro-LGBT cases, I need to first outline what I mean by the term "emotion". Affect, feeling, and emotion are rich concepts with different epistemological and ontological histories (see Abrams and Keren 2010). Affect is a term that can be located within the philosophical tradition of Gilles Deleuze and Baruch Spinoza to describe moments of action, non-conscious experience, or unstructured potentials. Affect is a kinetic concept – it captures a relationship between speed and duration (Deleuze and Guattari 1987: 31–3). Emotion is considered the narrative articulation of affect or a socialised description of the kinetic movements associated with affect (Ahmed 2004: 11). In other words, emotion is given a social intelligibility, while affect has an excess or remainder that resists representation (Clough 2007: 2). Emotion is also a relatively recent term to describe an individual's affective constitution; it has historically been referred to as "passions" or "moral sentiments" (Smith 2016: 3). Feeling, alternatively, is the personalised recognition of our affective and emotional histories. Feelings come to embody a biographical and psychological reality because they represent a more localised interpretation of our emotional lives and affective sensations. Feeling is political, too. Feeling is a means by which we recognise or understand experience and communicate politics (see Shouse 2004). For the purposes of this book, which draws from a specific trajectory of queer affect theory (discussed below), I do not pursue these theoretical distinctions in more depth and I rely for the most part on the term "emotion". In a similar vein to Ahmed, I prefer to use this term (rather than affect or feeling) because it captures how emotions are cultural expressions that circulate and crystallise through bodies, texts, and institutions (Ahmed 2004: 9).

To talk about emotion in law may seem queer to those who presume law is a system of objectivity and rationality divested of feeling. But, emotion circulates ubiquitously in law: from the emotional states of parties, to the "gut" reactions of juries or legal scholars, to passionate legislative debates. In thinking about emotion, rendering it into an object of scholarly enquiry, we seek to "see" what we (or others) "feel". However, academic analyses are fraught with some insecurity and uncertainty. We can never know authoritatively what others feel. So, if we cannot make an empirical claim to "know" feeling, how can we (as legal scholars) propose to analyse it? What sort of methodological approach should be adopted? For example, methodological approaches could include ethnographies of courtroom processes; fieldwork interviews with litigants, lawyers, and jurists; reviewing interrogatories; Hansard analysis of legislative debates; reviewing law reform processes in the parliamentary system; neurological or psychological studies of legal actors; or even personal reflections on legal analysis and advocacy. All of these methodological approaches are shaped by jurisdictional choices: a focus on federated legal systems (such as the interaction of state and federal laws); supranational or regional legal forums (such as matters from the European Court of Human Rights); comparative legal analysis of common law jurisdictions (such as comparing the United Kingdom (UK) and Australia); or international treaty making or customs of international law (such as international conventions or jurisprudence from the International Court of Justice).

With this in mind, I have chosen to focus specifically on judicial decisions to examine the textual enactment and circulation of emotion in case law in order to foreground how legal recognition channels and crystallises the emotions of parties through the prism of jurisprudence. In the analysis that follows, I render pro-LGBT cases as emotional texts. I situate "law" here as a field that exhibits literary or narrative tendencies. As James Boyd White argues, law is a disciplinary terrain generated through disparate narrative acts that include legislative enactments, litigation, testimony, and judicial pronouncements (White 1985: xi). These acts develop a "textual community" through "officially" designated actors such as lawyers, judges, and legislators working in "official" institutions such as courts, tribunals, and parliaments (see West 1988). My reason for attending to emotion and law in terms of case law's textual properties is that conversations about emotion in law tend to focus on the emotions of parties or the phenomenological experiences of judges, rather than exploring how emotion assumes legal significance through judicial reasoning (see Kennedy 1986). In other words, judicial decisions encode and propagate emotions at the level of the text and arrange the reach of ideas relating to inequality and discrimination (injury), sex and kinship (intimacy), and gender and sexuality (identity). While this method of analysis is retrospectively anchored (I look back on cases that have already been decided to figure enactments of emotion), it also speaks to the present and future (the emotional enactments in cases circulate within current law and shape terms through which future cases can be decided).[4] Activists, scholars, lawyers, and judges concerned with progressing the rights of LGBT people need to understand emotion analytically in cases to understand the politics of emotions in addressing the injuries, intimacies, and identities of LGBT people (Schacter 2005).

Feeling Queer Jurisprudence proceeds on two levels: emotion is both a political object of value in pro-LGBT cases and it forms the analytic register through which I queer the terms of injury, intimacy, and identity that take shape in such cases. The analytic scope of this reading relates to the performative dimensions of emotion, and the insights gained from this focus allow me to problematise how emotions shape, and generate attachments to, (hetero)normative ideas of identity, intimacy, and injury in the pursuit of legal progress. Eve Sedgwick describes the sort of analytic strategy I adopt here as a queer affect theory. Such a theory relies on "selective scanning" and "amplification" in order to resist a scholarly tendency to aggregate or taxonomise so as to "prove" an object (such as injury, intimacy, or identity) of thought conclusively (Sedgwick 2003: 135–6). I transpose Sedgwick's call to loosen the need for diagnostic analysis in favour of amplifying emotion analytically when "selectively" reading how it emerges in pro-LGBT cases. I take up the enactment of emotions to map what is at stake politically in using emotions to progress LGBT rights and show how mapping emotions opens up possibilities to rethink their role politically when it comes to defining the terms of legal progress. This analytic register takes emotions (like law) in terms of their textual enactments: they "glue" together legal ideas and social norms in judgments (Ahmed 2004: 5, 11). These emotional enactments arise from the contact between objects. In this book, I follow the contact between objects in case law (such as doctrines, facts, and norms) that give life to LGBT injuries, intimacies, and identities and the remedies deemed to repair them. Attending to case law in terms of these "contact zones", by focussing on their enactments, enables us to consider how we might loosen some of the emotional attachments that lawyers, activists, scholars, and judges have to make legal space for queer intimacies and identities (Ahmed 2004: 23).

Making readings of case law attentive to emotion – and to queer the consequences of such emotion – is politically necessary if we want to understand how pro-LGBT cases make visible and cover over queer intimacies and identities. As Kenji Yoshino argues, in relation to sexual minorities, ideas of gay visibility cannot be reduced to who is "in" or "out" of the proverbial closet. Rather, social norms allow sexual minorities to express some aspects of their sexuality in public while urging them to "cover" disorienting aspects of their sexuality (Yoshino 2002: 837). Borrowing from Yoshino's idea of covering in relation to sexual minorities, I argue that emotional enactments in law reform that enable new forms of recognition or visibility can work, paradoxically, to cover subjects that queer those enactments. I use covering to refer to legal movements or gestures that contain, obscure, limit, and obstruct. As I reminisced at the beginning of the chapter, joys of living free from discrimination were presented through marriage equality. Yet, these joys were sustained in part by obstructing and containing the legal space available to those individuals who turn away from being a marital subject or living in a dyadic relationship.

Queering how we read cases purporting to progress LGBT people – to understand their limits – demands that we move closer to feel them. Ahmed offers a poetic call to action:

> We have to work and struggle not so much to feel hurt but to notice what causes hurt, which means unlearning what we have learned not to notice. We have to do this if we are to produce critical understandings of how violence, as a relation of force and harm, is directed toward some bodies and not at others.
>
> (Ahmed 2004: 216)

This book as a whole seeks to explore this through a study of pro-LGBT cases. Instead of conceiving emotions as self-evident truths that "correct" injuries or progress intimacies or identities in the law, I want to reiterate how the arrangement of injury, intimacy, and identity through emotion in pro-LGBT cases works to regulate, as well as foreclose, the possibilities of recognising queer intimacy and identity.

By focussing analytically on what emotion is doing in case law, the queer readings and critiques I advance are not meant to suggest that courts "let go" of their responsibilities to adjudicate, or that the law removes itself from attempting to remedy LGBT exclusions. The political impetus of reading emotion is not about choosing a "side" among legal scholars and activists who condemn the law, those who urge us to embrace it, or even those who sit in between this ever-expanding spectrum of opinions (after all, existing activist-legal scholarship does not sit in neat binaries). Instead, my reading of emotion takes lawyers and judges, as well as activists and scholars, closer to their legal responsibilities to LGBT people by exposing what is made visible and what is covered over in pro-LGBT cases that purport to repair injury and further intimacy and identity. This reading makes it possible to use emotion both analytically and politically to contest the (hetero)normative ideas of injury, intimacy, and identity contained in pro-LGBT cases without abandoning law as a means of securing justice.[5]

By writing about emotion, I also want to foreground my own attachments and the emotions that arise as I respond to judicial decisions. My readings are subjective or partial and my own attachments to the legal interventions I consider have shaped how I organise the cases I discuss and how I make sense of them (see Butler 2005). I seek to avoid presenting an analysis of emotion in law at a level of abstraction that transforms it into a metanarrative. The scholarly contribution this book makes is to show the analytic and political importance of reading emotion when seeking to understand what emotions and queerness do in law. I am not interested in expelling or embracing emotion (if either were possible) in law as a means of pursuing legal justice for LGBT people and queers who do not identify with any specific label. Rather, I read emotion to better understand progressive legal interventions that recognise injury, intimacy, and identity. My outline of emotions in case law in the final section helps identify political convergences and tensions involving the impulses for progressive law reform that makes LGBT people visible, on the one hand, and possibilities of a queer(er) social justice, on the other hand.

Following feeling: injury, intimacy, and identity in pro-LGBT cases

Feeling Queer Jurisprudence does not simply explore emotional enactments in pro-LGBT cases; it is also a product of them. Pain, disgust, hate, anger, fear, and happiness have underpinned my own encounters with the judicial texts that form my queer catalogue of case studies. It is important to position my own emotional investment in pro-LGBT cases because, as a queer individual, I subscribe to the hope that legal progress will remedy experiences of injury and my intimacy and identity will be given greater support as a consequence of recognition. Yet, such emotional investments, as outlined below, can fail to address systemic LGBT subordination. In *Object Lessons*, Robyn Wiegman observes, "identity knowledges are animated by powerful political desires" (Wiegman 2012: 4). Such disciplinary logics are informed by the desire to reveal the way in which norms and dominant knowledge systems shape particular objects of enquiry (in my case, jurisprudence). It is difficult to separate my own investment in emotion from the investments that reveal the emotions that form the object of my scholarly enquiry. My own desires for justice animated this critical enquiry. I do not wish to eschew such desires. As such, I have chosen to pursue a reading of emotion at the intersections of law and queerness in order to analytically reorient focus towards how injury, intimacy, and identity are emotionally shaped in the pro-LGBT cases that I bring together and draw out the political possibilities and limits of emotion in legal interventions that promise a better future for LGBT people.

Some scholars query the claim that the injury LGBT people experience can be substantially eased, and queer intimacy or identity furthered, through the cultivation of "better" feelings such as hope and happiness (Berlant 1999: 53). Legal interventions that negate individual injuries without negating the conditions that make such injuries possible serve impoverished visions of social justice. Lauren Berlant asserts:

> Feeling politics takes all kinds: it is a politics of protection, reparation, rescue. It claims a hard-wired truth, a core of common sense. It is beyond ideology, beyond mediation, beyond contestation. It seems to dissolve contradiction and dissent into pods of basic and also higher truth.
> (Berlant 1999: 58)

Feelings can take the form of appeals to uncontested truths. Such appeals are dangerous because they place feelings beyond contestation or mediation. Berlant's discussion engages with the nature of public feelings to remind us that we must not simply try to replace "bad" feelings with "good" ones; we must also recognise the conditions that have elicited such negative feelings in the first place. Multiplying fixed representations about particular subjects without attending to the discursive conditions that make such subjects "knowable" limits our horizons of understanding (Scott 1991: 779–80). Measuring emotional experiences without interrogating the discursive terms that underpin them limits how we navigate the consequences of emotion. If we heed Berlant's caution then, we cannot afford to simply exclaim that feeling is the "emblem of true wisdom about injustice" (Berlant 1999: 74). Shifts in an individual's "bad feeling", without changes to the structural or discursive conditions that give rise to such feeling, render the emotive appeal to pursue effective legal remedies fleeting and counterproductive for those who desperately seek such remedies. This is why reading pro-LGBT cases using emotion is a useful intervention: it offers scholars a way to analytically register how "good" and "bad" emotions of individuals (defendants, victims, litigants) are crystallised at a structural level (jurisprudence) and then confront how these emotions politically shape the terms of legal progress.

Individual injuries, like the pain arising from them, ossify as objects. Wendy Brown provides a complementary critique on this process of "fetishisation" (of injuries) and cautions against the impetus to use state institutions to repair the injury that it has perpetuated (Brown 1995: 8–9). Brown invites her readers to consider the limits in institutional politics for "freeing" the individual subject. In a similar vein to Berlant, she argues that to mobilise critique from the position of injury is to reproduce a static relation between the subject who injures and the subject who is injured. While Brown acknowledges the material realities of injury, she does provoke us to think beyond the law as the panacea for injury. Specifically, she notes that we cede political possibilities by appealing to an affective structure of domination that "returns" pain when remedying the material vulnerabilities that it is complicit in creating (Brown 1995: 67).

Pro-LGBT law reform like hate crime legislation is an example of this because it hopefully promises the elimination of homo/transphobic pain and injury through punitive state action against homo/transphobes. Berlant argues that these promises are mediated affects that shape the present. Our sense of the present is aestheticised within a temporal genre that we are constantly revising (Berlant 2011: 4). While Berlant's analysis uses a set of literary and cinematic texts to explore the precarious role of optimism in building "better futures", she identifies a key question that is relevant to discussing the remedial power of pro-LGBT cases that attend to injury:

> In scenarios of cruel optimism we are forced to suspend ordinary notions of repair and flourishing to ask whether the survival scenarios we attach to those affects weren't the problem in the first place.
>
> (Berlant 2011: 49)

In thinking about remedying injury through pro-LGBT cases, "cruel optimism" brings into sharp relief the way in which the fantasies we have of legal rights, the demands we make of justice, and scholarly and activist attachments to ideas of equality may limit the ability to negotiate new modes of living (and legislating). Engaging with these emotional commitments analytically leads us to an "impasse" – do we (as scholars, activists, lawyers, and judges) break with these fantasies, pursue them further, or pause to think pedagogically about them? Ahmed advocates the latter by cautioning against the repudiation of injury or vulnerability in an attempt to "move on" from it (Ahmed 2010: 144). I take Ahmed's caution, along with Berlant's and Brown's critique of the public politics of fetishising injury, as an anchoring point to elaborate on the emotional relation of injury and reparation in progressive legal interventions. I do this by identifying how the individual emotions of parties in cases are jurisprudentially transformed through pro-LGBT cases that promise reparation from injuries. These emotional enactments sustain socio-legal arrangements that can discursively and materially harm LGBT people by obscuring certain forms of queer intimacy and identity.

Feeling Queer Jurisprudence develops and queers "the progressive story" in LGBT law reform movements. In the discussion above, I noted that queer could be used as a method to analyse injuries, intimacies, and identities that deviated from privileged social arrangements and as a politics to affirm the intimacies and identities of sexual and gender minorities. Here, I expand on the analytic and political dimensions of queer to characterise how I tell a non-linear story of recognition and why undertaking an emotional analysis of this story is politically valuable for LGBT people. I use emotion to queer the story of state recognition to capture movements in case law that turn against norms of heterosexual reproduction, domesticity, and family and challenge the consequences of legal interventions that assimilate LGBT people into these norms (see Bell and Binnie 2000: 13–5; Gonzalez-Salzberg 2019: 185). To build this argument in each chapter, I identify how specific emotions (disgust, hate, anger, fear, and love) of individuals of parties (LGBT victims and survivors alongside homo/transphobic perpetrators of violence and discrimination) have animated political claims for the legal recognition of LGBT people and then read emotion analytically through cases to explore how emotions crystallise jurisprudentially to arrange injury, intimacy, and identity.

This book begins the analysis by looking at the demand to limit state intervention in LGBT lives that centred on retracting criminal laws that injured LGBT people in private spaces, and I conclude the book by reflecting on calls for greater state intervention through laws that accommodate the intimacy and identity of LGBT people in public spheres. These paradoxical engagements with state intervention show how LGBT people move from being repudiated as sexualised "outlaws" to being embraced as domesticated "in-laws". By wading through various emotions and sub-disciplines of law to map the affective conditions of this trajectory, I provide my own narrative of pro-LGBT recognition. In doing so, I seek to further queer legal reflections by using emotion, rather than norms or doctrines, to organise the analytic and political impetus of critical legal scholarship. While this book deals specifically with deconstructing jurisprudence, it has implications beyond critical legal scholars. It has implications for activists, lawyers, and judges, too. Activists intervene in, or bring disputes to, court for consideration, lawyers frame the parameters of legal disputes through litigation, and judges ultimately decide those disputes. Queering enactments of emotions in these pro-LGBT cases not only offers a novel way for scholars to understand the scope of legal recognition available to LGBT people but also points to how activists, lawyers, and judges might loosen legal attachments to emotions as a way to make greater room for queer intimacies and identities. In other words, reading emotion in pro-LGBT cases opens up paths for scholars, activists, lawyers, and judges to understand the emotional terms of legal progress and parse their impacts on LGBT (and queer) people without having to let go of pressing demands for legal recognition and protection.

I begin my reading of emotion in Chapter 2 by following directions of disgust in cases dealing with sodomy, sadomasochism, and the "homosexual advance defence". From buggery in the bedroom to same-sex flirtations in public, activities that violate majoritarian (hetero)sexual ideas of intimacy and identity have been the subject of individual and penal revulsion. I begin with a precursor trigger for pro-LGBT reform, laws criminalising homosexuality, and register how individual and social disgust levelled at gay sex gets crystallised in law to criminalise homosexual intimacy and render gay men as threats to the "natural order". I then move to show how pro-LGBT sodomy decriminalisation cases contain legal aversions to homosexuality by moving gay sex to the bedroom and sentimentalising it through logics of privacy and conjugal intimacy. I use disgust analytically to foreground the limits of this legal progress by looking at how sentimentality functions problematically to repudiate queer intimacies such as consensual gay sadomasochism and unwanted sexual advances that enter into public view because they threaten the integrity of individual bodies and (hetero) social arrangements. I then extend the analytic frame to include cases that engender disgust when responding to the disgust of homophobes (as opposed to homosexuals), such as in the widely condemned "homosexual advance defence". The reading of disgust in this chapter shows why accounting for both the punitive and progressive directions this emotion can take is important to understand how gay intimacies (sodomy, sadomasochism, flirting) and identities (gay men) are arranged in law for the purposes of progressive recognition and homophobic repudiation. Mapping these juxtaposed enactments of disgust in law is politically necessary to make space for "disgusting" queer intimacies and identities that disrupt sentimental attachments to reproductive sexuality or social assimilation while challenging homophobic articulations of disgust that stigmatise gay people. In other words, reading disgust opens up analytic space for tracking the disparate kinds of LGBT intimacies and identities that the law is willing to recognise and this offers a political space from which to challenge the marginalisation of queer intimacies and identities.

In addition to (or alongside) disgust, hate has been galvanised in cases that target homophobic and transphobic violence. In Chapter 3, I narrate a specific shift in enactments of hate: case law moves from vigorously condemning the identities and intimacies of LGBT people as a threat to a (cis)gendered and (hetero)sexual order to despising those who inflict exceptional physical or sexual injuries on vulnerable LGBT people. In this chapter, I observe how exceptional forms of homophobic and transphobic hate have triggered legislative hostilities towards those who perpetrate such violence. I look at pro-LGBT hate crime legislation and cases in the United States (US) that crystallise these various expressions of hate. The *Hate Crimes Prevention Act of 2009*, for example, reveals how the government has a positive/public obligation to protect the intimacies and identities of LGBT people by punishing hateful subjects (homo/transphobes) that cause injury to them. I develop this analysis further by contrasting the litigation surrounding the separate murders of Gwen Araujo (in 2002) and Brandon Teena (in 1993). These cases highlight how hostile responses to transphobic hate can ossify commitments to harsh punishment of violent individuals who are "queer" to society while obscuring the role of violent institutions, such as police and prisons, in harming queer people (which includes both criminalised and LGBT populations). Reading hate analytically in pro-LGBT hate crime cases demonstrates how the emotion only recognises exceptional physical injuries (rape, murder) and identities (rapists, murderers) for the purpose of criminal sanction while obscuring more pervasive forms of legal and social violence. Registering this hate is politically important to highlight how activists and lawyers might challenge enactments of hostility in pro-LGBT cases to pursue alternate forms of accountability without abandoning the importance of legal interventions to protect LGBT people from violence.

The second half of this book turns to public law to expand critiques of how emotional enactments in criminal law eclipse a range of queer intimacies and identities that risk undermining a public order. By turning to public law, I register how emotions like anger, fear, and love make it possible to accommodate the injuries, intimacies, and identities of LGBT people in public spaces. I begin with anti-discrimination law in Chapter 4 and explore how anger has been central to mobilising law reform to address the individual and collective injury of discrimination. In Chapter 4, I read anger in pro-LGBT anti-discrimination cases from the US and Australia to show how individual anger manifests over discriminatory injuries that blocks the public expression of LGBT intimacies and identities. I register individual anger through refusals to legislate anti-discrimination law, allow gay men to serve as scout leaders, let an LGBT group march in a Gay Pride parade, and give space for LGBT children at camp. I show how this emotion gets refracted in judicial interventions that strike back against the pain of these injuries. I begin by reading anger analytically to delineate how pro-LGBT cases largely protect the identities and intimacies of LGBT people if they do not unsettle political guarantees of "free speech" or compromise protected religious sensitivities. Yet, on the other hand, reading anger also shows how pro-LGBT anti-discrimination cases that enact anger to limit religious or political objections to LGBT visibility also do so in ways that occlude queer (political) intimacies and (religious) identities. Registering these enactments of anger and loosening the attachments they generate are important if law is to make space for queer intimacies and identities that trouble institutional categories of sexuality.

Fear also emerges in pro-LGBT cases that seek to accommodate LGBT people fleeing violence from other countries. In Chapter 5, I navigate the ways in which an individual's "well-founded fear" of persecution is central to the grant of asylum under international law and explore how law generates new fears and anxieties through the adjudication of asylum claims. Here, I read fear analytically to map how sexual minorities who fear persecution are legally protected only to the extent their fears are "well-founded" and their claims for protection do not threaten the integrity of borders that strictly circumscribe LGBT injury, intimacy, and identity. By looking at the claims of same-sex attracted men and women, I show how fear crystallises in pro-LGBT refugee cases that mandate "discretion" to limit the scope of what counts as persecutory injury. I then map how courts anxiously authenticate intimacy and identity through ethnocentric stereotypes about popular culture, social visibility, and sexual practices to prevent impending threats (such as fraudulent claims) from coming too close and disrupting the integrity of the adjudication system. Reading fear here is politically useful to reveal how current legal progress fails to make space for intimacies and identities that are too queer (to be serious or credible). Reading emotion is necessary to confront the demands fear and anxiety make on legal recognition and pursue less anxious legal avenues for recognising the intimacies and identities of LGBT people fleeing persecution.

I conclude my examination of LGBT claims of public accommodation in Chapter 6 by reading how love, hope, and respect affirm LGBT intimacy and identity in US marriage equality cases. I focus on reading love analytically to show how individual expressions of romantic love are crystallised in pro-LGBT cases that affirm the personal and social well-being of LGBT people through a pursuit of liberty, equality, and dignity. Love through marriage elevates same-sex couples from the injury of relationship exclusion by idealising the quality of their intimacies and the equality of their identities. Mapping the emotional dimensions of these claims expose how love, hope, and respect shape the terms by which LGBT people and their relationships are legally affirmed. The positive emotions enacted in these cases cultivate attachments to a degendered version of the reproductive family. By reading love analytically, scholars, activists, and lawyers can begin to think politically about loosening legal attachments to make space for those who pursue queer intimacies that are transient or promiscuous and address how marital recognition obscures the injuries experienced by queer populations facing institutional economic and social marginalisation.

Reading emotion in pro-LGBT cases allows us, as scholars, to analytically navigate arrangements of injury, intimacy, and identity that emerge in jurisprudence that purports to progress the rights of LGBT people. Registering how emotion manifests in these interventions highlights that making law serve the needs or desires of LGBT people is not simply about critically engaging with legal doctrines to improve them, but is also about confronting and loosening attachments that shape, and secure, the reach of such doctrines in the first place. I conclude the book by bringing together the pro-LGBT cases discussed in each chapter to show why queer legal scholarship that offers analytic and political accounts of emotional jurisprudence is important if activists, lawyers, and judges are to advance reparative futures for LGBT people.

Notes

1 Some scholars refer to queer spaces as "counterpublics" (see Berlant and Warner 2000). Counterpublics interrupt public pursuits to define "normal" intimacies. They are creative spaces that challenge the privilege and sentimentality of heterosexuality. They are not reducible to communities formed around logics of domesticity, property, reproduction, and nationhood.
2 This book uses "queer" primarily as an analytic theory and political praxis. However, there are times where queer is used as a description of a subject position or identity (of people who do not conform to sexual and gender norms).
3 There are various forms of the LGBT* acronym. For example, some also include intersex and asexual. While inclusion is important, I do not use a more expanded acronym (such as "LGBTI" or "LGBTIA") in this book because the cases I discuss do not deal with intersex or asexuality. For a broader discussion on the challenges of labels in activist spaces and the problems of tokenism, see Thoreson (2014).
4 This also involves a "queer commitment" to a close reading of a small archive of texts (see Freeman 2010: xvii). Rather than analyse legal doctrines progressively or chronologically across entire subdisciplines of law, reading emotion queerly recasts case law

to bring together the past (prior emotions in cases), present (reading the emotions in cases), and future (speculating on the reach of emotions in cases) simultaneously.
5 This book does not use emotion as a way to "rewrite" legal decisions to make them queer. For examples of what "queer judgments" could look like, see Gonzalez-Salzberg (2019: 158–185) and Sharpe (2017: 417–435).

References

Abrams, K. and Keren, H., 2010. Who's Afraid of Law and the Emotions? *Minnesota Law Review*, 94, 1997–2074.
Acorn, A., 2004. *Compulsory Compassion: A Critique of Restorative Justice*. Vancouver: UBC Press.
Adler, L., 2018. *Gay Priori: A Queer Critical Legal Studies Approach to Law Reform*. Durham: Duke University Press.
Ahmed, S., 2004. *The Cultural Politics of Emotion*. Oxford: Routledge.
Ahmed, S., 2006. *Queer Phenomenology: Orientations, Objects, Others*. Durham: Duke University Press.
Ahmed, S., 2010. *The Promise of Happiness*. Durham: Duke University Press.
Ahmed, S., 2014. *Willful Subjects*. Durham: Duke University Press.
Arkush, D. J., 2008. Situating Emotion: A Critical Realist View of Emotion and Nonconscious Cognitive Processes for Law and Legal Theory. *Brigham Young University Law Review*, 2008(5), 1275–1366.
Ashford, C., 2011. Sexualities and the Law. *Sexualities*, 14(3), 265–72.
Bell, D. and Binnie, J., 2000. *The Sexual Citizen: Queer Politics and Beyond*. Hoboken: Wiley.
Belleau, M. C., Johnson, R. and Bouchard, V., 2007. Faces of Judicial Anger: Answering the Call. *European Journal of Legal Studies*, 1(2), 1–41.
Berlant, L., 1997. *The Queen of America Goes to Washington City: Essays on Sex and Citizenship*. Durham: Duke University Press.
Berlant, L., 1999. The Subject of True Feeling: Pain, Privacy and Politics. In Austin Sarat and Thomas Kearns, eds. *Cultural Pluralism, Identity Politics and the Law*. Ann Arbor: University of Michigan Press, 49–84.
Berlant, L. and Warner, M., 2000. Sex in Public. In Lauren Berlant, ed. *Intimacy*. Chicago: University of Chicago Press, 311–30.
Berlant, L., 2011. *Cruel Optimism*. Durham: Duke University Press.
Bondi, L., 2005. The Place of Emotions in Research: From Partitioning Emotion and Reason to the Emotional Dynamics of Research Relationships. In Joyce Davidson, Liz Bondi, and Mick Smith, eds. *Emotional Geographies*. Aldershot: Ashgate, 231–46.
Bower, L. C., 1994. Queer Acts and the Politics of Direct Address: Rethinking Law, Culture and Community. *Law & Society Review*, 28(5), 1009–34.
Brown, W., 1995. *States of Injury: Power and Freedom in Late Modernity*. Princeton: Princeton University Press.
Butler, J., 1994. Against Proper Objects. *differences: A Journal of Feminist Cultural Studies*, 6(2–3), 1–26.
Butler, J., 2005. *Giving an Account of Oneself*. New York: Fordham University Press.
Carbado, D. W., 2009. Black Rights, Gay Rights, Civil Rights. In Martha A. Fineman, Jack E. Jackson, and Adam P. Romero, eds. *Feminist and Queer Legal Theory: Intimate Encounters, Uncomfortable Conversations*. London: Ashgate, 223–44.

Case, M. A. C., 1995. Disaggregating Gender from Sex and Sexual Orientation: The Effeminate Man in the Law and Feminist Jurisprudence. *Yale Law Journal*, 105(1), 1–105.
Clough, P. T., 2007. Introduction. In Patricia Clough, ed. *The Affective Turn: Theorizing the Social*. Durham: Duke University Press, 1–33.
Crimp, D., 2002. *Melancholia and Moralism: Essays on AIDS and Queer Politics*. Cambridge: MIT Press.
Cvetkovich, A., 2003. *An Archive of Feelings: Trauma, Sexuality, and Lesbian Public Cultures*. Durham: Duke University Press.
Cvetkovich, A., 2012. *Depression: A Public Feeling*. Durham: Duke University Press.
Deleuze, G. and Guattari, F., 1987. *A Thousand Plateaus: Capitalism and Schizophrenia*. Minneapolis: University of Minnesota Press.
Duggan, L., 1994. Queering the State. *Social Text*, 39, 1–14.
Edelman, L., 2004. *No Future: Queer Theory and the Death Drive*. Durham: Duke University Press.
Eng, D., 2010. *The Feeling of Kinship: Queer Liberalism and the Racialization of Intimacy*. Durham: Duke University Press.
Freeman, E., 2010. *Time Binds: Queer Temporalities, Queer Histories*. Durham: Duke University Press.
Gatens, M., 1996. *Imaginary Bodies: Ethics, Power and Corporeality*. London: Routledge.
Gewirtzman, D., 2008. Our Founding Feelings: Emotion, Commitment, and Imagination in Constitutional Culture. *University of Richmond Law Review*, 43, 623–84.
Gonzalez-Salzberg, D., 2019. *Sexuality and Transsexuality under the European Convention on Human Rights: A Queer Reading of Human Rights Law*. Bloomsbury: Hart.
Halberstam, J., 2011. *The Queer Art of Failure*. Durham: Duke University Press.
Halperin, D. M. and Traub, V., 2009. Beyond Gay Pride. In David M. Halperin and Valerie Traub, eds. *Gay Shame*. Chicago: University of Chicago Press, 3–40.
Haritaworn, J., Posocco, S. and Kuntsman, A., 2014. Introduction: Queer Necropolitics. In Jin Haritaworn, Adi Kuntsman, and Sylvia Posocco, eds. *Queer Necropolitics*. London: Routledge, 1–28.
Harris, C. I., 1993. Whiteness as Property. *Harvard Law Review*, 106(8), 1707–91.
Hochschild, A. R., 1983. *The Managed Heart: Commercialization of Human Feeling*. Berkeley: University of California Press.
Hunter, S., 2015. *Power, Politics and the Emotions: Impossible Governance?* London: Routledge.
Johns, F., 2003. On Writing Dangerously. *Sydney Law Review*, 26, 473–80.
Kapur, R., 2005. *Erotic Justice: Law and the New Politics of Postcolonialism*. London: Cavendish.
Kennedy, D., 1986. Freedom and Constraint in Adjudication: A Critical Phenomenology. *Journal of Legal Education*, 36, 518–62.
LaFont, S., 2009. Not Quite Redemption Song: LGBT Hate in Jamaica. In David A. B. Murray, ed. *Homophobias: Lust and Loathing across Time and Space*. Durham: Duke University Press, 105–22.
Lange, B., 2002. The Emotional Dimension in Legal Regulation. *Journal of Law and Society*, 29(1), 197–225.
Lorde, A., 1984. *Sister Outsider*. Berkeley: Crossing Press.

Love, H., 2007. *Feeling Backward: Loss and the Politics of Queer History*. Durham: Duke University Press.

MacKinnon, C., 1987. *Feminism Unmodified: Discourses on Life and Law*. Cambridge: Harvard University Press.

Matsuda, M. J., 1989. Public Response to Racist Speech: Considering the Victim's Story. *Michigan Law Review*, 87, 2320–81.

Moran, L., 2009. What Kind of Field is "Law, Gender and Sexuality"? Achievements, Concerns and Possible Futures. *Feminist Legal Studies*, 17, 309–13.

Munoz, J. E., 2009. *Cruising Utopia: The Then and There of Queer Futurity*. New York: New York University Press.

Nussbaum, M. C., 2013. *Political Emotions: Why Love Matters for Justice*. Cambridge: Harvard University Press.

Nussbaum, M. C., 2016. *Anger and Forgiveness: Resentment, Generosity, and Justice*. New York: Oxford University Press.

Povinelli, E., 2011. Disturbing Sexuality. In Janet Halley and Andrew Parker, eds. *After Sex? On Writing since Queer Theory*. Durham: Duke University Press, 257–69.

Robson, R., 2007. Judicial Review and Sexual Freedom. *University of Hawai'i Law Review*, 30, 1–48.

Rosenblum, D., 1994. Queer Intersectionality and the Failure of Recent Lesbian and Gay "Victories". *Law & Sexuality: A Review of Lesbian and Gay Legal Issues*, 4, 83–122.

Schacter, J. S., 2005. Sexual Orientation, Social Change, and the Courts. *Drake Law Review*, 54, 861–83.

Scott, J. W., 1991. Evidence of Experience. *Critical Inquiry*, 17, 773–97.

Sedgwick, E. K., 2003. *Touching Feeling: Affect, Pedagogy, Performativity*. Durham: Duke University Press.

Sharpe, A., 2017. Queering Judgment: The Case of Gender Identity Fraud. *The Journal of Criminal Law*, 81(5), 417–435.

Shouse, E., 2004. Feeling, Emotion, Affect. *M/C Journal*, 8(6), 1–3.

Smith, T. W., 2016. *The Book of Human Emotions*. London: Profile Books.

Spade, D., 2011. *Normal Life: Administrative Violence, Critical Trans Politics, and the Limits of Law*. Brooklyn: South End Press.

Spindelman, M., 2013. Sexuality's Law. *Columbia Journal of Gender and Law*, 24(2), 87–252.

Stychin, C., 2000. Granting Rights: The Politics of Rights, Sexuality and EU. *Northern Ireland Legal Quarterly*, 50(2), 281–302.

Thoreson, R., 2014. *Transnational LGBT Activism: Working for Sexual Rights Worldwide*. Minneapolis: Minnesota University Press.

Tomsen, S., 2009. *Violence, Prejudice & Sexuality*. New York and London: Routledge.

Valdes, F., 2009. Queering Sexual Orientation: A Call for Theory as Praxis. In Martha A. Fineman, Jack E. Jackson, and Adam P. Romero, eds. *Feminist and Queer Legal Theory: Intimate Encounters, Uncomfortable Conversations*. London: Ashgate, 91–112.

Valverde, M., 2015. *Chronotopes of Law: Jurisdiction. Scale and Governance*. Oxford: Routledge.

West, R. Communities, Texts, and Law: Reflections on the Law and Literature Movement. *Yale Journal of Law & the Humanities*, 1, 129–56.

White, J. B., 1985. *Heracles' Bow: Essays on the Rhetoric and Poetics of the Law*. Madison: University of Wisconsin Press.

Wiegman, R., 2012. *Object Lessons*. Durham: Duke University Press.
Wiegman, R., 2017. Sex and Negativity; or, What Queer Theory Has For You. *Critical Inquiry*, 95, 219–43.
Wiener, R. L., Bornstein, B. H. and Voss, A., 2006. Emotion and Law: A Framework for Inquiry. *Law and Human Behavior*, 30, 231–48.
Williams, P. J., 1988. On Being the Object of Property. *Signs: Journal of Women in Culture and Society*, 14(1), 5–24.
Yoshino, K., 2002. Covering. *Yale Law Journal*, 111(4), 769–939.
Zanghellini, A., 2008. Queer, Antinormativity, Counter-Normativity and Abjection. *Griffith Law Review*, 18(1), 1–16.
Zalnieriute, M., 2017. The Anatomy of Neoliberal Internet Governance: A Queer Critical Political Economy Perspective. In Diane Otto, ed. *Queering International Law: Possibilities, Alliances, Complicities, Risks*. London: Routledge, 53–74.
Zylan, Y., 2011. *States of Passion: Law, Identity and the Social Construction of Desire*. Oxford: Oxford University Press.

Chapter 2

Directing disgust
Queerness and criminality

Introduction

Disgust and queerness emerge together in laws criminalising homosexual activity. Following disgust exposes the visceral recoil, or turning away, from sexual intimacies and identities that queer the reproductive, matrimonial, monogamous imaginaries that sustain the social order of heteronormative life (see Rubin 1984). This chapter uses disgust as an analytic register to foreground how social aversions to gay sex are channelled and crystallised in cases that recoil from recognising queer intimacies (sodomy, sadomasochism, flirting) and identities (gay men). Jurisprudential enactments of disgust position certain forms of gay sex as queer to a "natural order" because they are rendered polluting, contagious, and corrupting. I begin by reading disgust in the prosecution of Oscar Wilde for gross indecency to reveal how social aversions to homosexuality are refracted in law in order to criminalise queer intimacy (gay male sex) and queer identity (sodomite) that threatens to corrupt one's (heterosexual) character. Drawing on the English *Wolfenden Report* and US case law on the decriminalisation of homosexuality, I then track how progressive reform utilises the sentimentalising space of domesticity as a means to manage homophobic disgust and show how this emotionally repositions previously prohibited gay intimacies and identities to affirm them. Exploring the affective relationship between disgust and sentimentality in law, and how it gets articulated in private spaces, evinces how gay intimacy can be normalised and expunged of any associated abject queerness. I juxtapose this sentimentality with cases involving queer sadomasochism and homosexual advances, *R v Brown* (1994) and *R v Green* (1997). Reading emotion shows how pro-LGBT cases sentimentalise privacy and contain disgust to make visible the threat of prosecution (injury), affirm gay male sex (intimacy), and protect gay men (identity). However, this legal containment of disgust is precarious: disgust emerges to condemn sadomasochists and gay men who "flaunt" themselves (queer identity) by engaging in sexual practices involving body modification and flirting (queer intimacy) in private.

This chapter maps how enactments and containments of jurisprudential disgust arrange injury, intimacy, and identity across various cases dealing with criminalised forms of homosexuality. Reading homophobic articulations of disgust alongside more progressive attempts to contain or redirect it exposes how pro-LGBT cases recoil from, and expel, queer intimacies and identities that disrupt a public sexual order. Taking account of what disgust is doing differently in pro-LGBT cases – making greater critical room to reflect on it – becomes politically necessary for scholars, activists, lawyers, and judges who must respond to homophobic disgust to secure sexual freedom for LGBT people.

Disgust/queerness in private

Criminalising buggery

The "homosexual" occupies a historically abject position in English criminal law.[1] For example, in sentencing author Oscar Wilde for the crime of gross indecency (consensual oral sex with another man), Wills J remarked:

> The crime of which you have been convicted is so bad that one has to put stern restraint upon one's self to prevent one's self from describing, in language which I would rather not use, the sentiments which must rise in the breast of every man of honour who has heard the details of these two horrible trials.
>
> (Cited in Nussbaum 2004: 151)

Wills J's sentencing address exposed his aversion to the presence of homosexuality. Disgust prevented naming the "horrible" act itself. His disgust was crystallised in the judgment by holding that to even name the crime for which Wilde was charged would corrupt the dignity of honourable men. Wilde was initially charged with "soliciting" younger men and performing oral sex on them. Yet, the judicial "spitting out" of words did not refer to a specific criminal act but emerged through visceral recoil in relation to Wilde's contaminating homosexuality. Wilde's act (homosexual sex) was injurious to his character, in Wills J's account. Wills J's judgment enacted disgust through the recognition of a queer act or body, which is then pushed back or expelled because it was repulsive (Ahmed 2004: 88).

Wills J's words revealed how disgust cleaves to gay men and gay sex, as an expression of queer identity and intimacy.[2] In his 18th-century commentaries on the common law of England, jurist William Blackstone used disgust to make sense of homosexuality: sexual activity between men was an "offence of so dark a nature" that "the very mention" of it was "a disgrace to human nature" (Blackstone 1765–9: 4.15.215–6). Gross indecency, therefore, expressed social revulsion towards homosexuality. Male homosexuality and the homosexuals who performed such acts were a disgusting expression of sinful desires. Law crystallised these emotional expressions by figuring gay sex (intimacies) and gay men (identities) as a queer deviation from a natural order.

Wilde's act was queer because it disrupted this order by bringing "unnatural vices" into public view. Such "bad objects" (queer intimacies and identities) in the Wilde case were produced through judicial acts that spat them out in order to police them (Kristeva 1982: 45). In doing so, laws criminalising homosexuality refracted social disgust through legal punishment and produced (homo)sexualities that were queer in law: Wills J's judgment recoiled at the contamination of individual character or social order (injury to one's identity), manifested through the production of Wilde's homosexuality as a deviation (queer intimacy).

Buggery was often discussed in relation to a disparate range of queer intimacies covering non-reproductive forms of marital sex, including oral sex, anal sex, premarital sex, group sex, and even masturbation (Hoad 2007: 14). Anal sex, for example, was socially stigmatised as a debasing act against individual dignity. Anuses were construed as orifices for excreting wastes, not for penetration and sexual pleasure (Miller 1997: 100). Gay male sex was deemed lustful, wasteful, and violent (see Dalton 2000). As Leslie Moran observes in his examination of homosexuality in English criminal law, the lack of statutory specificity exposed the law's inability to define and "make sense" of queer intimacy and identity (Moran 1995: 5; Moran 1996: 39). While Moran details the discursive ways in which criminal laws police queer acts or bodies, I am interested in drawing out how legal expressions of recoil or revulsion in particular function to sustain queer criminality. Criminal law expels queer intimacies and identities through articulations of disgust.

Decriminalisation and privacy

In recent decades, gay and lesbian activism has confronted the social disgust levelled at homosexuality to advocate for decriminalisation (see Henderson 2000). Activists have heralded decriminalisation as instrumental in enabling the freedom of gay men to engage in intimacy and remedying state-sanctioned forms of injury (Stychin 1995: 2–3; Thomas 1992: 1460–92).[3] In common law jurisdictions, the *Wolfenden Report* on homosexual offences and prostitution is often cited as the first governmental document facilitating (legislative) decriminalisation of homosexuality (Committee on Homosexual Offences and Prostitution 1957). This report came about through an enquiry instigated in the United Kingdom in 1954 to review laws criminalising homosexuality and the treatment of persons convicted of such offences (Gleeson 2008: 401). Its most notable recommendation was that consensual homosexual acts undertaken by persons over the age of 21 should no longer be criminalised. Understandably, the document was celebrated as a progressive moment in law reform for sexual minorities, but it is important to consider how disgust features in the text to shape the terms of decriminalisation (Committee on Homosexual Offences and Prostitution 1957). Instead of "liberating" non-normative sexual intimacies, the legislative recommendations crystallised public disgust towards homosexuality to inscribe a boundary of "privacy" to sequester abject intimacies (Gleeson 2008: 405). In defining the parameters of current criminalisation, the Committee noted:

> In so far as the basis of this argument can be precisely formulated, it is often no more than an expression of revulsion against what is regarded as unnatural, sinful or disgusting ... But moral conviction or instinctive feeling, however strong, is not a valid basis for overriding the individual's privacy.
> (Committee on Homosexual Offences and Prostitution 1957: [54])

Here, the Committee refracted the "revulsion" individuals may feel towards "disgusting" sexual behaviour by containing disgusting behaviour within the spatial cover of the private. In doing so, the management of disgust through "individual privacy" enabled the Committee to expel acts "likely" to corrupt the public (Committee on Homosexual Offences and Prostitution 1957: [64]). In particular, it expressed concern that public homosexuality could be an inducement or indulgence for young boys. For this reason, the Committee reasoned that such "corruption" ought to incur legal sanction (Committee on Homosexual Offences and Prostitution 1957: [97]). It is important to note how the risks of "indulging" homosexual intimacy or "licensing" homosexuals were arranged in the text through the Committee's crystallisation of disgust over the sexual perversion of youth (Committee on Homosexual Offences and Prostitution 1957: [124]). The Committee invoked privacy to manage disgust – and to contain queer intimacies (homosexuality) and identities (homosexuals).[4]

Bowers and Lawrence – disturbing privacy

Privacy has worked to zone queer intimacies and identities away into a space hidden from public view. Queer and legal scholars have discussed at length how this articulation of privacy functions as a neoliberal logic to recognise, regulate, and contain sexual intimacies despite "liberating" them from criminal law. Privacy logic creates metaphorical closets that force people to manage their non-normative sexuality (see Sedgwick 1990; Stychin 1995), bolsters different modes of surveillance and policing in the home (see Suk 2009), and cultivates individual responsibilities of care (see Duggan 2003; Race 2009). This scholarship is useful because it captures how law discursively constructs homosexuality for the purposes of recognition and details how we might shift these discourses to make room for queer intimacies. Disgust, then, offers a rich analytic register to add to this scholarship by showing how law recognises gay male sex by using privacy and sentimentality to expunge it of its revolting qualities. Specifically, I draw on Lauren Berlant's understanding of sentimentality, as an attachment to nostalgic social fantasies, alongside US cases to highlight how gay sex is divested of its abject qualities through scenes of conjugal coupling (Berlant 1997: 48).

In 1979, Michael Hardwick was prosecuted after a police officer, who had targeted him previously for working at a gay bar, "discovered" Hardwick having oral sex with another man when he forcefully entered his home (using an outdated warrant). It is not necessary to detail the background of the case, other than to note that the specific prosecution of Hardwick reflected a broader policing strategy that involved the targeting of openly gay men in Georgia (see Thomas 1992).

Even though Hardwick's sex was contained in the bedroom, the Supreme Court of the United States was unable to manage its disgust. The majority of justices upheld the statutory ban on sodomy by noting the lack of a constitutional guarantee for what it termed "homosexual sodomy":

> No connection between family, marriage or procreation on the one hand and homosexual activity on the other has been demonstrated ... Against this background, to claim that a right to engage in such conduct is "deeply rooted in this Nation's history and tradition" or "implicit in the concept of ordered liberty" is, at best, facetious.
>
> (*Bowers* 1986: 193–4)

The majority narrated the nation through a sentimentalised history of heterosexual reproduction. Homosexuality became facetious; it was expelled from the view of "ordered liberty". Much of the majority's reasoning in the case transposed the prohibition against sodomy into a mechanism to guard against (homo)sexual conduct that risked infecting the national public by undermining family, marriage, and procreation.

When *Bowers* was overruled by *Lawrence v Texas* (2003) almost two decades after it was handed down, divesting gay sex of disgust was key to constitutional recognition of intimacy. In this case, John Lawrence and Tyrone Garner were the subject of prosecution for "deviate sex" in Texas after police responded to a neighbour's call that erroneously suggested that Garner was brandishing a gun. While the invalidation of the Texas sodomy law should be celebrated, the reasoning of the case encapsulated the sanitising power of the domestic space to expunge disgust by diverting "deviate sex" into the conjugal bedroom. The constitutional principle of liberty in this case was domesticated rather than expanded – that is, queer intimacy was confined to domestic space (such as the bedroom) rather than given a broader public licence (Franke 2004: 1401). Kennedy J held:

> When sexuality finds overt expression in intimate conduct with another person, the conduct can be but one element in a personal bond that is more enduring. The liberty protected by the Constitution allows homosexual persons the right to make this choice.
>
> (*Lawrence* 2003: 567)

Instead of confronting the issue in terms of anal or oral sex, Kennedy J opted to recognise "enduring" intimacy without the disgust associated with sodomy in earlier cases (Ball 2010: 224). Kennedy J echoed the Committee on Homosexual Offences and Prostitution's reasoning on decriminalising homosexual activity by noting the absence of minors, public conduct, and prostitution in the case (*Lawrence* 2003: 578). Kennedy J oriented the decision around a sentimentalised scene of same-sex relationships in the home and, in doing so, severed disgust from gay sex that had previously (as in *Bowers*) been expelled from constitutional inclusion. Jurisprudential disgust continued to repudiate queer sex acts that were promiscuous, orgiastic, and uncontrollable while judicial sentimentality functioned to move homosexual intimacies that were conjugal and enduring away from the space of legal abjection and into the home.

Lawrence went further than the *Wolfenden Report* by ushering in the possibility of sanitising, not simply containing, disgust once it entered the domestic sphere. Private "indulgences" could be transformed into valuable intimacies. Such possibilities were deftly highlighted in Scalia J's ferocious response to the majority:

> What a massive disruption of the current social order, therefore, the overruling of *Bowers* entails.
>
> (*Lawrence* 2003: 591)

Scalia J's notion of homosexuality as a social contaminant was not particularly spectacular. It largely echoed the ruling by the Texas Court of Appeals that same-sex sexual behaviour could be classed as "more offensive" than the cross-sex variety (*Lawrence* 2001: 356). However, despite the formal overruling of *Bowers*, the majority's reasoning in the case resonated with the majority in *Bowers*. Specifically, homosexuality (at least in a domesticated form) could be assimilated by sentimental tropes of reproductive conjugal intimacy thought central to the protection of liberty in *Bowers* (Spindelman 2004: 1629). Affective similarity became key to the legal possibilities of privacy. Martha Nussbaum, for example, celebrates the decision as a "rejection of the politics of disgust" (Nussbaum 2010: 89). I would add that judicial sentimentality worked here to expunge gay sex of the social disgust previously associated with it. Instead of orienting around the sex act itself, the majority was able to pursue a liberty doctrine through a spatialisation of privacy that showcased romanticised intimacy rather than making space for disturbing acts of sodomy. The Court's sentimentality arranged (homosexual) intimacy in the home to enable decriminalisation but, in doing so, covered over abject dimensions of queer sex.

While the outcomes of *Bowers* and *Lawrence* were different, scholars can read emotion to track how the relationship between disgust and sentimentality featured in both cases to limit the expression of queer intimacies and identities. Homosexuality was no longer emotionally tied to disease or contagion, but became sentimentalised to resemble heterosexual partnerships (see Glick 2011). Zoning sodomy through relational and spatial sentimentalities (such as the home) kept it from disturbing or disgusting others (Eng 2010: 30). Whether judgments seek to criminalise or decriminalise homosexuality, reading emotion is analytically useful to grasp how sentimentalising moves to recognise gay sex within a scene of conjugal intimacy work alongside the containment of disgust to limit legal space to affirm queer intimacies that threaten normative emotional fantasies about domesticity and privacy. In *Bowers*, disgust was crystallised by a majority decision that felt sodomy would disturb a constitutional order founded on reproductive heterosexuality. In *Lawrence*, the redirection of disgust away from gay sex by using privacy as a space of sentimentality shielded it from criminal sanction. Specifically, the crystallisation of sentimentality – rendering gay sex a nostalgic idea of everyday social act of personal bonding – in *Lawrence* countered judicial disgust evinced in *Bowers* to render gay sex legal (see Berlant 1997).

Disgust/queerness in public

The above discussion highlights how gay sexual freedom is made possible when disgust can be legally contained or expunged. I now turn in this chapter to read how disgust in relation to sadomasochist practices resists containment and criminalises sadomasochism under the rubric of "public interest" (as shown in *Brown*). Rather than eschew or (re)arrange disgust directed towards queer intimacy, which has been the subject of much legal scholarly critique and LGBT activism, I show how following disgust analytically opens up space to confront legal attachments that repudiate non-(re)productive intimacies and identities.

Queering sadomasochism

Sadomasochism is not a discrete sexual practice. Rather, it is a diverse constellation of activities that involve "leathersex, bondage, erotic torture, flagellation, verbal humiliation, fist-fucking, and watersports" (Califia 2000: 171). *R v Brown* (1994) has become a legal authority on this topic – particularly when it comes to the limits of consent and sexual privacy. *Brown* emerged from "Operation Spanner", a broader policing movement around drugs in Manchester, England during 1987. As a result of the investigation, a number of men were charged with assault occasioning actual bodily harm after videotapes were uncovered showing them participating in a range of sexual and body modification acts. Per sections 20 and 47 of the *Offences Against the Person Act 1861*, the UK House of Lords had to consider whether consent could be used as a defence to acts occasioning actual bodily harm and wounding (such as a breaking of the skin). The "actual bodily harm" in this case ranged from nailing pierced foreskins to wooden boards, to incisions on the scrotum, to hot wax play. "Public interest" became a key anchor for judicial discussion in this case in order to determine whether these sadomasochist acts could be excepted from criminal liability. Legal scholarship has already considered the doctrinal technicalities of this point (see Tolmie 2012). However, tracking disgust helps explain how distinctions between public and private blur and eclipse legal recognition of queer intimacies and identities.

In refusing to exempt sadomasochist practices from liability, the Court held that the appellants "participated in the commission of acts of violence against each other ... [for] sexual pleasure ... engendered in the giving and receiving of pain" (*Brown* 1992: 552). In articulating what constituted the specific act of wounding, the jurisprudence in this case makes palpable the Court's revulsion towards socio-sexual "deviance" by transforming the participants' painful indulgences into an abject social injury. Lord Templeman wrote:

> The violence of sadomasochistic encounters involves the indulgence of cruelty by sadists and the degradation of victims ... Pleasure derived from the infliction of pain is an evil thing. Cruelty is uncivilised.
>
> (*Brown* 1994: 237)

Disgust crystallised in the Court's expression that violence in sex was evil. Lord Templeman's reasoning pointed to how wilfully intrusive, non-sentimental sexual practices were an "evil thing" to be expelled. His abject characterisation of the sadomasochistic act (intimacy) focussed on the "indulgence of cruelty" and the sensations of pain (injury) that were associated with it. This emotional arrangement tied sadomasochist intimacy to sexual injury and, in doing so, backgrounded consent as a relevant consideration when sexual intimacies promoted "cruelty" and threatened "civility" (Gurham 2011: 125). Sadomasochism (and sadomasochists), as it emerged in this case, disturbed the organisation of sexual intimacy within a cultural imaginary of genital (read: heterosexual penile/vaginal) penetration. By making visible the judicial enactment of disgust, we can draw out how this sexual activity could not be sentimentalised as an "enduring" intimacy, as Kennedy J did to the act of homosexual sodomy in *Lawrence*. If the right to protected private sex was sentimentally imagined to be conducive to romance, genital pleasure, and orgasmic acts, then the act of sadomasochism failed to conform to this emotional fantasy. Sadomasochism was a queer intimacy that caused harm because it was a "cruel" sexual expression that "injured" a "civilised" (public) order. Pejorative terms such as "indulgence" and "degradation" were annexed to the representation of sadomasochistic sex to render the sex of the appellants perverse. Moreover, the "indulgence" exhibited by the appellants evoked judicial revulsion towards sadomasochism. Judicial disgust made visible how aggression, indulgence, and violence queered the romantic or sentimental imagining of sexual intimacy.

Much like earlier legal reluctance apparent among US judges towards decriminalising sodomy, queer sadomasochism generated judicial recoil because it failed to appeal to conjugal ideals of "loving" sex. Lord Templeman held:

> In my opinion sadomasochism is not only concerned with sex. Sadomasochism is concerned with violence. The evidence discloses that the practices of the appellants were unpredictably dangerous and degrading to the body

and mind and were developed with increasing barbarity and taught to persons whose consents were dubious or worthless.

(*Brown* 1994: 235)

Sadomasochism derived its "barbarous" qualities from its "concern with violence". Judicial disgust was not expressed in response to the actual harm perpetrated or to the individual experience of pain, but it crystallised through the Court's figuration of dangers that threatened the boundaries of the (social) body. In other words, the recoil levelled at sadomasochism was not about the sex involved, but rather about the violence and disorder it engendered – it took the sex too far. Such "unpredictable" violence was "degrading". By recoiling at the thought of "genital torture" – rather than critically confronting what specific injury was disgusting – the Court was unable to confront the queer intimacies present in sadomasochism (*Brown* 1994: 236).

Marking the body in "violent" ways creates queer possibilities for pleasure by using "strange parts of the body" (Foucault 1984: 165). Group sadomasochism dislocates love and bonding from sex, "leaving only (dangerous) enjoyment" (Bibbings and Allridge 1993: 360). Rather than reproduce the sentimentalised fantasies of romance, love, and monogamy, the dynamic positions and erotic roles in sadomasochism create greater fluidity in sexual intimacy and identity. Moran notes that sadomasochism is not so much about cruelty and revenge as it is about "prior agreement and contract" (Moran 1995: 238). This construction of sadomasochism runs counter to that offered in *Brown* and illuminates how disgust functioned in *Brown* to deride queer intimacies or identities while actively working to "take over" them. The judicial assessment of actual bodily harm expressed disgust by appropriating the pain of individuals (regardless of consent) to construct a social injury while eclipsing the fact that the participants were willing and did not feel disgust about what they were doing.

The Court's disgust was entrenched by the fact that the participants refused to see their conduct as disgusting. Consenting to bodily or erotic modifications became more of a transgression against the social order than the actual physical act of wounding. Adapting the words of Nussbaum, we can say that the antecedent judicial abjection of homosexual sex was revived to understand the "assault" (Nussbaum 2010: 41). Disgust amplified injury beyond just a medical diagnosis of infection – the judgment directed attention to the social problematic of exchanging bodily fluids and uncontrolled behaviours. Thus, what was considered "actual" (to the individual) is more accurately construed as "social" because harm was emotionally arranged beyond physical injury. Unlike the aversion exhibited in Wilde's case to describe sodomy, here the Court was willing to go a little further in detailing the offences. From the "nailing of foreskin" to "hot wax", Lord Jauncey concluded that while the actual injuries in this case did not warrant medical treatment, such degenerative intimacies were a queer intrusion to public integrity:

> Wounds can easily become septic if not properly treated, the free flow of blood from a person who is HIV positive or who has AIDS can infect another and an inflicter who is carried away by sexual excitement or by drink or drugs could very easily inflict pain and injury beyond the level to which the receiver had consented.
>
> (*Brown* 1994: 246)

Judicial revulsion at the prospect of sadomasochist intimacy led the Court to conflate the sexual practices of gay men with HIV, substance use, and the transmission of bodily fluids. In doing so, queer intimacy became potentially infectious. It was a "danger" to which one could not freely consent. These sexual practices were judicially figured in relation to intoxicants or substance use, either drugs or alcohol. Judicial recoil from homosexual sadomasochism manifested through moral panics surrounding homosexuality and disease. Sadomasochist promiscuity coupled with uncontrolled "sexual excitement" risked infection. Wounding that resulted in the exchange of blood and semen became a "muck" that shattered the "integrity of the body's seal" (Miller 1997: 58). This abject formulation legitimated sexual policing with reference to the AIDS crisis, homosexual sex, and (injecting) drug users. Loss of control became symptomatic of homosexual sadomasochism (Moran 1999: 45). If we recall the discussion of *Lawrence* above, we can also observe how these cases reproduced an affective demarcation between the sentimental and the disgusting homosexual intimacy. The former practised conventional sexual coupling, while the latter was queer because it sought to disturb the idea of sex as a form of genital intercourse. Homosexual sadomasochism fell into the latter category with risks that the Court felt compelled to repel. Consent was not included as a "defence" (or a means of containment) because jurisprudential revulsion positioned the intimacy as a threat to the public.

This emotional differentiation between private and public queer sexual acts was reproduced in subsequent cases dealing with assault occasioning actual bodily harm.[5] In *R v Wilson* (1997), a comparable UK case concerning consent and actual bodily harm, a man was found not liable for assault occasioning actual bodily harm when he consensually branded his spouse's buttocks with a knife. In that case, the court distinguished between the sexual acts through a number of sentimentalising manoeuvres:

> We are abundantly satisfied that there is no factual comparison to be made between the instant case and the facts of ... *R v Brown* ... Mrs Wilson not only consented to that which the appellant did, she instigated it. There was no aggressive intent on the part of the appellant. On the contrary, far from wishing to cause injury to his wife, the appellant's desire was to assist her in what she regarded as the acquisition of a desirable piece of personal adornment ....
>
> (*Wilson* 1996: 50)

Disgust offers a lens for understanding why this distinction was possible. The Court in *Wilson* distinguished *Brown* on the basis that "injury" was incidental to, rather than the motivation for, sexual intimacy. Such a distinction, however, was largely a reflection of how disgust organised the legal concept of actual bodily harm differently. In a similar emotional tread to *Lawrence*, domestic space was sentimentalised as a zone that could enable intimacy. While the matrimonial "home" was not necessarily a zone free from legal interference, it did function as the literal and metaphorical "scene" for intimate coupling. Far from being disgusting, the physical act of cutting and branding was articulated within the home space as an "adornment". It was a "desirable" mark of marital (and patriarchal) solidarity. Even though the cutting involved in *Brown* was different, the definition of wounding (or tattooing) established in that case as the breaking of the skin that was more than "transient or trifling" was clearly evident in this case (*Brown* 1994: 233). Both raised the possibilities of infection. Yet, only *Brown* brought this concern to the forefront (Gurham 2011: 129). The "public interest" references revealed judicial need to contain disgust relating to unusual forms of queer sexual intimacies while preserving a nostalgic commitment to matrimonial heterosexual behaviour.

Following disgust reveals the law's moral commitments to self-preservation and the reassertion of the public order through the spitting out of queer intimacies. *Brown* was an invitation for the Court to act paternally to prevent the contaminating spread of queer intimacies and identities. In doing so, the sentimentality that proved key to securing freedom for sodomy in *Lawrence* by severing disgust from such practices resurfaced in *Brown* to condemn queer individuals who refused to domesticate their intimacies and identities. The judicial refusal to affirm consent in *Brown* evinced an aversion to thinking about disgusting and troubling sex. Disgust captures how legal recognition of (conjugal) gay intimacy in the bedroom is possible through the repudiation of (sadomasochist) queer intimacy.

Redirecting disgust from homosexuality to homophobia

In the final sections of this chapter, I turn to *R v Green* (1997) to map how disgust moves from the homosexual to the homophobe as a way to condemn lethal injuries suffered by sexual minorities while covering over systemic forms of homophobia. In May 1993, Donald Gillies, aged 36, was killed by Malcolm Green, aged 22 at his home in Mudgee, Australia. The two men were acquaintances at the time. On the night in question, Green was invited to stay over at Gillies's home. At some point during the night, Gillies got into bed with Green and proceeded to rub his shoulders and back. Gillies then allegedly tried to grope him. Green responded to intimate touching with lethal violence. According to the medical evidence, Gillies was punched 35 times and then stabbed in the face with a pair of scissors at least 10 times. In accounting for his actions, Green pleaded that Gillies made an unwanted sexual advance towards him and that this triggered his latent rage towards his father, who had allegedly sexually assaulted his sisters (*Green* 1997: 338–9). Green confessed, but argued that it was manslaughter because of Gillies's provocation. In accepting Green's assertions of Gillies's behaviour, the High Court of Australia had to determine whether an "ordinary person in the position of the accused" would have been induced to form an intent to kill or inflict grievous bodily harm when considering the "homosexual advances" of the deceased.[6]

Provocation and the gay panic defence

Homosexual advances have a notorious history in criminal law. In essence, the homosexual advance defence (HAD) trades on emotions such as rage and disgust – that is, the defendant must establish an emotional "trigger" that prompts an unlawful killing, and this emotion must then be translated for the judge or jury (according to the relevant statute) in order for them to determine if the offender can be (partially) exculpated for the crime. In common law jurisdictions, the doctrinal (as distinct from more social) foundations of "gay panic" are drawn from a number of existing criminal law defences, including insanity, diminished capacity, provocation, and self-defence (Lee 2008: 477–9). In the 1980s, the declassification of homosexuality as a mental illness precipitated a shift away from defining the defence in terms of a defendant's mental incapacity. Instead, the pathological panic used to legitimate the defence for a number of years gave way to disgusted provocation (Smyth 2006: 906). Coupling HAD with provocation rather than pathology demonstrated the way in which a person's susceptibility to emotion (such as disgust) could crystallise a legal claim to mitigate responsibility for murder (see Crofts and Loughnan 2014). These emotions typically included outrage, fear, humiliation, and disgust (Steinberg 2005: 504). HAD, under its new doctrinal cover, allowed a defendant to be convicted of manslaughter instead of murder where the person could demonstrate that the gravity of the same-sex advance constituted sufficient provocative conduct that would cause an ordinary person in the circumstances to lose control.

Homophobic violence was attributed to the emotions of "ordinary men". By redirecting the focus from the queerness of the perpetrator to the queerness of the victim, the contemporary use of HAD has further advanced the stereotypes of gay men as sick, effeminate, predatory, and monstrous (Smyth 2006: 906). As Adrian Howe and Robert Mison argue, the success of the defence depends on the extent to which these stereotypes can engender emotions of hatred and revulsion towards the victim to which the judge(s) and/or jurors can relate (Howe 1997: 344; Mison 1992: 136). For example, the disgust of the perpetrator at the prospect of a same-sex advance is recognised and crystallised through judicial disgust towards same-sex intimacy. Howe notes that the inability to see the homophobic sentiments that are embedded in law reveals the "privilege of unknowing", an ignorance that uncritically accepts the assumption that gay men are dangerous and predatory (Howe 2000: 98). Alternatively, Joshua Dressler, who shares Howe's assessment of how emotion is transmitted, argues contra Howe for the retention of provocation to acknowledge the cultural context in which homophobic violence exists (Dressler 1995: 755).

These arguments invite us to reflect on how (progressive) criminal law attributes responsibility for homophobic violence. Disgust provides an analytic register for this task. As noted above, much has already been written on the litany of cases that deal with HAD across the various common law jurisdictions in which it has been used. This scholarship carefully details the problematic doctrinal articulation of HAD within the terms of provocation (see Howe 1997; Mison 1992) while also drawing attention how it legitimises homophobic violence and toxic masculinities (see Lunny 2003; McDonald 2006; Tomsen 2006). These critiques also express disgust towards a homophobic legal system.[7] I take these critiques as a starting point to think about what it is at stake in redirecting disgust from homosexuals to homophobes in order to punish them. I take this up, alongside my earlier consideration of sodomy and sadomasochism, to show how "successful" HAD cases crystallise the disgust of the homophobe to render the gravity of provocation (injury) caused by a gay man (identity) making an "aggressive" advance (intimacy). When this disgust is redirected, towards the defendant, it is used to condemn a homophobe (identity) who, when confronted with an unwanted flirtation (intimacy), performs an exceptional act of violence to cause death (injury). While much of the critical legal scholarship oscillates between arguing for the end of homophobic legal defences and affirming the importance of provocation to recognise the cultural context of homophobia, reading emotion maps progressive and homophobic articulations of disgust to expose how these emotional judicial enactments sustain the institutional marginalisation of LGBT people.

Departures of disgust in Green

Much public admonition has been directed towards the outcome in *Green*, provoked by the chilling words Green spoke after he was charged with the murder of Gillies. In his statement to the police, Green said, "Yeah, I killed him, but he did worse to me ... he tried to root me" (*Green* 1997: 391). Green's revulsion at the thought of gay sex presented Gillies's attempt to solicit sex from him as more morally reprehensible than Green's decision to kill him. The New South Wales Court of Criminal Appeal is the departure point for discussing the "grossness" of advancing same-sex flirtations. Smart J held:

> Some ordinary men would feel great revulsion at the homosexual advances being persisted with ... They would regard it as a serious and gross violation of their body and their person ... Some ordinary men could become enraged and feel that a strong physical re-action was called for. The deceased's actions had to be stopped.
>
> (*Green* 1995: 24)

Smart J's obiter revealed how a gay advance was a queer intimacy because it tore at the bounded rationality of the male subject through a violation of their bodily and sexual integrity (see Naffine 1997). By conflating homosexual advances with "revulsion", and aversion to them with "ordinariness", Smart J transformed gentle touching into a disgusting act. In Smart J's own words, it "had to be stopped". The judicial reasoning here relied on refracting Green's disgust towards Gillies and depersonalising it through legal references to what "ordinary" (read: heterosexual) men would do. Smart J's revulsion brought the queer body (Gillies) into view as a threat (to Green). Smart J focussed on "ordinary men" in order to justify the fact that such "feeling" could call for a "strong physical retaliation". Disgust marked out how the "body" of heterosexual masculinity was easily violated. Yet, Smart J's movement from a more distanced account of "ordinary men" to a more forceful personalised statement that "the deceased's actions had to be stopped": disgust moved from the defendant to the judge and was crystallised in the judgment. Tracking the judicial crystallisation of Green's disgust to solidify the claim of provocation shows how disgust "overtook" Green's body and Smart J's judgment while it "took over" (to expel) the queer intimacy and identity that gave rise to it – Gillies's and his sexual advance (Ahmed 2004: 85).

The castigating majority – exceptionalising queer advances

Green's violent rebuke of Gillies's unwanted solicitation and Smart J's abjection of that solicitation was mirrored in the High Court of Australia's condemnation of a "homosexual advance". Homophobic disgust became referable to this "ordinary" person. If we track disgust in *Green*, we can observe that the success or failure of the defence can be ascribed to emotionally divergent understandings of "ordinariness" and whether what was recurringly described as the "sexual interference" by Gillies towards Green could lead a reasonable jury, properly instructed, to feel disgust and make a finding of provocation. The concurring judgments of Brennan CJ, Toohey and McHugh JJ narrated Gillies's advances as "persistent" in order to defend against the threat of queer intimacy – that is, Gillies's non-violent sexual advances were seen as a microcosm for how same-sex intimacies could trouble the integrity (of identity) of the person. In this particular case, same-sex intimacies were judicially referred to as "sexual interferences" read against an accused's background of alleged third-party family sexual abuse (*Green* 1997: 342). Brennan CJ held:

> It was essentially a jury question, a question the answer to which depended on the jury's evaluation of the degree of outrage which the appellant might have experienced. It was not for the Court to determine questions of that kind, especially when reactions to sexual advances are critical to the evaluation. A juryman or woman would not be unreasonable because he or she

might accept that the appellant found the deceased's conduct "revolting" rather than "amorous".

(*Green* 1997: 346)

While there was an explicit reference to anger and juries, the qualifying sentences shaped the evaluation of outrage through legal recognition of Green's disgust and judicial crystallisation of that disgust. Labelling the conduct of the deceased "unreasonable" and "revolting" rather than "amorous" expressed judicial recoil at a homosexual advance. Brennan CJ's disgust in the judgment constructed a scene that foregrounded queer intimacy with negativity. Unwanted same-sex sexual advances were judicially figured to disgust the ordinary person and to provoke that person to understandable outrage.

Brennan CJ relied on Green's testimony to frame Gillies's non-violent touching as innately intrusive or aggressive: "Here, the deceased was the sexual aggressor of the appellant" (*Green* 1997: 346). Gillies's flirtatious moves became injurious ones. Interestingly, the erasure of comparable scenarios involving women who were groped by men is telling of the way disgust rendered a "sexual advance" in queer terms (*Green* 1997: 345). For example, despite the pervasive sexual harassment of women, the law is often reticent to consider such "common" acts as aggressive or dangerous (Ramakrishnan 2011: 294–8). While we should be cautious about making jurisdictional generalisations when it comes to the ease of establishing HAD, we should interrogate the ways in which HAD crystallises disgust to unsettle social norms that privilege heterosexual men as penetrating subjects, rather than penetrated objects. As Brennan CJ pointed out, "the real sting of provocation could be found not in the force used by the deceased but in his attempt to violate the sexual integrity of a man who had trusted him" (*Green* 1997: 345). In *Green*, the physically gentle nature of the touching was obscured by the abject figuration of queer advances as intimacies that were sexually violating. Despite Brennan CJ's attempt to distinguish force from violation, the abjection of homosexuality bled them together when considering Brennan CJ's earlier use of the term "aggression" to qualify the same-sex advances made to Green. Moreover, little effort was made in the judgment to distinguish between wanted and unwanted same-sex intimate activity. Much of the obiter here used disgust as a means of recoiling from, and turning back, purportedly aggressive queer sexual advances.

Despite his attempts to emphasise the sexual nature of Gillies's conduct, rather than its homosexual character specifically, McHugh J's recoil at Gillies's conduct obscured the way in which queer "sexual" contact in this case was rendered public or (hyper)visible. Same-sex advances were impugned, while heterofamilial relationships attracted no emotional scrutiny. The latter point is particularly important to emphasise because in this case the alleged sexual violence that made Green "especially sensitive" arose from a violent heteropatriarchal dynamic whereby Green claimed that his father had consistently sexually abused his sisters. McHugh J, much like Lord Templeman in *Brown*, tried to decouple private sexuality from public violence:

> [T]he fact that the advance was of a homosexual nature was only one factor in the case. What was more important from the accused's point of view was that a sexual advance, accompanied with some force, was made by a person whom the accused looked up to and trusted.
>
> (*Green* 1997: 370)

The act of "gentle" touching became a glaring problem of a "persistent" sexual character. Specifically, Gillies's unwanted advances were marked as queer to the normative space of reproductive heterosexual relations. In this case, the "force" of the touch was considered in terms of the "special sensitivity" Green had on the basis of alleged child abuse perpetrated against his sisters. Even though McHugh J followed the issues relating to Green's alleged history of abuse more closely, he rendered homoerotic touching as a socially revolting breach of socially acceptable homosociality. Despite the importance of family abuse in underscoring the gravity of the provocation, McHugh J's reasoning departed from this line of reasoning to stigmatise touching as something perverse insofar as it related to (unacceptable) homoeroticism rather than (acceptable) homosociality (Tomsen 2006: 402). Gillies had abused his position of being "looked up to" by seeking to express his homosexual desire towards Green. The "force" of Gillies's conduct (touching on the shoulders and back) was emotionally felt in this judgment. The literal (sexual advance) and metaphorical (legal response) "touch" was intimately tied to the abject sexual meaning ascribed to Gillies's homosexuality and Green's heterosexuality.

Taken together, Brennan CJ's and McHugh J's concurring judgments reveal how enactments of disgust problematised the coherence of criminal law doctrines relating to personal responsibility and the "objective" way in which the ordinary person was understood (*Green* 1997: 346–7). By reading HAD in terms of disgust, scholars can see why the Court accepted, unproblematically, the "unusual" sexuality of the victim in the case, and in doing so suggested that ordinary persons were susceptible to homophobic prejudices. To make such a defence plausible, the defendant must express a disgust that can be recognised. The "special sensitivities" used to mitigate (or at least understand) the disgust of the perpetrator were crystallised through judicial revulsion towards advances of homosexual intimacy and identity. By conflating terms such as "advance" and "aggression" and coupling them with revulsion rhetoric, the concurring judgments secured the Court's emotional inability to separate non-violent and violent intimacies in relation to homosexuality. In particular, for Green, his disgust over unwanted homosexual advances was articulated through a history of child sexual assault in relation to his siblings. Disgust confused, rather than clarified, what exactly acted as the tipping point for provoking lethal violence in this case. The judgment can be read as presenting Green's provocation through two abjected forms of intimacy. The Court construed sexual violation through its rendering of a "queer friendship" (Gillies's abuse of Green by flirting with him) and "queer kinship" (the abuse Green and his siblings endured from his father). Judicial revulsion at these queer forms of touching conflated heterosexual abuse with homosexual desire (Tomsen 2009: 93–5). Taken together, these queer intimacies were judicially repudiated in order to accommodate the homophobic susceptibilities of "ordinary" heterosexual men.

The compassionate dissent – exceptionalising homophobia

Despite the majority's use of disgust to render homophobia as an ordinary response, homophobia can be framed as an exceptional or unusual social bias. Kirby J's dissent took a different emotional route with disgust to do this. In particular, he found that the majority judgments were disturbing because they were unable to see (or sense) that gay intimacy could be non-violent. Kirby J held that non-violent sexual advances were problematic, but not provocatively disgusting as a matter of criminal law. Kirby J began by detailing the minutiae of the brutal attacks and followed with an overview of the development of provocation law to critique the way in which the jurisprudence of the majority prejudicially allowed the ongoing abjection of homosexual intimacy and identity as a threat in need of containment, which assumed reasonable or ordinary persons were homophobic. Kirby J held:

> For the law to accept that a non-violent sexual advance, without more, by a man to a man could induce in an ordinary person such a reduction in self-control as to occasion the formation of an intent to kill, or to inflict grievous bodily harm, would sit ill with contemporary legal, educative, and policing efforts designed to remove such violent responses from society, grounded as they are in irrational hatred and fear.
> (*Green* 1997: 408)

His dissent made explicit reference to the broader context of homophobic violence sparked by hatred and fear. While sentencing legislation recognised that sexual orientation may be an aggravating factor in relevant "hate crimes", it could simultaneously mitigate the charge of murder to manslaughter in those very same circumstances (Golder 2004: 4). Drawing upon the broader institutional and legal efforts to address this, Kirby J surmised that the existence of HAD would "sit ill" with broader reform projects. Judicial concern was focussed on identity: gay men were the victims of violence and not the perpetrators of it. HAD "sickened" the law. Read alongside the "irrational" emotions of hatred and fear directed towards queer identities, in contradistinction to the majority, Kirby J expressed disgust towards a defence that legitimised homophobia and this formed this basis to stop HAD from advancing. Kirby J redirected disgust away from Green's behaviour to the law itself. For Kirby J, HAD fostered abject prejudice by exceptionalising same-sex advances at the expense of the rights of sexual minorities to live free from violence.

Kirby J held:

> In my view, the "ordinary person" in Australian society today is not so homophobic as to respond to a non-violent sexual advance by a homosexual person as to form an intent to kill or to inflict grievous bodily harm.
>
> (*Green* 1997: 409)

Kirby J's judgment moved against the disgust articulated by the majority by suggesting that a non-violent sexual advance – even given the appellant's specific circumstances – could not create an excusable intent to kill or inflict grievous bodily harm. The ordinary person was not homophobic. Coupled with Kirby J's previous comments about the role of law in remedying violence against gay men, the common law was recuperated as a place for eliminating homophobia.

Kirby J's redirection of disgust, however, generated different legal consequences. He sought to equate the potential "offensiveness" of heterosexual and homosexual advances:

> Any unwanted sexual advance, heterosexual or homosexual, can be offensive. It may intrude on sexual integrity in an objectionable way. But this Court should not send the message that, in Australia today, such conduct is objectively capable of being found by a jury to be sufficient to provoke the intent to kill or inflict grievous bodily harm.
>
> (*Green* 1997: 416)

By construing the same-sex advance as indistinguishable from the heterosexual kind, Kirby J's dissent covered over the way disgust enabled the majority to reason towards the existence of HAD in the first place. In *Green*, the differences in interpretation arose due to the affective positioning of heterosexuality (as a norm) while recoiling from "unusual" homosexuality (as queer). Reading emotion shows that the distinguishing doctrinal feature of HAD is the extent to which culpability for murder could be mitigated simply by saturating the jurisprudential space with revolting representations of the homosexual subject as a disorienting threat, which backgrounds the subject's status as a victim. In *Green*, queer intimacy and identity could only be imagined in relation to this norm where they were threatening or dangerous. For the majority, Gillies's act generated a disgust that could be excused as provocation. For the dissent, Green's act of lethal violence was disgusting to a community seeking to remedy violence against sexual minorities who seek to express their intimacy and identity.

By following disgust, through both its progressive and homophobic enactments in *Green*, we can see how jurisprudence crystallises disgust to individualise injury (whether it is the touch of homosexuality or the harm of homophobia) while occluding social conditions that make those disgusting injuries possible. While other scholarly critiques focus on discourse and doctrine to offer recommendations for law reform in relation to HAD, reading emotion allows scholars to observe how disgust can enable progressive condemnation of homophobic injury while evaluating how that disgust is capable of obscuring queer intimacies and identities.

Queering disgust

Following disgust through the above cases highlights that it is a series of emotional enactments, not simply a set of homophobic social norms or narrow legal doctrines, which obstruct (by criminalising) the recognition of queer intimacies. This section shifts from the analytic tracking of disgust to evaluate the politics of using disgust to remedy homophobic injury and further same-sex intimacy and gay identity. In *Lawrence*, sex was enabled insofar as disgust could be contained or expunged. *Lawrence* showed that sex that conformed to sentimental ideas of intimacy could work to cover over the previous disgust exhibited towards homosexuality that rendered it judicially unpalatable in *Bowers*. Alternatively, the framing of privacy in the *Wolfenden Report* attested to the fact that homosexual intimacy and identity were tolerable to the extent that "offensive" conduct that generated disgust could be contained in a private zone. In *Lawrence*, covering over disgust when construing same-sex intimacies allowed the law to judicially ingest gay intimacies without risking sickness or recoil (Ahmed 2004: 94). Such legal progress was made possible by the shifting emotions in jurisprudence – moving from disgust in public to sentimentality in private.

However, the containment and redirection of disgust within private spaces placed queer intimacies (non-conjugal, polyamorous, sadomasochistic) and queer identities (sadomasochists) outside the reach of legal protection. For lawyers and judges interested in pursuing greater sexual freedom, reading emotion shows how legal affirmation of gay sex (i.e. sodomy) is sustained by homophobic aversions to queer intimacy (i.e. sadomasochism). Rather than attempting to abandon disgust, law must reckon with the ways such emotion arranges injury, intimacy, and identity. Disgust facilitated forms of legal containment that decriminalised homosexuality while sequestering such intimacies and identities from public view. Sentimentality emerged as an antidote to homophobic disgust by rendering both the injurious impact of sodomy laws and the value of same-sex intimacy through a spatial separation of "good" (domesticated) gay intimacy from "bad" (sadomasochist) queer intimacies. Activists, lawyers, and judges who wish to make space for sexual freedom must confront the containing gestures of disgust and sanitising moves of sentimentality through their judicial crystallisation to avoid foreclosing intimacies and identities that queer those affective terms of recognition.

An analytic focus on jurisprudential articulations of disgust can further the political potential of anti-homophobic critiques by problematising how private/

public binaries are emotionally sustained and undone. *Brown* implied that privacy rights could be circumscribed and would not guard against hypervisible, disgusting kinds of queer sexual behaviour. Specifically, Lord Jauncey's judgment framed sadomasochist sexual practices as ones that rendered the public/private distinction porous. Even when undertaken in private spaces, homosexual intimacies must conform to a sentimentalised imaginary of romantic or monogamous intimacy in order to avoid injuring public health sensitivities. Here, the jurisprudential enactments of disgust worked to police the boundaries between public and private. On the one hand, the activities undertaken in *Brown* occurred within a home and the wounding was confined to the individuals who consensually participated in the activity. Yet, on the other hand, judicial disgust amplified the scope of sexual injury and rendered it into something capable of disrupting a heterosexual order through tropes relating to sexually transmitted infections, youth corruption, and violent incivility.

Taken together, the sodomy and sadomasochism cases reveal some of the (hetero)normative consequences of expunging disgust from law: queer intimacies and identities domesticated through normative ideas of monogamous and enduring partnerships are covered over within the private space, zoned away from corrupting the public. Cases with different outcomes dealing with gay sex can be read through their shared emotional content. Reading emotion in cases such as *Lawrence* alongside *Brown* demonstrates how disgust can bring scholars, activists, lawyers, and judges closer to making room for queer sexual possibilities in the law. Janet Halley critiques the normative construction of abjection, victimhood, and negativity, arguing that a queer theory of law can enable us to think productively about negative emotions (Halley 2004: 25). Instead of suggesting that negative emotions only work to actively "disapprove" of prejudice (or a practice), Halley invites scholars to consider how discomforting sexual practices can create new avenues for sexual politics that do not descend into moralising about their negativity. Reading disgust enables an analytic focus on how negativity and antinormativity relate to legal progress. My readings of *Lawrence* and *Brown* make visible how law recognises some gay bodies and desires by attaching them to sentimentality and repels some queer intimacies and identities by attaching them to disgust. Reading emotion becomes a political strategy for lawyers and judges who wish to loosen those emotional attachments to make greater room for sexual freedom.

Disgust is an emotion that "sticks" ideas of waste and contamination to objects that are purported to bring such ideas about (Ahmed 2004: 89–90). In *Green*, using disgust to juxtapose Kirby J's dissent with Brennan CJ's and McHugh J's judgments captures the difficulties of conceiving disgust and homosexual intimacy or identity in static terms. In thinking about progressive demands to abolish HAD, I defer to a cautionary note offered by Cynthia Lee: a statutory exclusion of HAD will enable homophobia to persist in other, less visible, ways. Lee notes that the only way to contest emotional stereotypes of gay men as deviants or predators is to draw attention to the cultural (as well as legal) currency that enables such investments (Lee 2003: 247–59). For Lee, the focus on the technical aspects of HAD (and their abolition) obscures broader concerns about how homophobia is articulated in legal defences. In taking this caution seriously, reading emotion lets scholars recognise the affective value of (abolishing) homophobic defences in criminal law while identifying how lawyers and judges might confront emotional attachments to contest homophobic injury. Statutory abolition of HAD, for example, risks covering over institutional forms of homophobia that contribute to queer injury and impede intimacy and identity. If HAD derives its judicial force from disgust, then detaching from it will require more than a shift in statutory interpretation. Writing on the recent murder of US high school student Lawrence King by a fellow classmate, David Perkiss argues that anti-gay hostility can only be addressed by confronting the law (and its complicity) rather than through a single legal act of rhetorical repudiation (Perkiss 2013: 784). In other words, making HAD more visible by providing greater context to social manifestations of bigotry could better enable a jury to critically reflect on its import (see Lee 2003).

Eliminating homophobia in law, however, demands more than a self-reflexive discursive engagement. It necessitates confronting the politics of homophobic abjection. To illustrate this, I want to return to my reading of disgust through the lens of "touch" in *Green*. Here, I refer to "touch" in the way that it has been theorised by Ann Cvetkovich – as a concept that reaches across the emotional and physical, indicating that emotions can impress upon us in a way that feels physical (Cvetkovich 2003: 51). In her work, Cvetkovich details how affects associated with trauma and melancholy, partly catalysed by the AIDS crisis, circulate to create public cultures (Cvetkovich 2003: 47). In the analysis above, I touched on how judicial enactments of disgust shaped the public terms by which homosexual intimacy and identity could be understood as both an injury to social and bodily integrity and as expressions to protect against an individual's exceptional violence. I want to take this further here to show how disgust in *Green* manifested through varied (and conflicting) forms of literal and metaphorical touching. Emotional readers of the case could observe that disgust shaped HAD in two distinctive ways: it condoned violent homophobia (Brennan CJ, McHugh and Toohey JJ) and condemned it (Gummow and Kirby JJ). Disgust circulated (albeit differently in each judgment) in all the judgments in *Green*. Green's disgust of Gillies's advance was used to mitigate the heinous nature of killing, the High Court crystallised Green's homophobic disgust in order to "weight" Gillies's conduct and consider whether it amounted to provocation (and some discerning readers of the case were disgusted by the use of homophobic sentiment to partially excuse an act of homicide). In its homophobic articulation, disgust directed at literal touch (Gillies advance on Green) pressed the Court to protect the integrity of Green's masculinity. In its progressive repudiation, disgust directed at literal touch (Green's stabbing of Gillies) pressed a dissenting minority to protect the integrity of a gay community that experienced homophobic violence with impunity.

Reading disgust allows scholars and activists to challenge pro-LGBT reform agendas that redirect disgust from gay men to condemn homophobes. Instead of severing disgust from law, the dissenting judgment in *Green* illustrated that disgust has the capacity to attach to new norms or ideas. Kirby J's dissent typified an alternative politics to the disgust rhetoric relied on by the majority. Specifically, Kirby J's dissent directed disgust towards the majority's belief that a homosexual advance alone could ever be enough to constitute legal provocation. While that approach sought to work against homophobia, Kirby J's judgment exposed how the problematic mobilisation of disgust worked by sticking disgust to some objects, while leaving other (possibly harmful) objects – such as laws denying equality to same-sex couples – without its visceral taint. By localising Gillies's sexual advance, Kirby J attempted to excise the revulsion that underpinned Green's violence from the rest of society. Green became what Ahmed calls the "affect alien" or "hateful homophobe" (Ahmed 2010: 41–2). Far from being ordinary, Green's homophobia was aberrant or "alien" to the community. Its presence discomforted the law. In making this argument, Kirby J reimagined society as progressing towards the elimination of homophobia through both legal and educative "efforts". Both Green's homophobia and the homophobia legitimated by the majority were alien to Kirby J precisely because they sat "ill" with other social changes (*Green* 1997: 408).

Much of the legal scholarship that I discussed earlier implicitly urges an emotional reader of this case to ask what then should we do with the disgust that confronts the court when it seeks to adjudicate the sorts of horrific homophobic acts that occurred in *Green*. Dan Kahan argues, in contrast to Nussbaum, that disgust should be cultivated in the law for progressive responses to crime. Disgust can be used as an emotion capable of rendering moral judgment. Specifically, Kahan argues that since disgust inheres in law regardless of changing social norms, it is futile to repudiate disgust (Kahan 1999: 65). Instead, disgust should be directed towards objects or individuals "worthy" of its emotional force. Kirby J specifically took up this point of redirection or appropriation in a dissent that stated that what "sat ill" was not Gillies's conduct but the idea that the law should give credence to homophobia. Instead, he suggested that disgust should not be ceded to those who use it as an instrument to oppress. Kahan would likely approve of Kirby J's progressive appropriation of disgust because he effectively redirected disgust from the oppressed to the oppressor: he made homophobes accountable for their homophobia.

However, Kirby J's refusal to entertain the ordinariness of homophobia covered its pernicious circulation. Specifically, disgust was used here as a public enactment for the moral condemnation of Green because his homophobia was seen as a failure to come "forward" with the rest of ordinary (read: non-homophobic) people. Homophobia, not homosexuality, was backward. Moreover, *Green* could be used as an example to generate a different kind of legal disgust if adjudicated through a "hate crime" paradigm (discussed in the next chapter). Homophobic disgust, as HAD necessitates, may no longer be referable to the "ordinary person", but that does not mean that it has simply been expunged from legal circulation. In fact, by suggesting that homophobia is a non-issue in the broader community, cases that follow a similar emotional tread to *Green* can cloud judicial perceptions of just how pernicious and pervasive homophobia remains. Indeed, a cursory examination of the rates of homophobic violence, vilification, and harassment around the time that the case was decided in New South Wales reveals that it persisted at terrifyingly common (or even "ordinary") levels (see NSW Attorney General's Department 2003). Homophobia was far from exceptional in the mid-1990s, any more than it is today. Additionally, an affective focus on physical violence against sexual minorities as the measure of homophobia can also eclipse the verbal, psychological, and symbolic injuries that operate affectively to shape queer identities and intimacies (Mason 2002: 74–6). Kirby J's progressive appropriation of disgust in order to direct it to homophobic individuals, rather than homophobic institutions, rendered the dissent emotionally indifferent to the ubiquity of homophobia: society was not as progressive as Kirby J would have thought. As Cvetkovich argues, homophobic violence is "shocking" not simply because it is sensational, but because it points to systemic manifestations of violence that are yet to be recognised (Cvetkovich 2003: 273). Reading emotion cautions lawyers and judges against a politics of appropriation that exceptionalises homophobia using disgust because such emotional attachments cover over the legal maintenance of homophobia. Scholars, activists, lawyers, and judges have to confront and loosen these attachments to eliminate the circulation of homophobia more broadly.

Conclusion

Activists and scholars must interrupt celebratory accounts of progress in cases that redirect disgust as a way to embrace gay intimacy and identity. Reading emotion in contrasting cases like *Lawrence*, *Brown*, and *Green* made clear how the containment of disgust in private space, through sentimentality, obscured forms of queer intimacy (sadomasochism or non-conjugal forms of gay sex) that could injure (hetero)social orders. These cases ambivalently mobilised disgust alongside desire and perversity to criminalise queer intimacies and identities associated with homosexuality. By following disgust, I was able to frame the affective relationship between cases decriminalising sodomy and criminalising sadomasochism and map the forms of legal progress possible in each. I then examined how disgust was embraced for progressive purposes to end the "homosexual advance defence" and how this disgust rendered gay injury, intimacy, and identity as both ordinary and exceptional. Reading emotion in pro-LGBT cases is necessary in order to analytically register the disparate forms of injury, intimacy, and identity disgust arranges in law and taking account of disgust is politically valuable to challenge what this arrangement keeps hidden or criminalised. Instead of celebrating legal redirections of disgust as paradigmatic of progressive jurisprudence, reading emotion brings scholars and activists closer to understanding how disgust obscures homophobic injury. Making space to confront legal attachments to disgust, rather than redirecting or containing them, is important if lawyers and judges are to address homophobic injury without abjecting queer intimacies and identities in the process.

I turn in the next chapter to consider pro-LGBT hate crime cases aimed at eliminating homo/transphobic injury and enabling queer intimacies and identities through "hateful" criminal laws.

Notes

1 For a more detailed discussion of "the homosexual" as a relatively recent social, historical, and political category, see Foucault (1977).
2 This point connects into the broader legal proscriptions against buggery that avoided naming specific acts.
3 Lesbian, queer, and bisexual women suffered social and legal violence outside buggery criminalisation (see Robson 1998: 59–60). While jurisprudence on decriminalisation cites non-discrimination and equality, the right to sexual privacy has been a key anchoring point for successful litigation and law reform in this area (see *Dudgeon* 1981; *Lawrence* 2003; *Naz Foundation* 2009; *Toonen* 1994).
4 Ten years after the *Wolfenden Report* was published, England passed the *Sexual Offences Act 1967* to implement the Committee's recommendations and partially decriminalise homosexuality.
5 Subsequent judicial citations of *Brown* highlighted the way in which senses of contagion and danger underscored responses to non-matrimonial sexual intimacies (irrespective of whether or not they were homosexually oriented). *R v Meachen* involved the fisting of a woman who was drugged, while *R v Konzani* involved a promiscuous man spreading HIV in the community. When *Meachen* and *Konzani* are read alongside *Brown* in terms of disgust, they highlight how individuated forms of injury (literal wounding) can be emotionally understood in broader social terms (metaphorical wounding of civility).
6 During the trial, the primary judge refused to direct the jury to consider the question of provocation per (now amended) s 23(2)(b) of the *Crimes Act 1900* (NSW). See also, New South Wales Legislative Council Select Committee on the Partial Defence of Provocation (2013).
7 Disgust is not isolated to homophobic violence. Other areas of criminal law, such as those dealing with lethal and non-lethal violence, engender disgust (see Dan Kahan 1999: 63–79).

References

Ahmed, S., 2004. *The Cultural Politics of Emotion*. Oxford: Routledge.
Ahmed, S., 2010. *The Promise of Happiness*. Durham: Duke University Press.
Attorney General's Department of New South Wales. 2003. *You Shouldn't Have to Hide to Be Safe: A Report on Homophobic Hostilities and Violence against Gay Men and Lesbians in New South Wales* (December), www.lawlink.nsw.gov.au/lawlink/cpd/ll_cpd.nsf/vwFiles/Hide2BSafeExec.pdf/$file/Hide2BSafeExec.pdf (accessed 5 August 2016).
Ball, C., 2010. *From the Closet to the Courtroom: Five LGBT Rights Law Suits That Have Changed Our Nation*. Boston: Beacon Press.
Berlant, L., 1997. *The Queen of America Goes to Washington City: Essays on Sex and Citizenship*. Durham: Duke University Press.

Bibbings, L. and Alldridge, P., 1993. Sexual Expression, Body Alteration, and the Defence of Consent. *Journal of Law and Society*, 20(3), 356–70.
Blackstone, W., *Commentaries on the Laws of England* (1765–69).
Califia, P., 2000. *Public Sex: The Culture of Radical Sex.* San Francisco: Cleis Press.
Committee on Homosexual Offences and Prostitution, 1957. *Report of the Committee on Homosexual Offences and Prostitution.*
Crofts, T. and Loughnan, A., 2014. Provocation, NSW Style: Reform of the Defence of Provocation in NSW. *Criminal Law Review*, 2, 109–25.
Cvetkovich, A., 2003. *An Archive of Feelings: Trauma, Sexuality, and Lesbian Public Cultures.* Durham: Duke University Press.
Dalton, D., 2000. The Deviant Gaze: Imagining the Homosexual as a Criminal through Cinematic and Legal Discourses. In Carl Stychin and Didi Herman, eds. *Sexuality in the Legal Arena.* London: The Athlone Press, 69–83.
Dressler, J., 1995. When "Heterosexual" Men Kill "Homosexual" Me: Reflections on Provocation Law, Sexual Advances, and the "Reasonable Man" Standard. *Journal of Criminal Law and Criminology*, 85(3), 726–63.
Duggan, L., 2003. *The Twilight of Equality: Neoliberalism, Cultural Politics and the Attack on Democracy.* Boston: Beacon Press.
Eng, D., 2010. *The Feeling of Kinship: Queer Liberalism and the Racialization of Intimacy.* Durham: Duke University Press.
Foucault, M., 1977. *The History of Sexuality (Volume 1): The Will to Knowledge.* London: Penguin.
Foucault, M., 1984. Sex, Power and the Politics of Identity. In Paul Rabinow, ed. *Ethics: Subjectivity and Truth.* New York: The New Press.
Franke, K. M., 2004. The Domesticated Liberty of *Lawrence v. Texas. Columbia Law Review*, 104(5), 1399–1426.
Gleeson, K., 2008. Freudian Slips and Coteries of Vice: The Sexual Offences Act of 1967. *Parliamentary History*, 27(3), 393–409.
Glick, M. H., 2011. Of Sodomy and Cannibalism: Dehumanisation, Embodiment and the Rhetorics of Same-Sex and Cross-Species Contagion. *Gender & History*, 23(2), 266–82.
Golder, B., 2004. The Homosexual Advance Defence and the Law/Body Nexus: Towards a Poetics of Law Reform. *E Law: Murdoch University Electronic Journal of Law*, 11(1), 1–67.
Gurham, D., 2011. Legal Authority and Savagery in Judicial Rhetoric: Sexual Violence and the Criminal Courts. *International Journal of Law in Context*, 7(2), 117–37.
Halley, J. I., 2004. Queer Theory by Men. *Duke Journal of Gender Law and Policy*, 11, 7–54.
Henderson, E. M., 2000. I'd Rather Be an Outlaw: Identity, Activism, and Decriminalisation in Tasmania. In Carl Stychin and Didi Herman, eds. *Sexuality in the Legal Arena.* London: The Athlone Press, 35–50.
Hoad, N., 2007. *African Intimacies: Race, Homosexuality and Globalisation.* Minneapolis: University of Minnesota Press.
Howe, A., 1997. More Folk Provoke Their Own Demise (Homophobic Violence and Sexed Excuses – Rejoining the Provocation Law Debate, Courtesy of the Homosexual Advance Defence). *Sydney Law Review*, 19, 336–65.
Howe, A., 2000. Homosexual Advances in Law: Murderous Excuse, Pluralized Ignorance, and the Privilege of Unknowing. In Carl Stychin and Didi Herman, eds. *Sexuality in the Legal Arena.* London: The Athlone Press, 84–99.

Kahan, D. M., 1999. The Progressive Appropriation of Disgust. In Susan A. Bandes, ed. *The Passions of Law*. New York: New York University Press, 63–79.

Kristeva, J., 1982. *Powers of Horror: An Essay on Abjection*. New York: Columbia University Press.

Lee, C., 2003. *Murder and the Reasonable Man: Passion and Fear in the Criminal Courtroom*. New York: NYU Press.

Lee, C., 2008. The Gay Panic Defense. *UC Davis Law Review*, 42, 471–566.

Lunny, A. M., 2003. Provocation and "Homosexual" Advance: Masculinized Subjects as Threat, Masculinized Subjects under Threat. *Social & Legal Studies*, 12(3), 311–33.

Mason, G., 2002. *The Spectacle of Violence: Homophobia, Gender and Knowledge*. London and New York: Routledge.

McDonald, E. 2006. No Straight Answer: Homophobia as Both an Aggravating and Mitigating Factor in New Zealand Homicide Cases. *Victoria University of Wellington Law Review*, 37, 223–48.

Miller, W. I., 1997. *The Anatomy of Disgust*. Cambridge: Harvard University Press.

Mison, R. B., 1992. Homophobia in Manslaughter: The Homosexual Advance as Insufficient Provocation. *California Law Review*, 80(1), 133–78.

Moran, L., 1995. Violence and the Law: The Case of Sado-Masochism. *Social & Legal Studies*, 4, 225–51.

Moran, L., 1996. *The Homosexual(ity) of Law*. London and New York: Routledge.

Moran, L., 1999. Law Made Flesh: Homosexual Acts. *Body & Society*, 5(1), 39–55.

Naffine, N., 1997. The Body Bag. In Ngaire Naffine and Rosemary Owens, eds. *Sexing the Subject of Law*. Pyrmont: Law Book Co of Australasia, 79–93.

New South Wales Legislative Council Select Committee on the Partial Defence of Provocation. 2013. *The Partial Defence of Provocation* (April), http://rlc.org.au/sites/default/files/attachments/Partial%20defence%20of%20provocation_Final%20report.pdf (accessed 5 August 2016).

Nussbaum, M. C., 2004. *Hiding from Humanity: Disgust, Shame and the Law*. Princeton: Princeton University Press.

Nussbaum, M. C., 2010. *From Disgust to Humanity: Sexual Orientation & Constitutional Law*. Oxford: Oxford University Press.

Perkiss, D. A., 2013. Panic Defense at Trial: Lessons from the Lawrence King Case. *UCLA Law Review*, 60, 778–824.

Race, K., 2009. *Pleasure Consuming Medicine: The Queer Politics of Drugs*. Durham: Duke University Press.

Ramakrishnan, K. B., 2011. Inconsistent Legal Treatment of Unwanted Sexual Advances: A Study of the Homosexual Advance Defense, Street Harassment, and Sexual Harassment in the Workplace. *Berkeley Journal of Gender, Law & Justice*, 26, 291–355.

Robson, R., 1998. *Sappho Goes to Law School: Fragments in Lesbian Legal Theory*. New York: Columbia University Press.

Rubin, G., 1984. Rethinking Sex: Notes for a Radical Theory on the Politics of Sexuality. In Carol Vance, ed. *Pleasure and Danger: Exploring Female Sexuality*. Boston and London: Routledge, 143–79.

Sedgwick, E., 1990. *The Epistemology of the Closet*. Berkeley: University of California Press.

Smyth, M., 2006. Queers and Provocateurs: Hegemony, Ideology, and the "Homosexual Advance" Defense. *Law & Society Review*, 40, 903–30.

Spindelman, M., 2004. Surviving *Lawrence*. *Michigan Law Review*, 102, 1615–67.
Steinberg, V. L., 2005. A Heat of Passion Offense: Emotion and Bias in "Trans Panic" Mitigation Claims. *Boston College Third World Law Journal*, 25, 499–524.
Stychin, C. F., 1995. *Law's Desire: Sexuality and the Limits of Justice*. London and New York: Routledge.
Suk, J., 2009. *At Home in the Law: How the Domestic Violence Revolution Is Transforming Privacy*. New Haven and London: Yale University Press.
Thomas, K., 1992. Beyond the Privacy Principle. *Columbia Law Review*, 92, 1431–516.
Tolmie, J., 2012. Consent to Harmful Assaults: The Case for Moving away from Category Based Decision Making. *Criminal Law Review*, 9, 656–71.
Tomsen, S., 2006. Homophobic Violence, Cultural Essentialism and Shifting Sexual Identities. *Social & Legal Studies*, 15(3), 389–407.
Tomsen, S., 2009. *Violence, Prejudice & Sexuality*. New York and London: Routledge.

Legislation

Crimes Act 1900 (NSW).
Offences Against the Person Act 1861 (UK).
Sexual Offences Act 1967 (UK).

Cases

Bowers v Hardwick, 478 US 186 (1986).
Dudgeon v United Kingdom, App No 7525/76 (ECtHR, 22 October 1981).
Lawrence v Texas, 41 SW 3d 349 (2001).
Lawrence v Texas, 539 US 558 (2003).
Naz Foundation v Government of NCT of Delhi (2009) 160 DLT 277.
R v Brown [1994] 1 AC 212.
R v Green (unreported, New South Wales Court of Criminal Appeal, 8 November 1995).
R v Green (1997) 191 CLR 334.
R v Konzani [2005] 2 Cr App R 14.
R v Meachen, 2006 WL 3006904.
R v Wilson [1997] QB 47.
Toonen v Australia, Communication No 488/1992, UN Doc CCPR/C/50D/488/1992 (1994).

Chapter 3

Healing hate

Queer violence and punishment

Introduction

Disgust directed towards LGBT people rarely features in isolation of other emotions. It accompanies a range of feelings, such as pity, anger, contempt, and hatred. Reading disgust made visible how the law addressed the harms of criminalising homosexuality (injury) and affirmed the liberty of same-sex couples to engage in conjugal sex (intimacy) while containing sexual activities or advances that unsettled public sensitivities (queer intimacy) and punishing exceptional homophobes who threatened that (queer identity). This chapter explores further the affective dimensions of punishing homo/transphobia by reading emotion to show how and why homo/transphobic "hate" has become the subject of legislative and judicial attention in attempts to respond to the violence that LGBT people face. Specifically, I read emotion analytically to trace how the hate directed towards LGBT people is recognised and refracted through pro-LGBT hate crime cases that express hatred towards homo/transphobes to remedy homo/transphobic injury and use this analysis to address the politics of hate in healing homo/transphobia.

I begin by outlining what is meant by homo/transphobic hate and how this has become an object of legal interest. The consequences of this hate are typically understood in relation to the physical assault, rape, or homicide inflicted on LGBT people. This chapter goes further to map the discursive and symbolic dimensions of anti-LGBT hatred and foregrounds its crystallisation in law to explore the extent to which "progressive" articulations of hate protect LGBT intimacy and identity from injury. I begin this mapping by foregrounding the competing emotional claims in the *Hate Crimes Prevention Act of 2009* (US) and its associated "pro-LGBT criminalisation" jurisprudence: LGBT people move from objects of derision with no positive value to vulnerable subjects in need of protection, while homo/transphobes become unredeemable threats to the social order.

This chapter then moves back in time to consider hate in the criminal and civil litigation in response to the murder of Brandon Teena. Brandon Teena, a queer/trans person who was raped and subsequently murdered for reporting the crime, has become an activist emblem for the urgency of hate crime legislation. However, in considering the erasures of sexual violence in the criminal judgments alongside the civil litigation that exposed the state of Nebraska, USA, for its inadequate protection of Teena, I look at (the limits of) the ways in which both individuals and institutions can be made accountable for homo/transphobic injury without emotionally enhanced penalties. In teasing out emotional terms of the civil and criminal cases, I look at how the lack of judicial loathing directed to those who killed Teena meant, at least in part, that the police and community could be held to account for their complicity in Teena's death. I then broaden discussions of pro-LGBT hate crime cases by demonstrating that reading emotion allows scholars to track how hate brings into focus excessive forms of physical violence (injury) to condemn exceptional perpetrators (identity) while obscuring those who disrupt carceral systems and refuse legal labels (queer identity). Reading emotion exposes how legislative reduction of homo/transphobic hatred to the individual and judicial hostility directed at stigmatising the homo/transphobic offender covers over the ways homo/transphobic hate is institutionalised.

Following expressions of hate in pro-LGBT hate crimes cases enables scholars to confront "unremarkable" forms of social injury and examine the political costs of maintaining hate against offenders. I conclude that the emotional appeal of criminalisation as a means of remedying LGBT pain confuses the source of homo/transphobic injuries. By building on the previous chapter, I evaluate how emotional pathologisation of homo/transphobic bigotry, and the personalisation of hate exhibited towards offenders through enhanced legal punishments for homo/transphobic violence, can ultimately eclipse how homo/transphobia is institutionalised in law by this refracted hate. Reading emotion analytically equips scholars to politically critique the terms in which homo/transphobic injury is progressively "healed" by legal interventions. In doing so, this critique shows how scholars, activists, lawyers, judges, and legislators might loosen current insistence on hatefully condemning violent individuals to avoid reproducing disparate forms of injury against sexual and gender minorities that pro-LGBT hate crime cases seek to guard against.

Homo/transphobic hate and the emotional architecture of hate crime law

Homo/transphobic hate

Homo/transphobic hate is a term I use to encapsulate expressions of violence against LGBT people. I use both Stephen Tomsen's and Gail Mason's work as a starting point to argue that this hate is an intense dislike of a group/object that is articulated through/by individuals and institutions. Tomsen argues that while homo/transphobic hate is sometimes pathologised as an individual expression of fear or anxiety, it remains a highly ambivalent and dynamic phenomenon

(Tomsen 2009: 17). Mason suggests that hate is a means of reinforcing the exclusion or containment of queer intimacies and identities through acts of violence (Mason 2005a: 586; Tomsen 2009: 30). Hatred manifests through different spaces, people, and objects (Mason 2005b: 841). Mason suggests that hate mobilises through expressions of closure: to say that one "hates" another means in effect that one finds no redeeming quality in that other. Hate is an investment in a body that is denied any positive value (Ahmed 2004: 45). Much discussion of anti-gay hatred fixates on homo/transphobia and concentrates on gay or trans "bashing", which is typically physical assault – though it also includes rape and homicide (see Ruthchild 1997). However, as discussed in Chapter 1, homophobic violence manifests in affective ways that are not reducible to a punch or a kick. It materialises in the fear that makes LGBT people manage their visibility in public, in the shame that forces individuals to remain in the proverbial "closet", and in the sadness that comes with social exclusion and isolation (Mason 2007: 265). Hatred is apparent in the production of these LGBT exclusions through social hostility to non-heteronormative sexual or gendered differences or identities, the community contempt exhibited towards such differences, and individual desires to "close off" or eradicate such differences that are deemed to lack any positive value. In this chapter, I follow the recognition of homo/transphobic hate – as an expression of closure and exclusion that denies positive value to individuals – in legal interventions that refract hate from LGBT people to homo/transphobes in order to punish them.

The affective architecture of hate crime responses

The marking out of identity differences, acts of injury, and the intimacy between victims and offenders is key to the recognition of "hate" in pro-LGBT criminal law reform. In recent decades, the recognition of homo/transphobic violence has precipitated public demands for criminal law to deal with what is colloquially referred to as "hate crimes". This demand reflects a remarkable shift in the positioning of LGBT identities in the criminal law (see Chapter 2): homosexual criminalisation is replaced by a criminalisation of (some) homophobes. As Ely Aharonson observes, the shift towards criminalisation can be understood in terms of citizenship: hate crimes are typically imagined as a threat to the state's interest in equality, and thus "pro-minority criminalisation" becomes a strategy for reasserting ideals of egalitarian citizenship (Aharonson 2010: 289). These reforms also go beyond concepts of citizenship: community unity or harmony is at stake in hate crime violence. Mason argues that hate crime is an extralegal category that occupies enormous currency in political vernacular. Specifically, it is used to label acts of physical violence, sexual assault, or verbal abuse directed towards subordinated minorities (Mason 2007: 250). Communities, in addition to individual citizens, are seen as "injured" by such crimes. The hostility exhibited against specific individuals becomes transformed into a general fear of violence to those who belong to the targeted minority community. Such symbolic violence can be glimpsed in the way hate crimes "closet" people in the community or force LGBT individuals to manage their (homo)sexual visibility in order to minimise their risk of violence (Mason 2002: 29).

Hate crime legislation can serve as an emotional enactment to reaffirm social orders and police borders of social inclusion (Aharonson 2010: 291). Criminalisation seeks to affirm respect and recognition for subordinated minority identities and intimacies. Specifically, the recognition of hate in violence perpetrated against LGBT people is refracted through legislative responses to the injury by hatefully repudiating the queer identities of the perpetrators of that violence. The specific use of the term "hate" (as opposed to "bias") to characterise such crimes has been the subject of continuing legal debate. In some jurisdictions, "hate" has been legally defined as a "set of emotions that involve extreme ill will towards another person or group of persons" (Mason 2002: 42). Yvonne Zylan, in a slightly different vein, suggests that the emotional investments generated by loathing become institutionalised as a psychological or corporeal feeling that animates contempt towards sexual "others" (Zylan 2011: 115). By focussing on the enactment of hate through ideas of closure – a closure effected through the mobilisation of hostility towards specific bodies – this chapter maps out how the legal crystallisation of hate, unlike disgust or even anger (the subject of the next chapter), manifests as an unrelenting attachment to the negativity of homo/transphobes that produces punitive legal parochialism.

The Hate Crimes Prevention Act of 2009

In the United States (US), following the brutal murders of James Byrd Jr. and Matthew Shepard, there was overwhelming activist mobilisation to demand federal penalties for racist and homophobic violence (see Human Rights Campaign 2010). It is important to note that while the US Congress had previously enacted the *Hate Crimes Statistics Act of 1990*, the federal impetus to investigate hate crimes was largely reserved to data collection rather than individual prosecutions (as the acts in question were otherwise criminal already at a state level). Such legislation was subject to enormous critique for its discretionary application and for its lack of punitive effects (Jacobs and Potter 1997: 8; Maroney 1998: 594–6). The legislation also failed to account for gender-identity-motivated violence. Hate crime was being recorded, but little was being done at a federal level to prevent it. Legislation was introduced following the two highly publicised homicides as an attempt to supplement the perceived statutory deficiencies (18 USC § 249). US President Barack Obama, in commemorating the enactment of the *Hate Crimes Prevention Act of 2009*, emphasised that "no one in America should ever be afraid to walk down the street holding the hands of the person they love" (White House 2009).[1] He continued, "we must stand against crimes that are meant not only to break bones, but to break spirits" (*ibid*). Here, love and hope were invoked to "stand" against the fears and injuries generated by hate crime.

Reading this presidential pronouncement through its emotional register lets scholars observe how claims to optimism and futurity mark a contrast to the treatment of the "homosexual advance" discussed in the previous chapter. Instead of (partially) locating responsibility for death on the victim's sexually assertive or "threatening" behaviour, hate crime laws work to refuse what Kirby J referred to in *Green* as the "ills" of homophobia and what Obama referred to here as the crimes that "break spirits". Hate crime law was invoked as both the recognition of the "seriousness" of such violence and the remedy capable of "healing" insecurity within the community (in this instance, the gay and lesbian community). Obama's celebration of hate crime legislation operated at the level of metaphor: same-sex intimacy and identity was particularised through sentimental and uncontroversial tropes such as love and "holding hands". The non-explicit intimate bonds between two people were marked out as worthy of protection. In other words, gay and lesbian people who "love" by exhibiting romantic intimacies or domesticated identities were to be protected from the brutality of injury.

Criminalising hate crime requires more than holding individual offenders accountable for ill feeling or acts of violence. Legislative responses seek to secure the civil rights of subordinated groups through punitive sanctions directed against violent bigots. Hate crime laws transport an anti-discrimination agenda into the criminal law (Kohn 2002: 270). Hate crime laws (much like the hate crimes themselves) are symbolic statements rather than mechanisms of "crime control" (Jacobs and Potter 1997: 38). They signify a number of emotional investments primarily by invoking a public urgency to address homophobia and restore social order (Moran 2004: 928–9). In the *Hate Crimes Prevention Act of 2009*, the non-incorporated "findings" note that hate crime "disrupts the tranquillity and safety of communities" (18 USC § 249). The findings also go on to state that such violence "devastates not just the actual victim and the family and friends of the victim, but frequently savages the community sharing the traits that caused the victim to be selected" (*ibid*). The legislation purports to recognise the intimate associations between the victims, their families, and the broader community to which the victims belong. In doing so, it imagines the national community as tolerant and inclusive and emotionally casts those who would be liable under the Act as "savage" interlopers.

The legislation's emotional articulation of bigoted violence is a process in which homophobes, instead of homosexuals, are rendered queer threats to the community. In discussing the *Hate Crimes Prevention Act of 2009*, Obama's analogising of hate crime with "savagery" stigmatised offenders as barbaric or uncivilised, while his comments sentimentalised the community as a homogenous site of "tranquillity". In sentimentalising the community as always already safe and welcoming, Obama's words cast those who expressed homophobia as lacking in self-control and deserving of enhanced punishments (Moran and Skeggs 2004: 35). These individuals become emotionally queer to the community by virtue of their "savage" ill feeling towards homosexuality, and that hate threatens an otherwise "tranquil" community. In *Bennett v Texas* (1992), for example, the defendant appealed his sentence for murdering a gay man on the basis that it was excessive. On appeal, the court affirmed the trial decision, noting that the "excessive" violence (in this case, anal injuries), punished with a term of incarceration of 60 years, was an appropriate sentence rather than an "excessive" one (*Bennett* 1992: 22). While the case predated the existence of specific hate crime legislation, it is interesting to note how "excessive" violence was construed as disruptive to the social order and needed to be contained through enhanced (but legally appropriate) penalties. By redirecting hostility from the victim to the perpetrator, a type of mobilisation encouraged by Kirby J in *Green* and Dan Kahan in relation to disgust, *Bennett* showed how homophobia was relatively easy to delineate when it was hostilely described in terms of a single offender who is "wilful" and exceptional in the community (Ahmed 2012: 37–9).

Pro-LGBT, pro-hate: hate crime jurisprudence in the US

In 2002 in California, Gwen Araujo was brutally assaulted and murdered when a few of her acquaintances discovered that she had putatively "male genitalia". The perpetrators, a group of men who were socialising with the victim at the time, were convicted of second-degree murder (*Merel* 2009: 2). I begin with this homicide because it speaks provocatively alongside *Green*: Araujo was murdered because the queering of a social investment in bodies (in this case, the social assumption that women do not have penises) triggered a lethal response. As various legal scholars note in their respective reflections of the case, Araujo was targeted for allegedly "deceiving" others about her gender and for possessing a body that did not conform to a normative idea of "femaleness" (see Buist and Stone 2014; Lloyd 2012; Steinberg 2005). After uncovering Araujo's "real sex", the offenders repeatedly beat her until she died. As in *Green*, the violence was "excessive". In seeking to mitigate responsibility, the defendants, José Merel and Michael Magidson, sought to advance the claim that the discovery that they had had sex with a trans person had triggered an uncontrollable panic that, in the circumstances, could be understood (Buist and Stone 2014: 42; Steinberg 2005: 517). Homophobia and transphobia were fused in this brutal event: the defendants' fears over having an intimate relationship with a woman who did not conform to normative gender expectations were marked by heteromasculine anxieties that such intimacy would, in turn, make them both "gay".[2]

In the above case, it was revealed that the appellant, Michael Magidson, "was enraged and wanted to hurt" Araujo (*Merel* 2009: 8). The jury in the case had rejected the provocation proposition that would have reduced the charge to manslaughter, but had remained divided on whether Araujo's murder constituted a hate crime.[3] On appeal, the convictions were affirmed but the judicial analysis of the appellants' actions revealed how the combination of the perpetrators' disgust directed at Araujo's body and the hatred engendered by the idea that they were "tricked" by a "man" into having sex emotionally triggered the murder. José Merel (the second perpetrator) had looked at Araujo and "saw her as a man, and went out of the room and cried" (*Merel* 2009: 6). Sadness was invoked, alongside disgust and hostility, during his act of lethal violence. While the judgment was unclear as to the particular object of his sadness, Merel's statement arrived following a discussion of Araujo's alleged deception of the men as to her biological status. Merel seemed to cry over both the murder and the fact that he had engaged in sex acts with a "man". The Court's "progressive" refusal to recognise Merel's individual emotions as excuses for murder were subtended by the Court's inability to connect these individual emotions to broader social biases that stigmatise trans women as deceptive.

Following the initial trials, California enacted the *Gwen Araujo Justice for Victims Act* (2006), which barred future defendants from relying on "societal bias" (such as transphobia) when advancing a claim for provocation. The reason for this was simple: while Araujo's death was treated as murder rather than manslaughter, it was not considered a hate crime. Yet, the hostility and rage exhibited by individuals over the idea that a woman could possess a penis revealed homo/transphobic attachments that the Court failed to consider in any detail. The refusal to dismiss "trans panic" reiterated the idea that trans people were deceiving the world about their "true gender" (Steinberg 2005: 518). Such deficiencies precipitated demands for a statutory remedy.

Hate crime laws, like the one prompted by Araujo's murder, have developed disparately from various victim and civil rights movements (Maroney 1998: 578–82). Such laws vary across state jurisdictions in terms of their enactment, enforcement, education, and effect. Legal attempts to intervene in hate violence range from introducing provisions for the specific reporting and gathering of statistics about the prevalence of identity-motivated violence, to increasing penalties for existing crimes where hate or bias was a motivating factor, to creating specific categories of hate crime offences. Yet, the enactments that underpin these legal attempts are far from uniform. This is particularly perceptible in the way hate crime laws split the individual from the institution when considering the types of offences, the grading or classification of bias acts, the use of police discretion, the role of prosecutorial or judicial guidelines, and the kinds of identities and intimacies that ought to be specifically protected (Haggerty 2001: 46). While a history of institutional inaction in responding to a particular crime is acknowledged in these laws, the affective focus on individual punishment crystallises expressions of hostility towards homo/transphobes without making space for addressing social accountability for homo/transphobia.

Identifying hateful intent

The emotional interests of the state in delineating definitional narrowness for hate crime laws are privileged over the queer experiences of both perpetrators and victims of homo/transphobic violence. By transposing my earlier political discussion of the *Hate Crimes Prevention Act of 2009* into the judicial arena,

I now examine how the legislation has criminalised "wilful" bodily injury (and death) "because of" the victim's actual or perceived sexual orientation or gender identity (18 USC § 249(a)(2)). This hate crime law mobilises hostility against "wilful" offenders while leaving the social will untouched in terms of responsibility for LGBT exclusion. It is interesting to note the use of the word "wilful" here – it designates "wilfulness" on the part of the individual or offender. The "wilful" offender is one who obstructs the harmonious social fabric by bringing social intolerance into the fold (Ahmed 2014: 42). In doing so, such offenders are made inassimilable – queer to a purportedly tolerant society. The legislation crystallises hostility towards perpetrators of homo/transphobic violence by assuming a causal tether between LGBT identity and injury through the hatred motivating violence against LGBT people.

In the leading case upholding the validity of the law, the US District Court refused standing to a conservative family association on the basis that causing "headaches and stomachaches" to sexual minorities (a risk posed by the views that this group espoused) did not form a "particular interest" that would generate a threat of prosecution (*Glenn* 2010: 21). While the Court upheld the validity of the federal hate crime statute, it did so noting that, for any federal prosecutions to succeed, federal authorities would need to demonstrate a malicious intent to cause bodily injury (not merely recklessness or negligence) that excluded emotional shock or disorienting queasiness. This position was affirmed on appeal to the US Sixth Circuit Court of Appeals, where the majority held that the appellant's fear of prosecution was misplaced (*Glenn* 2012: 425). The appellant accepted that homophobic speech was violent, while the Court was quick to decouple the two. Criminalising hate crime was given limited scope: it extended to intentional physical violence while expressly excluding pernicious forms of hate speech and other psychic injuries. The Court privileged the physical over the emotional when it came to injury, acts over speech when it came to intimacy, and the immutable over the fluid when it came to identity. It is also important to note that in *Glenn* the emotional tether that bound LGBT identity to injury – the idea of hateful "wilfulness" – was given little critical attention by the Court and instead was treated as self-evident.

There remains considerable critical legal discussion over the best way of understanding the animus motivating hate crimes for the purposes of both eliminating it and holding individuals (legally) accountable for the perpetration of such crimes. As James Jacobs and Kimberley Potter argue, reading anti-gay violence by reference to a causal explanation of individual hatred or "animus" confuses the complex interaction of opportunities and institutions (Jacobs and Potter 1997: 2). Criminalisation privileges intentionality, rather than the subconscious emotional dimensions of animus, to punish offenders (Blake 2001: 123; Zylan 2011: 136). The legal focus on hate alone tends to obscure the complex economy of emotions. On the one hand, hateful violence produces identities of vulnerability by spreading intimidation and fear among those who identify with the social position of the victim. On the other hand, the recognition of such hate is used to individualise anti-LGBT hostility through hostile legislative responses to punish offenders. Taken together, this crystallisation and refraction of hate enacts literal and symbolic violence against the identities of those they purport to protect by defining the intent of those who hate (homo/transphobes) and entrenching the hated (LGBT people) within a narrow emotional prism of violence and victimhood.

Reading emotion makes apparent the relationship between victimhood and offending in pro-LGBT hate crime cases: the pitied victimised LGBT object has its value pitted against the hated homo/transphobic object, and the law works as the instrument to emotionally measure the value of both objects. Bringing together the jurisprudence surrounding the *Hate Crimes Prevention Act of 2009* with a broader public insistence on criminalising homo/transphobic violence, scholars can observe how hate crime generates "emotional thinking" within the terms of law, alongside the emotional public claims calling for criminalisation (Mason 2007: 255; Mason 2014: 76). In particular, the labelling of violence as a "hate crime" is contingent on law's capacity to recognise the "hate" of perpetrators, generating compassion or pity for the victim who is subject to such hate, and refracting that hostility against the acts of the perpetrators. Obama's words welcoming the *Hate Crimes Prevention Act of 2009* are apt here: "we sense where such cruelty begins ... the moment we fail to see in another our common humanity" (White House 2009). Compassion becomes a key emotional enactment for securing moral claims for respect and recognition (Mason 2007: 254). Victims must be palatable objects amenable to becoming the subject of sentimental narratives involving a "common humanity" in order to garner support (Mason 2014: 80–2). The characterisation of a particular act of injury as a "hate crime" is "compelled" by the extent to which perpetrators and victims can generate pity and concern stereotypically associated with their respective intimacies and identities. Hate crimes and the hostile legal interventions that deal with them arrange the terms through which LGBT identities and injuries are recognised for inclusion and protection. Yet, mapping this affective arrangement exposes how LGBT intimacies and identities cannot be too "queer" or they risk being emotionally excluded from legal narratives about homo/transphobic violence.

By reading emotion, it is apparent how emotions serve as anchoring points for legislative recognition of LGBT injury. In contrast to cases dealing with sodomy and sadomasochism criminalisation, such as *Bowers* and *Brown* discussed in Chapter 2, pro-LGBT hate crime cases redirect the meanings of criminality, anxiety, and deviance from homosexuals to homophobes. Yet, such progressive legislative articulations of hate relied on a personalising narrative of hate (see my earlier discussion of Kirby J's reasoning in *Green*) that crystallised hostility towards hateful perpetrators while obscuring the institutional entrenchment of homophobia. Hate crime laws may emotionally render LGBT victims visible and punish anti-LGBT offenders, but they do so at a cost – the covering over of institutional accountability.

Hating and healing: the case(s) of Brandon Teena

Reading emotion in the above cases enables scholars to foreground how hate and hostility shape legal recognition of LGBT injury and identity while condemning offenders as queer deviations to a tolerant public. I want to contrast that discussion by moving back in time to read emotion in the criminal and civil cases that dealt with the murder of Brandon Teena. I use this as a case study because it was not legally marked in terms of a "hate crime". Teena's death brought to the fore the routine injury to which trans people are subject through Teena's queer intimacies and identities. Reading emotion here allows scholars to contrast different legal presentations of (trans)gender identities and the transphobic injuries that shape the protection of those identities.

In her real-crime novelisation, Aphrodite Jones provides a confronting account of the events surrounding John Lotter and Tom Nissen's rape and murder of Brandon Teena in a small town in Nebraska in 1992.[4] This case has been the subject of enormous legal, public, and activist interest.[5] Teena was a martyr at the altar of trans rights, "Brandon Teena was a latter day Joan of Arc" (Jones 1996: 247). Much critical scholarship that touches on this case details how physical (rape, murder) and symbolic (misgendering) injuries manifest through transphobic desires (of Teena's killers, the police, the community) to contain/label gender nonconforming identities (see Buist and Stone 2014; Duggan 2004; Hale 1998; Juang 2006; Ohle 2004). My interest in this case is directed at drawing out emotional enactments in the criminal and civil litigation in order to analyse the judicial (re)distribution of responsibility for transphobia among individual and institutional actors. My reading foregrounds how the lack of jurisprudential hate towards transphobes – refusing to characterise transphobia as an exemplary act of hatred – meant that both Teena's killers and the state could be held accountable for Teena's death.[6]

Individual responsibility – the punishment of Lotter and Nissen

The murder of Teena was not a random act of violence. Unlike other "typical" hate crimes, Teena's murder galvanised enormous public interest due to the personal and communal intimacies between those involved in the crime: Teena's "friendship" with both Lotter and Nissen, Teena's fraught relationship with local law enforcement over fraud (writing bad cheques), and Teena's varied romantic trysts with women from his local community. Lotter and Nissen interacted with Teena on a number of social occasions. They had mutual friends and family. Lotter and Nissen worked in concert to sexually assault Teena and murder him. In Jones's account of the events, the associations between such individuals and institutions provide a melodramatic impetus for an otherwise banal story of life as a trans person in the small town of Falls City, Nebraska (see Jones 1996). I begin with these scenes of intimacy and community because homo/transphobic violence is not strange – it is situated and experienced in specific spaces and relationships that are familiar.

My interest in the criminal judgments relates to the emotions that were absent – largely, the lack of hostility in relation to Teena's sexual assault and the transphobia that underpinned it. Both Lotter and Nissen were charged with, and convicted of, first-degree murder. Yet, the Nebraska Supreme Court's gendering of Teena as a female and the scant attention the Court paid to Teena's sexual assault reproduced the forms of trans erasure that occurred during Teena's rape. In refusing to recognise transphobic bias to repudiate it, the Court was unable to contextualise the sexual assault as a hostile act of gender policing. In *Nebraska v Lotter* (1998), the Court recounted the material facts of Teena's rape and murder by reversing Teena's personal identification as a man: Teena was gendered as a "she" and as an individual who "presented herself [sic] as a man" (*Lotter* 1998: 603). Implicit in this framing was the assumption that anatomical "femaleness" (presumably reducible to possessing an anatomically unaltered vagina) determined one's gender identity. This is not unique: trans people continue to be misgendered and spoken for or "dis(re)membered" within the legal system (Hale 1998: 319; Ohle 2004: 250). Although the judgment made only a few explicit references to Teena's trans identity, much of the Teena's sexual injury was sidelined in the decision. It was discussed insofar as it established a motive for the murder. While it was not surprising that the sexual assault was subordinated to the murder (Teena was no longer a complaining witness and the indictment only related to the murder), it revealed the troubling ways in which an absence of specific hate crime laws could limit discussions of homo/transphobia. The judicial failure to express condemnation of the transphobic hate animating the violence obscured the Court's policing of Teena's gender.

Given the refusal to engage with the transphobic hostilities of the rape itself, and the Court's reiteration of a number of gender stereotypes, it was surprising that the Court went on to dismiss Lotter's claim for mitigation on the basis of external pressures, noting that the "pressure" was created by Lotter's own behaviour. Yet, while this judicial statement did not rely on particularly potent hostility towards Lotter, it did rather banally suggest that the hatred exhibited towards Teena was an emotion of Lotter's own making. We can see echoes here of Kirby J's judgment in *Green*: the "pressure" or "provocation" of having a masculine identity challenged was not sufficient to warrant mitigating murder as manslaughter. Such biases were individual "ills" for which individuals must be held accountable. They were not victims of deception, but rather calculated offenders who deserved to be punished for murder. However, as pointed out in my critique of Kirby J's dissent in *Green* in the previous chapter, Lotter and Nissen were not presented in the appellate jurisprudence as unredeemable hated objects or "savages" (to use the language of the *Hate Crimes Prevention Act of 2009*). The absence of judicial crystallisations of hate, which function as an intense hostility towards an object (such as a homo/transphobe) with no redeemable value, meant the violence inflicted against Teena was not just a matter of Lotter and Nissen's responsibility. The Court did not engage the matter of transphobia directly. But, the absence of enhanced criminal sanctions that could refract judicial hate towards Lotter and Nissen made space for the subsequent civil decisions that considered the role other institutional actors (particularly the local police) played in enabling Teena's murder.

Institutional accountability – state compensations for negligence

The state's failure to protect Teena from injury following his rape became the subject of extensive civil litigation about the emotional impact Teena's death had on his mother.[7] Jo-Ann Brandon's tort claim pursued against Sheriff Charles Laux (in his capacity as an agent for the state of Nebraska) on the basis of Teena's "wrongful death" illustrated a refusal to confine responsibility to Lotter and Nissen. Here, the state also switched position in the litigation: it moved from acting as the prosecuting party seeking to hold Lotter and Nissen accountable for murder, to having to defend its own culpability for failing to protect Teena following the allegations of sexual violence and threats to his life. Brandon, Teena's mother, initiated the civil litigation and argued that Lotter and Nissen's murder was an act of "hate" against "women who dressed like men" and an extension of the sexual assault (*Brandon* 1997: 873). The Court dismissed the federal suit, noting that Laux was not unreasonable for failing to arrest Lotter and Nissen, or for failing to warn Teena about the fact that such arrests had not taken place (*Brandon* 1998: 540).[8] While the Court recognised the possibility of institutional accountability in the state appeal, the jurisprudence still failed to grasp Teena's gender identity, his intimacy with others, and his experiences of transphobic injury. In *Brandon v County of Richardson* (2000), the Court pronounced that Teena (or Brandon, in the Court's reverse gendering) "presented herself [sic] as a man" (*Brandon* 2000: 611). Compacting the discussion of a "gender identity disorder" alongside Teena's childhood sexual abuse presented the two as correlated (if not causally linked).

However, despite these conflations, the Court pursued a more rigorous analysis of Laux's conduct by bringing to the fore the way "disbelief" and "deception" structured the institutional injury that Teena endured. The Court began by noting Laux's dehumanising reference to Teena as an "it" when he first interviewed Teena about his sexual assault (*ibid*). This reference was expanded through the Court's confronting account of Laux's questions to Teena, which expressed ongoing disbelief. Laux stated: "I can't believe that if he pulled your pants down and you are female that he didn't stick his hand in you or his finger in you" (*Brandon* 2000: 612). Laux's titillation with the sexual violence was driven by his perverse curiosity about Teena himself: "Why do you run around with girls instead of, ah, guys being you are a girl yourself?" (*ibid*). Laux's statement presumed Teena's gender identity, which was necessarily assumed to be a heterosexually oriented one. Sexual and gender nonconformity was covered over by Laux's disbelief. Much of his questioning revolved around Teena's credibility. Laux aligned Teena's previous convictions for forgery to his identity, arguing that he "had been deceiving people in the community" about his gender (*Brandon* 2000: 613). The Court referenced Laux's hostile treatment of Teena without making Laux himself the subject of hate. Moreover, even though the Court did not use the specific language of transphobic injury, the reasoning enabled a broader reflection about the role of policing institutions in its ongoing perpetuation because the Court was not affectively focussed on rendering Laux (or Lotter and Nissen) queer aberrations to be judicially expelled or eradicated as the sole bearers of homo/transphobia.[9]

Most strikingly, the Court's evocative recognition of emotional distress, while sentimentalising at times, was mobilised through an analysis of trauma rather than hate. Teena's life was given compensable value by holding the state to account for its contribution to his trauma. The legal tests animated powerful emotions: outrage, atrocity, and intolerance. Hate and animus were absent from this common law formulation. Following a discussion of existing case law, the Court held Laux's conduct to be negligent in terms of the legal obligations that state officials owed to citizens who came within their duty of care. Laux was a representative of Nebraska's law enforcement agency with a relationship to Teena, who was a complainant seeking assistance from the state to remedy his sexual assault through the arrest of Lotter and Nissen (*Brandon* 2000: 620). Laux was in a position of power to do this. Moreover, Laux was aware of Teena's state of distress and fear. Institutional intent was established through an analysis of power and pain.

The Court expressed contempt a number of times when determining the "outrageous" character of Laux's conduct. The Court chastised Laux for repeatedly using "crude" and "dehumanising" language in reference to Teena (*Brandon* 2000: 625). The tone of Laux's interview of Teena was "intimidating". The analysis proceeded to note that Laux's dislike of Teena was due to his "negative attitude" towards Teena's gender identity and Teena's failure to respond to his prurient questioning. The Court also moved to recognise that a reasonable investigation of a sexual assault complaint did not exhaust the duty of the county to protect Teena from the threat posed by Lotter and Nissen. By rendering both Laux's contempt towards Teena's gender identity and the county's inaction that resulted from his complaint of sexual injury, the Court expressed its own contempt for such "utterly intolerable" behaviour (*Brandon* 2000: 624). Unlike hate crime legislation discussed earlier that recognises homo/transphobic hate in exceptional terms and refracts hate through hostile legal penalties aimed at punishing exceptionally "evil" homo/transphobic offenders, Laux's behaviour was made "intolerable" here as a proxy for the state's intolerance towards Teena's gender identity and experience of sexual violence. Despite the judicial contempt for Laux's conduct, this contempt was not about making Laux a loathed subject. The Court's remedy for his conduct was directed against the state – not Laux as an individual. Institutional accountability for transphobic sexual injury was maintained alongside that of Lotter and Nissen by refusing judicial enactments that expressed loathing of, in order to refuse value to, individuals. Laux's responsibility was valued at $7,000 (*Brandon* 2002: 837). While this was limited in financial terms, the case at least acknowledged institutional responsibility for the murder of Teena through its contempt for the rape investigation rather than loathing towards Laux.

Queering hate

Reading hate analytically in the Teena litigation and hate crime legislation enables scholars to critique how pro-LGBT hate crime cases produce emotional exceptions that obstruct queer intimacies and identities. As Sarah Lamble articulates, "queer investments in punishment" are central to the production of LGBT rights claims (Lamble 2014: 152). This "taming" of identity and injury satisfies legal demands to fix LGBT people and those who abuse them into a crude legal binary of victim/perpetrator (Adler 2018: 72). I expand on this argument, and arguments about individuating identity and injury, to show that "queer investments in punishment" are made possible through legal expressions of hate. An analysis of emotion makes clear how hate in pro-LGBT cases narrow legal attention to forms of homo/transphobic injury that can be repudiated as both individual and exceptional. Reading emotion reveals how pitied LGBT people (victims) and hateful homo/transphobes (perpetrators) are emotionally co-constructed, as exceptionally vulnerable and exceptionally violent respectively. Reading emotion lets scholars account for how hate secures the recognition of vulnerable LGBT injury, intimacy, and identity through the hostile repudiation of homo/transphobic offenders. Loosening these hostile attachments in law becomes necessary for activists, lawyers, judges, and legislators who wish to make space to address the structural realities of homo/transphobic injuries and queer intimacies and identities that do not fit within the narrow emotional prism of hate crime law.

Making homo/transphobic violence an exceptional matter

As I argued in relation to the *Brandon* cases, the capacity to situate violence in an "ordinary" community meant that outrage, instead of loathing, could be used to effect institutional accountability. In refracting hate to carve out exceptional responses to homo/transphobia, hate crime laws work to patrol emotional responses and produce "covers" for structures that subordinate queer intimacies and identities. Legislative inclusion of specific identity categories is contingent upon whether a history of hate-motivated violence, like that faced by Gwen Araujo, can be rendered emotionally visible to the public. Legislatures must be able to "recognise" minorities and be "moved" to add them (though this operates in a mutually constitutive rather than unidirectional way). The homo/transphobic hate motivating homicide or assault is crystallised as exceptional and refracted in hate crime laws – it is not an "ordinary" act. In *New York v DeLee* (2013), hate crime was punishable to the extent that it sent a "powerful message" about the injury of intolerance and discrimination (*DeLee* 2013: 1146). The emotional visibility of homophobic injury relied on crystallising quite generalised associations between homosexual identity, intimacy, and injury. While Bruce MacDougall cautions against the casual ways in which homosexuality is seen as violent, I would flip this caution to the way homosexuality is seen as victimised by violence (MacDougall 2000: 148). Moreover, despite the promising moves for institutional accountability in the *Brandon* cases, the associations that were made in that litigation between Teena's gender identity and his "disorder" or vulnerability limited the ability for such identities to be considered ordinary or acceptable. Framing LGBT discrimination alongside LGBT identity through vulnerability risks reproducing ideas that such minorities can only be protected from homo/transphobia through recourse to hostile legal remedies that punish those who abuse vulnerable LGBT people. Yet, emotional appeals to a legal order capable of reasserting the rights of sexual or gender minorities by closing down and expelling (certain) homo/transphobes obscure the ways safety for such groups (and the forms of insecurity against which those ideas are defined) are contingent on social conditions (Moran and Skeggs 2004: 11). The refusal to frame homo/transphobic vulnerability or trauma within a broader institutional context of negation and subordination affectively reduces homo/transphobic violence to an individualised injury and marker of LGBT identity.

Hate crime legislation encourages a problematic legal punitivism by privileging the emotions associated with particular (homophobic or racist) individuals over the social harms effected by oppressive institutions. As Aharonson observes, "pro-minority criminalisation" works by recasting victimisation as an injury that can be remedied by the state. Noting the historical context in which hate crime legislation operates alongside broader political movements for minority rights and recognition, Aharonson suggests that hate crime laws tend to disproportionately burden already marginalised groups (Aharonson 2010: 293). In the Teena cases, Lotter and Nissen were both from impoverished backgrounds marked by family abuse. While this certainly does not excuse the violence, Lisa Duggan notes that mobilising public loathing against the offenders worked to sustain fantasies about the violence and "otherness" of working-class masculinity because those prosecuted were disproportionately working class (Duggan 2004: 38; Halberstam 2005: 25). In addition, as evident in *Glenn*, cases that rely on distinguishing speech from violence, or the wilful from the unintentional, risk erasing the experience of homophobic injury. Framing injury in terms of a "hate crime" can often act as a vehicle for managing public outrage or social resentments by rendering unlawful the "emotional harm" suffered by the victim (and the community to which the victim belongs).

These laws also use hate for a punishing (legal) vengeance: under these laws, homophobes are made deserving of exemplary punishment as directed by law (Moran and Skeggs 2004: 40). Public demands to punish Lotter, Nissen, Merel, and Magidson may have stemmed from a desire to "feel" justice. A tension arises at the heart of desiring punishment through the law: injury generates outrage that demands legal ways to strike out against offenders, yet at the same time the refraction of hate or loathing in punitive judicial interventions should caution activists and legislators against returning one form of injury with another (an "eye for an eye") (Murphy 1999: 167). Echoing the emotional impetus of the *Hate Crimes Prevention Act of 2009*, the channelling of public contempt through law reform satiates desires for vengeance "in the name of equality" without ending structural subordination (Spade 2011: 127). This powerful exchange of emotion enables "popular fears and resentments" to manifest legally through the construction of "othered" identities – "savages" deemed to be "disruptive" to both social and political harmony (Charles 2012: 91). Such anxieties reveal how both the victim and the perpetrator can be injured by a legal system that is invoked to deliver justice. Hate directs public interest in pursuing collective vengeance (towards an individual offender), while blocking empathy that may seek to recognise the broader context of the injury.

Even though criminal law generally operates by transforming an individual injury into a wrong against the state, hate intensifies this by transposing an individual crime into a broader history of hate-motivated violence. However, in this process of hateful intensification, the relations between individual and institutional injury are severed. Using the acts of violent offenders (such as Lotter, Nissen, Merel, and Magidson) to individuate the injury of LGBT people (such as Teena or Araujo) works to obscure the social conditions of their suffering (such as the violent social denial of Teena and Araujo's gender or demeaning legal presentation of their genders as deceptive). By turning to the state's monopoly over violence through the vehicle of the criminal law, the state's historical (and ongoing) responsibility for maintaining heteronormative regimes is redeemed through a single act of legal hatred in relation to individual offenders that expels them (through incarceration or death) from the otherwise socially tolerant community. If we read the *Brandon* cases emotionally and reflect on the possibility of the civil routes being sidelined through the use of enhanced criminal penalties, it becomes clear how legal loathing can fixate activist and lawyerly attention to individuals while leaving institutions untouched by outrage. This becomes a hate-cultivating process of (first creating and then) expunging the identities of the exceptionally "bad" offenders and covering over institutional accountabilities for remedying injury. Scholars, activists, lawyers, judges, and legislators need to confront the consequences of such hate in law, and loosen their emotional attachments to it, to make space for recognising and protecting queer identities that do not fit an emotional prism that defines LGBT people in terms of their vulnerability or queer intimacies that are subordinated by (hetero/cis)normative social and legal norms.

Addressing accountability – making space for queer intimacies and identities

LGBT demands for state sanctions against homo/transphobic injuries and hateful expressions are troubling because they conflate the elimination of inequalities with individual punishment (Maroney 1998: 569). In thinking back to the *Hate Crimes Prevention Act of 2009*, I am reminded that legislation is presented as the opposite of, and antidote to, violence (Kaplan 2008: 49; Moran and Skeggs 2004: 19). However, such oppositional claims underwrite the homophobic injury of law by emotionally overstating the identities of offenders and simplifying and sequestering the intimacy (of violence) between offenders and victims. While criminalisation may be seen as "a public expression of caring for minorities", reducing the obligation to "care" to incarceration limits broader opportunities for social change (Haritaworn 2010: 79). Obama's words when celebrating the introduction of the *Hate Crimes Prevention Act of 2009* point to this directly: communities can be sentimentalised to "cover" over bigotry by invoking hateful homophobes or transphobes as queer objects (that cause injury) to be expelled from the community through enhanced criminal penalties. By rendering homo/transphobia as an emotional rather than social problem, punitive sanctions become appealing emotional covers (rather than actual solutions) to an invidious structural injury. Reading emotion makes it possible to contest this by exposing how pro-LGBT hate crime cases can reproduce the homo/transphobic injury they purport to challenge in the first place by misattributing responsibility for violence solely to individual offenders. Seeking to remedy the social impact of hate crime through the individuation of punishment conflates individual action with institutional change. LGBT individuals and homo/transphobes share one common legal trajectory: they have both at different (though overlapping) times been hated as "outlaws" (Burrington 1994: 257; Mogul, Ritchie, and Whitlock 2011: 10). Specifically, appropriating hate for hate crime law often underestimates the emotional (as well as structural) complexity of the act it seeks to remedy and the complicity of the law in punishing queerness.

Reading hate analytically demonstrates how hate functions politically as a way of preserving a (hetero)normative social order. Homo/transphobic hate can be expressed as "cleansing" – preserving the social order by eradicating queer intimacies (Tomsen 2009: 56). Hate cannot be easily deterred. As some analyses of hate crime statutes make clear, the varying rationales of punishment, combined with the causal explanations that subtend them, assume that hate can be juridically codified and sanctioned (Zylan 2009: 34–7). Tomsen suggests that insisting on a strict causal relationship between pathological homophobic feelings and violence is a "fool's beacon" because it distracts us from seeing non-exceptional forms of homophobic violence (Tomsen 2009: 41). While I do not share Tomsen's characterisation of such acts as "foolish", I do agree that his analysis should caution us against reading either (homo)sexual orientation or violence in physically and emotionally exceptional terms. In *Merel*, the Court's inability to critically reflect on transphobia was not due to the absence of "inclusive" hate crime laws. Rather, it resulted from the court's failure to understand how "deception" was being advanced on the basis of normative ideas of sexual anatomy, gender identity, and sexual orientation. Recognising Merel's and Magidson's hate of trans bodies and refracting that hate through judicial condemnation of Merel and Magidson, however, covered over the ongoing injuries perpetrated against trans bodies that are always already construed as inauthentic or fraudulent.

Legislative and judicial expressions of hate narrow queer identities and intimacies in terms of their proximity to violence or injury – that is, LGBT anti-violence legal or policy initiatives repeatedly construe queer individuals as "at risk" and in need of state intervention (Stanko and Curry 1997: 514). Queer intimacies and identities are eclipsed here through an emotional double bind. On the one hand, they are sexually threatening or disturbing figures that need to manage their sexual or gender visibility. Yet, on the other hand, they are poor victims in need of paternalist protection. Even in the various *Brandon* cases, the proximity of trans identity to vulnerability was continually reinforced through the associations between Teena's gender and the sexual abuse he suffered. In relation to the *Lotter* and *Nissen* cases, I showed that pro-LGBT hate crime cases sought to hold individuals accountable for a brutally transphobic homicide, but only did so by disregarding the gendered experiences of sexual violence.

The above readings of hate in pro-LGBT hate crime cases highlight why progressive scholars, activists, and legislators need to loosen hateful attachments when pursuing legal sanctions, both as a means of recognising specific individual injuries and as part of a broader strategy for advancing the eradication of homo/transphobia. In *Glenn*, I noted the ways in which queer bodies were rendered visible in a way that subordinated their identity or intimacy to injury. The act of naming "hate" in an attempt to recognise and remedy LGBT suffering became, ironically, a rhetorical manoeuvre that reinforced the coupling of queerness with violence and homophobia with individuals. These intimate couplings produce violence against LGBT people by pitifully positioning both their identities and their intimacies primarily in proximity to injury. Pushing this further, anti-homo/transphobic hate points to LGBT people as objects in need of perpetual rescuing from vulnerability, while homo/transphobes attract exemplary punishment. Both victim and perpetrator become objects shaped by exemplary enactments of emotion (pity and hate respectively). Loosening the emotional tether that binds them together – by eschewing the overdeterminations of hate – is necessary to make space for queer intimacies and identities that resist pity, vulnerability, and violence.

Alternatively, reading the absence of hate in the Brandon Teena cases highlighted how law could provide greater institutional accountability for transphobic injury. Moving away from expressions of hate show scholars, activists, lawyers, judges, and legislators how it is possible to use law in ways that address both the injurious individual and collective dimensions of homo/transphobia. *Bowles v Florida* (1998) provides an illustrative example of how a failure to consider the individual and institutional dimensions of homophobic violence can obscure the nature of injury. This case involved an appeal of a Florida trial court's decision to allow evidence of the offender's homophobia (from previous conversations) for the purposes of sentencing (*Bowles* 1998: 771). In this case, the defendant, Gary Bowles, was sentenced to death for the murder of Walter

Hinton, a man in Florida who had allowed Bowles to live with him. At trial, the prosecution alleged that Bowles murdered Hinton because he loathed homosexuals. Bowles was a sex worker who disliked sex with men but did it to generate an income (and he had boasted in earlier conversations that he enjoyed "rolling faggots"). The Court held that the evidence of his homophobia, introduced to prove the aggravating elements of the murder, was admissible because it could be tethered to his particular act (Bowles dropped a concrete slab on Hinton while he slept) and to his state of mind at the time (Bowles blamed homosexuals for his ex-girlfriend's decision to have an abortion). Such judicial allowances, however, relied on framing violence as an individual problem. The trial court's decision was overturned on appeal: the references to homophobic prejudice were ultimately deemed unduly prejudicial (*Bowles* 1998: 772). However, ignoring the homophobic hate of individuals in its entirety covers over the homophobic elements of crime while eclipsing institutional accountability. The argument to make institutions receptive to injury (disruptions to carceral systems), queer intimacy (relationships between victims/survivors and offenders), and queer identity (those who do not have fixed labels), like my argument about *Green*, is not designed to background individual responsibility. As my reading of emotion in both *Lotter* and *Nissen* highlighted, loosening legal attachments to hate is not a call to supplant individual responsibility with institutional accountability, which is a different form of erasure. Lotter and Nissen needed to be held accountable for their crimes to avoid displacing their perpetration of transphobic violence on some abstract institution – or, worse, on Teena himself. But, in making space to recognise the transphobic hate animating the crime, my recasting of the Teena cases using hate highlighted that activists and judges must be cautious about refracting hate to offenders in ways that reduce transphobic hate to an exceptionally violent offender who is queer to an otherwise tolerant (read: non-transphobic) community.

Conclusion

Mobilising hate from LGBT people to homo/transphobes does little to challenge the structures that enable anti-LGBT violence. Fetishising hate and injury in pro-hate crime activism does not challenge social exclusions (see Haritaworn 2013; Spade and Willse 2000). This does not mean criminal law is futile (see Simmons 2012). Reading emotion demonstrated that, when hateful and hostile expressions are made visible, scholars could map the ways in which progressive interventions make possible the recognition of homo/transphobic violence through the covering over institutional homo/transphobic injuries that obstruct the expression of queer intimacies and identities. Making pathological claims about homo/transphobic hate and the refusal to grasp its refraction in pro-LGBT cases limit progressive critiques of heteronormative regimes that continue to marginalise LGBT individuals.

Queer legal scholarship must account for emotion to address the disparate ways in which hate injures LGBT people and undermines their intimacies and identities in law. Reading emotion to understand progressive legal interventions targeting hate crime showed that seeking to remedy homo/transphobic injury through refracted legal expressions of hate eclipsed the possibility of addressing both individual and institutional injuries that LGBT people suffer. Following (the absence of) emotion in the Teena cases highlighted alternative routes in pursuing accountability for injury: the cases revealed how the absence of hate meant responsibility could be ascribed to a number of actors. Giving an account of emotion in pro-LGBT cases – to see what injuries, intimacies, and identities it makes visible and obscures – makes space for scholars and activists seeking accountability.

The next chapter follows anger to consider how homo/transphobic discrimination is dealt with in institutional contexts. By reading emotion in pro-LGBT anti-discrimination cases, I shift the focus of this book to public law to analyse the affective ways law recognises discrimination and accommodates LGBT intimacy and identity in public.

Notes

1 The White House, during the current Trump administration, has removed this press release from its website.
2 Accusations of deception or fraud have also been used successfully to prosecute trans and gender nonconforming people in the context of sexual encounters (see Sharpe 2018).
3 This chapter does not detail the complexities of the trial relating to the murder of Gwen Araujo. For a detailed examination, see Lloyd (2012: 820–2).
4 There remains uncertainty about the appropriate pronouns to use when referring to Teena (or Brandon). The wide-ranging interviews Jones conducts with Teena's friends, family, and neighbours reveal one remarkably banal fact about the events: no-one interviewed shared the same perspective on the best way to "label" Teena's identity and the most appropriate way to describe his intimacies with his killers. While I do not wish to reproduce the same discursive violence I am critiquing, based on my reading, I glean a preference for male pronouns in the literature I have read. Therefore, I refer to Teena as a man. However, it is important to acknowledge Teena's gender fluidity. For a more detailed discussion of the ambivalence around naming and gendering Teena, and the "colonising" impulses to claim Teena as a trans man or butch lesbian, see Hale (1998).
5 While the discussion in this chapter focusses on the murder of Teena, it is important to note that Lotter and Nissen murdered Teena along with Lisa Lambert and Philip DeVine. The erasure of DeVine from this narrative has prompted critical analysis on the association of blackness, freedom, and death in public cultures (see Snorton 2017: 177–98).
6 I do not want to overstate that the laws in Nebraska provided adequate remedies for the crime because they disengaged the crime from the question of hate. The absence of specific language to talk about trans intimacies and identities left much of the judicial discussion in the criminal cases bereft of critical nuances about the complex positioning of sexual violence in the context of gender nonconformity.
7 Under Nebraskan law, intentional infliction of emotional distress required the plaintiff to prove that (i) there was intentional or reckless conduct; (ii) the conduct was so outrageous in character and so extreme in degree as to go beyond all bounds of decency and be regarded as atrocious and utterly intolerable in a civilised community; and (iii) the conduct caused emotional distress so severe that no reasonable person should be expected to endure it (*Brandon* 2000: 621).
8 This decision was subsequently affirmed in *Brandon v Lotter* (1998), where the Court expressed caution about ex post facto review of discretionary police decisions

(*Brandon* 1998: 541). Despite the dismissal of the federal claims, the Nebraskan cause of action was upheld. On appeal to the Nebraska Supreme Court, Brandon's claim was allowed and referred back for merits assessment by a trial court.

9 The Court in *Brandon* (2000) drew attention to Laux's institutional responsibility and denied his claim for contributory negligence under Nebraskan law. In the initial determination, the damages for which Laux was liable were reduced by 85 per cent due to the individual actions of Lotter and Nissen. However, insofar as Laux was responsible for an intentional tort (the infliction of emotional distress on Teena), contributory negligence was no defence to it. Even in the context of Laux's negligence in failing to protect Teena, the Court revealed its contempt for Laux's claim for mitigation. The Court stated that it would be "irrational" for a court to reduce the police department's liability for an intervening act (Lotter and Nissen's violence) that was precisely the act against which the department had a duty to protect (*Brandon* 2000: 613).

References

Adler, L., 2018. *Gay Priori: A Queer Critical Legal Studies Approach to Law Reform*. Durham: Duke University Press.

Aharonson, E., 2010. "Pro-Minority" Criminalization and the Transformation of Visions of Citizenship in Contemporary Liberal Democracies: A Critique. *New Criminal Law Review*, 13, 286–308.

Ahmed, S., 2004. *The Cultural Politics of Emotion*. Oxford: Routledge.

Ahmed, S., 2012. *On Being Included: Racism and Diversity in Institutional Life*. Durham: Duke University Press.

Ahmed, S., 2014. *Willful Subjects*. Durham: Duke University Press.

Blake, M., 2001. Geeks and Monsters: Bias Crimes and Social Identity. *Law and Philosophy*, 20(2), 121–39.

Buist, C. L. and Stone, C., 2014. Transgender Victims and Offenders: Failures of the United States Criminal Justice System and the Necessity of Queer Criminology. *Critical Criminology*, 22, 35–47.

Burrington, D. D., 1994. Constructing the Outlaw, Outing the Law, and Throwing Out the Law. *Utah Law Review*, 1, 255–67.

Charles, C., 2012. *Critical Queer Studies: Law, Film, and Fiction in Contemporary American Culture*. Surrey: Ashgate.

Duggan, L., 2004. Crossing the Line: The Brandon Teena Case and the Social Psychology of Working-Class. *New Labor Forum*, 13(3), 37–44.

Haggerty, B. P., 2001. Hate Crimes: A View from Laramie, Wyoming's First Bias Crime Law, the Fight against Discriminatory Crime, and a New Cooperative Federalism. *Howard Law Journal*, 45, 1–75.

Halberstam, J., 2005. *In a Queer Time and Place: Transgender Bodies, Subcultural Lives*. Durham: Duke University Press.

Hale, J., 1998. Consuming the Living, Dis(re)membering the Dead in the Butch/FTM Borderlands. *GLQ*, 4, 311–48.

Haritaworn, J., 2010. Queer Injuries: The Racial Politics of "Homophobic Hate Crime" in Germany. *Social Justice*, 37(1), 69–89.

Haritaworn, J., 2013. Beyond "Hate": Queer Metonymies of Crime, Pathology, and Anti/Violence. *Jindal Global Law Review*, 4(2), 44–78.

Human Rights Campaign. 2010. Questions and Answers: The Matthew Shepard and James Byrd, Jr. Hate Crimes Prevention Act, www.hrc.org/resources/entry/questions-and-answers-the-matthew-shepard-and-james-byrd-jr.-hate-crimes-pr (accessed 5 August 2016).

Jacobs, J. B. and Potter, K. A., 1997. Hate Crimes: A Critical Perspective. *Crime & Justice*, 22, 1–50.

Juang, R. M., 2006. Transgendering the Politics of Recognition. In Paisley Currah, Richard M. Juang, and Shannon Minter Price, eds. *Transgender Rights*. Minneapolis: University of Minnesota Press, 242–61.

Jones, A., 1996. *All She Wanted: The True Story of "Brandon Teena"*. New York: Pocket Books.

Kaplan, M., 2008. Hate Crime and the Privatization of Political Responsibility: Protecting Queer Citizens in the United States? *Liverpool Law Review*, 29, 37–50.

Kohn, S., 2002. Greasing the Wheel: How the Criminal Justice System Hurts Gay, Lesbian, Bisexual and Transgendered People and Why Hate Crime Laws Won't Save Them. *New York University Review of Law and Social Change*, 27, 257–80.

Lamble, S., 2014. Queer Investments in Punitiveness: Sexual Citizenship, Social Movements and the Expanding Carceral State. In Jin Haritaworn, Adi Kuntsman, and Sylvia Posocco, eds. *Queer Necropolitics*. London: Routledge, 151–71.

Lloyd, M., 2012. Heteronormativity and/as Violence: The "Sexing" of Gwen Araujo. *Hypatia*, 28(4), 818–34.

Maroney, T. A., 1998. The Struggle against Hate Crime: Movement at a Crossroads. *New York University Law Review*, 73, 564–620.

Mason, G., 2002. *The Spectacle of Violence: Homophobia, Gender and Knowledge*. London and New York: Routledge.

Mason, G., 2005a. Being Hated: Strange or Familiar? *Social & Legal Studies*, 14(4), 585–605.

Mason, G., 2005b. Hate Crime and the Image of the Stranger. *British Journal of Criminology*, 45, 837–59.

Mason, G., 2007. Hate Crime as a Moral Category: Lessons from the Snowtown Case. *Australian and New Zealand Journal of Criminology*, 40(3), 249–71.

Mason, G., 2014. The Symbolic Purpose of Hate Crime Law: Ideal Victims and Emotion. *Theoretical Criminology*, 18(1), 75–92.

MacDougall, B., 2000. *Queer Judgments: Homosexuality, Expression, and the Courts in Canada*. Toronto: University of Toronto Press.

Mogul, J. L., Ritchie, A. J. and Whitlock, K., 2011. *Queer (In)Justice: The Criminalization of LGBT People in the United States*. Boston: Beacon Press.

Moran, L., 2004. The Emotional Dimensions of Lesbian and Gay Demands for Hate Crime Reform. *McGill Law Journal*, 49, 925–59.

Moran, L. and Skeggs, B., 2004. *Sexuality and the Politics of Violence and Safety*. London and New York: Routledge.

Murphy, J. G., 1999. Moral Epistemology, the Retributive Emotions, and the "Clumsy Moral Philosophy" of Jesus Christ. In Susan A. Bandes, ed. *The Passions of Law*. New York: NYU Press, 149–90.

Ohle, J. M., 2004. Constructing the Trannie: Transgender People and the Law. *Journal of Gender, Race & Justice*, 8, 237–80.

Ruthchild, C., 1997. Don't Frighten the Horses! A Systemic Perspective on Violence against Lesbians and Gay Men. In Gail Mason and Stephen Tomsen, eds. *Homophobic Violence*. Sydney: Hawkins Press, 1–14.

Sharpe, A., 2018. *Sexual Intimacy and Gender Identity 'Fraud': Reframing the Legal and Ethical Debate*. London: Routledge.

Simmons, K. C., 2012. Subverting Symbolism: The Matthew Shepard and James Byrd, Jr. Hate Crimes Prevention Act and Cooperative Federalism. *American Criminal Law Review*, 49, 1863–912.

Spade, D., 2011. *Normal Life: Administrative Violence, Critical Trans Politics, and the Limits of Law*. New York: South End Press.
Spade, D. and Willse, C., 2000. Confronting the Limits of Gay Hate Crimes Activism: A Radical Critique. *Chicano-Latino Law Review*, 21, 38–52.
Snorton, C. R., 2017. *Black on Both Sides: A Racial History of Trans Identity*. Minneapolis: University of Minnesota Press.
Stanko, E. and Curry, P., 1997. Homophobic Violence and the Self "At Risk": Interrogating the Boundaries. *Social & Legal Studies*, 6(4), 513–32.
Steinberg, V. L., 2005. A Heat of Passion Offense: Emotion and Bias in "Trans Panic" Mitigation Claims. *Boston College Third World Law Journal*, 25, 499–524.
Tomsen, S., 2009. *Violence, Prejudice & Sexuality*. New York and London: Routledge.
White House Press Release. 2009. Remarks by the President at Reception Commemorating the Enactment of the Matthew Shepard and James Byrd, Jr. Hate Crimes Prevention Act (28 October 2009), www.whitehouse.gov/the-press-office/remarks-president-reception-commemorating-enactment-matthew-shepard-and-james-byrd- (accessed 5 August 2016).
Zylan, Y., 2009. Passions We Like … and Those We Don't: Anti-Gay Hate Crime Laws and the Discursive Construction of Sex, Gender, and the Body. *Michigan Journal of Gender & Law*, 16, 1–48.
Zylan, Y., 2011. *States of Passion: Law, Identity and the Social Construction of Desire*. Oxford: Oxford University Press.

Legislation

Gwen Araujo Justice for Victims Act 2006 (CA).
Hate Crimes Prevention Act of 2009 (US).
Hate Crimes Statistics Act of 1990 (US).
Political Subdivisions Tort Claims Act 1969 (NE).

Cases

Bennett v Texas, 831 SW 2d 20 (1992).
Bowles v Florida, 716 So 2d 769 (1998).
Brandon v County of Richardson, 566 NW 2d 776 (1997).
Brandon v County of Richardson, 624 NW 2d 604 (2000).
Brandon v County of Richardson, 653 NW 2d 829 (2002).
Brandon v Lotter, 157 F 3d 537 (1998).
Glenn v Holder, 738 F Supp 2d 718 (2010).
Glenn v Holder, 690 F 3d 417 (2012).
Nebraska v Lotter, 586 NW 2d 591 (1998).
Nebraska v Nissen, 560 NW 2d 157 (1997).
New York v DeLee, 108 AD 3d 1145 (2013).
People v Merel, 2009 WL 1314822 (Cal Ct App, 12 May 2009).
R v S (G) (1991) 5 OR (3d) 97.

Chapter 4

Animating anger
Queer discrimination and accommodation

Introduction

While criminal law has addressed individual injury through punitive sanctions, its remedial or restorative power to address homo/transphobic injury is limited. Reading hate foregrounded how the refraction of hostility to punish homo/transphobes functioned to sustain the state's failure to recognise its complicity in perpetrating violence while strengthening institutional intolerance of queer intimacies and identities. In this chapter, I read emotion to show how anger can enable, rather than inhibit, legal interventions to remedy painful experiences of LGBT discrimination (injury) while recognising the right of LGBT people to be visible (identity) and associate with others (intimacy) in public. Anger animates individuals to strike back against the pain caused by a status quo that sustains inequality and pushes beyond such injury to advance justice. This anger is crystallised and refracted through equality laws that render a particular form of discrimination legally intolerable. Specifically, this chapter shows how jurisprudential enactments of anger work to push sexual intimacies and identities away from the injuries of exclusion and discrimination. Reading anger – as an expression that strikes back against pain and pushes away from injury – draws attention to the difficulties, and limits, of publicly accommodating LGBT people who form sexually deviant associations (queer intimacy) and express non-conforming religious sexualities (queer identity) that risk disrupting established social, political, and religious institutions. Reading emotion analytically allows scholars to grasp how these jurisprudential expressions of anger arrange the terms through which law recognises injury and accommodates LGBT intimacy and identity. Making analytic space to follow the disparate dimensions of anger is politically necessary for scholars, activists, lawyers, and judges who wish to loosen emotional attachments in law that fail to accommodate queer intimacies and identities.

I begin by considering how discrimination triggers individuals' experiences of anger. I focus on how anger is expressed through personal and social demands for legal change to eliminate LGBT discrimination. I then use the *Romer v Evans* (1996) litigation in the United States (US) to show how individual anger at discriminatory injury is crystallised in jurisprudence and animates LGB identities that push back against that injury. I then overlay two US "public accommodation" discrimination cases, *Hurley v Irish-American Gay, Lesbian and Bisexual Group of Boston* (1995) and *Dale v Boy Scouts of America* (2000), in order to show how the absence of anger to recognise the right of LGB people to form expressive associations (queer intimacy) and be "out" in a "straight" workplace (queer identity) limits the reach of legal accommodation.

In the final part of this chapter, I consider *Christian Youth Camps Ltd v Cobaw Community Health Services Ltd* (2014) in Australia to track how progressive judicial expressions that crystallise and refract the anger of LGBT people narrow objections to accommodate queer intimacies and identities. Here, I analyse how progressive articulations of anger generate broader thresholds of what constitutes unlawful discrimination but, in doing so, can sometimes reproduce divisions that cover over intersectional injuries, intimacies, and identities (that is, those that do not fit within a lawful/unlawful binary) when pro-LGBT cases try to accommodate them. Making space to mobilise and critique anger is valuable for scholars seeking to expose the reach of pro-LGBT cases when dealing with discrimination, and this exposure makes room for lawyers, activists, and judges to confront judicial attachments to anger that confine or cover queer intimacies and identities.

Animating LGBT anger and discrimination law

Anger is tied to the experience of injury. From the Stonewall Riots in New York City to the Gay and Lesbian Mardi Gras in Sydney, collective anger at moral persecution has been instrumental in protesting homophobic persecution (Stychin 1998: 13–5). In writing about the development of queer social movements, Lauren Berlant notes that collective rioting gave rise to an "expanded politics of erotic description" where anger generated new ways of imagining sexual politics and communities (Berlant 1999: 149). Rioting here both expressed, and was expressed by, anger. My outline of the legal scholarship analysing *Bowers* and *Brown* in Chapter 2, for example, demonstrated how individual people's anger framed responses to the criminalisation of sodomy and sadomasochism. The homophobic disgust mobilised to expel queer intimacies was met with activist anger that such decisions could be made. Perceived discrimination generates anger that pushes people to action. Experiences of police invading queer social spaces, for example, have led to riots. As Michael Fader, an activist from the 1969 Stonewall Riots, observes:

> It was like the last straw. It was time to reclaim something that had always been taken from us ... [I]t was total outrage, anger, sorrow, everything combined, and everything just kind of ran its course. It was the police who were doing most of the destruction. We were really trying to get back in and break it free ... [T]here was something in the air, freedom a long time overdue, and we're going to fight for it.
>
> (Cited in Schiavi 2011: 63)

As this account indicates, anger generated action against injury during the Stonewall Riots. In Fader's account, this is expressed in his reflection that the Stonewall Riots were a refusal to tolerate continued policing. The police raid on Stonewall, a gay bar in New York City, was the "last straw" that energised activists to "get back in and break it free". Anger (alongside sorrow) was an impetus to fight and break (it) away from injury. Audre Lorde writes compellingly about this energising push of anger: "focused with precision it can become a powerful source of energy serving progress and change" (Lorde 1984: 127). For both Fader and Lorde, anger arises at the moment of coming up against something intolerable: people are pushed to strike back against (a perceived) injury. Instead of seeking to "cover" injury or render it palatable to others, anger represents a refusal to tolerate it by repudiating the pain of an injury through a desire to ease that hurt (Ahmed 2004: 175; Nussbaum 2016: 17).

The anger expressed by LGBT people has been a means of claiming greater social inclusion and accommodation. Rather than fetishise or localise identity or injury, this emotion has directed individuals to call for new visions of social justice across a range of minoritarian differences (sex, race, class, age, disability, and so on). Dismantling heterosexism, patriarchy, capitalism, ableism, colonialism, and whiteness became rallying points for those who were dispossessed by one or more of these interlocking structures. While identity politics played a vital role in animating queer struggles against heteronormativity, the refusal to fix those identities or differences along discrete or essentialist lines enabled the building of coalitions. Unlike pain, which risks fetishising injury and identity, anger was an organising emotion for groups such as Queer Nation and ACT UP to challenge social and political structures that marginalised queers (referring also to diverse populations like sex workers, those who use drugs, incarcerated populations who were marginalised for failing to conform to social norms) for being immoral and perverse (Berlant 1999: 151–5; Cvetkovich 2003: 156–60).[1] For these groups, anger was an expression of pain (of injustice), but it was also about mobilising against the cause of such pain. Specifically, these groups enabled the exchange of activist anger, and these points enabled connections between gay men, injecting drug users, sex workers, and black women living with HIV. Anger marked out moments of injury, while energising activists to move away from the injurious source of such anger to further their expressions of queer intimacies and identities (Crimp 1992: 12).[2]

LGBT anger is not reducible to claims for legal inclusion. As noted in earlier chapters, many activists and scholars vociferously critiqued the assumption that justice could be secured through legal systems that have served to entrench homo/transphobia. However, part of the anger directed towards unjust modes of sexual governance translated into specific activist demands to correct deficiencies in legal and administrative structures. While not uniform or universal in reacting to this anger, over time, a number of jurisdictions were pushed to implement laws and policies that not only prevented state interference in LGBT lives, but also enabled state intervention against the discriminatory acts of individuals and non-state institutions against LGBT people (Koppelman 1996: 8; Rosenblum 1994: 91; Taylor, Lewis, Jacobsmeier, and DiSarro 2012: 78–9). Anti-discrimination legislative schemes effectively crystallised and refracted this anger. Specifically, they became a kind of regulatory lightening rod: they were designed, for the most part, to censure bigotry by striking back against acts of unjust discrimination where one individual had been unjustifiably treated on the basis of a protected characteristic (when compared to an individual who did not possess that characteristic).

B(e)aring animus: the pro-LGBT case of *Romer*

In addition to individual and collective expressions of anger, legal interventions that condemn LGBT discrimination crystallise and refract anger as a means to register and remedy forms of LGBT injury. *Romer v Evans* (1996), for example, is an important case because it marked the first time that the highest appellate body in the US recognised that discriminatory animus against sexual minorities was unlawful. In *Romer*, the Supreme Court of the US refused to validate a constitutional amendment that would strip the Colorado legislature of the ability to create protections and programmes to support LGB people. The animus of the amendment precipitated the Court's anger over discrimination (*Romer* 1996). Much of the legal scholarship about *Romer* discusses the doctrinal problems with Amendment 2 (see Amar 1996; Koppelman 1996), how the law functioned as a political conflict over public expressions of homosexuality (see Dailey and Farley 1996; Keck 2009), and how the jurisprudence vindicated social and democratic equality for LGB people (see Schacter 1997). While these critiques point to the difficult task of balancing conflicts over LGB rights, I recast *Romer* through anger to show how the case undertakes this balancing exercise in emotional terms. Judicial enactments of anger legitimise the invalidation of a law that stigmatises and excludes LGB people and, in doing so, strikes back against the pain inflicted on LGB people to push forward the intimacies and identities of some LGB people away from injury.

In 1992, a group of activists submitted a petition to amend the Colorado Constitution. Commonly referred to as "Amendment 2", the measure proposed in the petition was designed as a way to nullify sexual orientation anti-discrimination ordinances that had recently been introduced in the Colorado cities of Denver, Aspen, and Boulder. The Amendment also sought to prevent the future enactment of similar legislation across the state (Dailey and Farley 1996: 260). Amendment 2 stated:

> Neither the State of Colorado, through any of its branches or departments, nor any of its agencies, political subdivisions, municipalities or school districts, shall enact, adopt or enforce any statute, regulation, ordinance or policy whereby homosexual, lesbian or bisexual orientation, conduct, practices or relationships shall constitute or otherwise be the basis of or entitle

any person or class of persons to have or claim any minority status, quota preferences, protected status or claim of discrimination. This Section of the Constitution shall be in all respects self-executing.

(*Romer* 1993: 1)

When the District Court of Colorado had to decide on the substantive merits of the constitutional violation claim – whether Amendment 2 fettered the participation of a specific class of (LGB) persons in political processes – anger was apparent in the Court's exploration of animus. When the measure was passed in Colorado, the cities of Denver, Boulder, and Aspen filed suit seeking an injunction from the Supreme Court of Colorado to prevent the enforcement of a hostile amendment that violated fundamental civil rights. In responding to the suit, supporters of Amendment 2 pushed back against this claim arguing this was not a measure of exclusion but a measure designed to prevent "special rights" being granted to LGB people.[3] In defending the measure, witnesses noted that, "Amendment 2 was a defensive reaction to fend off state-wide militant gay aggression" (*Romer I* 1993: 1285). In brushing aside the angry "defensive" rhetoric of Amendment 2 proponents, the District Court of Colorado struck back against the animus in Amendment 2 by recognising the "irrationality" of the biases that gave rise to it. The Court held that "if one wished to promote family values, action would be taken that is pro-family rather than anti some other group" (*Romer I* 1993: 8). Recognising the (homo/biphobic) anger of the measure's supporters and refracting that against them fatally flawed Amendment 2. In other words, the Amendment's references to LGB people in exclusionary terms were expressions of animus rather than rationality.

Romer showcased competing enactments of anger when it came to recognising the bigoted anger of Amendment 2's supporters and refracting that anger to remedy the stigmatising injury of Amendment 2. The Colorado Supreme Court focussed on Colorado's disproportionately "hostile" abrogation of a constitutional right to (LGB) political participation that lacked a narrowly tailored response to a compelling state interest (*Romer II* 1993: 1350). Yet, accounting for the absence of anger in the Court's implicit acceptance of "pro-family" mandates and religious objections as "legitimate interests" reveals how it was possible to disregard histories of homophobic discrimination. Ironically, while the argument that LGB people should never be treated as a "special group" for anti-discrimination purposes did not pass constitutional muster for the purposes of validating Amendment 2, the Court refused to see this group as a "suspect class" (akin to racial minorities) with an insidious history of discrimination and political dispossession (*Romer II* 1993: 1341).

The jurisprudence of the Supreme Court of the US directly addressed these erasures by narrowing the holding of the Colorado Supreme Court and identifying that the core issue was whether Amendment 2 served any rational purpose in relation to a legitimate state interest (*Romer* 1996: 1629). The Court held that Amendment 2 was solely a public manifestation of animus and as such lacked any rationality or connection with a governmental interest. In denying state support for sexual minorities, the amendment privileged a negativity that lacked any rational foundation. In a judgment that did not adopt exceptionally emotive language, the majority held that the prohibitory language of Amendment 2, coupled with an identifiable class of people, created an "inevitable inference" that the law was designed to harm an unpopular minority (*Romer* 1996: 1628). This animosity was an injury that pushed the Court to strike back against this hostile injury. Kennedy J held that Amendment 2 closed off the possibility of LGB people seeking recognition (let alone support) from the legislature. Instead of repealing or reforming existing anti-discrimination laws, Amendment 2 was designed to prevent any future state or local action on behalf of an LGB population (*Romer* 1996: 1623). Here, the Court rejected the claim that Amendment 2 prevented the passage of "special rights". In a reflective judgment, Kennedy J observed that what made anti-discrimination protections seem "special" was that they did not need to be invoked by majorities that "already have them or do not need them" (*Romer* 1996: 1627). The Court recognised how anger could manifest differently for different groups: those historically disenfranchised were less likely to get angry because they were not subject to marginalisation. This recognition of anger ran counter to the controlling decision of *Bowers*, which held that sexual minorities did not have the right to pursue their intimacy without state interference. While Kennedy J would later overrule that decision, here, he recognised the (understandable) anger of marginalised LGB people alongside the (irrational) anger animating Amendment 2. His judgment refracted the former against the latter and created a judicial space in which it was possible to condemn the stigma of animus-based laws that injured sexual minorities.

In contrast, Scalia J's dissent reversed the judicial anger present in the majority's decision. He began by framing Amendment 2 as a "cultural conflict" rather than a "fit of spite" (*Romer* 1996: 1629). Scalia J condemned the majority for "imposing" its "elitist" values on the general American public. Scalia J's indignation was directed towards a judgment that dared to confuse the protection of majoritarian cultural values with anger or animosity. Scalia J stated that such a claim had been simply fabricated by a majority eager to privilege the position of homosexuals. He detailed the "heated political disputes" over homosexuality and warned of confusing this passionate debate and the associated public reprobation of homosexuality with anger and animosity. In other words, he held that moral opprobrium towards homosexuality was not a prejudiced act. Scalia J's heated dissent highlighted that to say regulation of homosexuality (as *Bowers* provided at the time) was an act of animus was a shameful insult to the law.

Romer is a striking decision because of how anger was crystallised and refracted through different enactments. It moved from LGB people who got angry over the inequality that animated the push for anti-discrimination protections to those who pushed back against the presence of these measures by rejecting what they deemed to be a "special" imposition. However, although the Court read the latter as "animus" rather than a rational response, it did not include

LGB people in the constitutional space of "equal protection". It was merely the affective "breadth" of the animus of Amendment 2 (by recognising a specific minority only to deny them any protection) that rendered it constitutionally unacceptable (Schacter 1997: 379). In sum, the anger in response to the "bare animus" against LGB people failed to acknowledge the fact that the anger of sexual minorities reached into their experiences of banal forms of discrimination and criminalisation. While wide-reaching pre-emptive prohibitions against anti-discrimination protections for sexual minorities were deemed unconstitutional, there was no corresponding jurisprudential striking back to guarantee sexual minorities protection from unjust discrimination. A refusal to angrily register the invidious histories of discrimination that underscored the animosity or "private biases" of Amendment 2 meant that LGB people were denied status as a "suspect class" worthy of heightened protection.

Reading anger shows how pro-LGBT anti-discrimination cases both overdetermine and understate the vulnerability of LGBT people to injury. In Chapter 3, I showed how group categorisations for the purposes of hate crime criminalisation were problematic because they refracted hate against homo/transphobes to render LGBT identities and intimacies in terms of their vulnerability or proximity to injury. Reading anger analytically in *Romer* showed that the recognition of "irrational" animus-motivated anger that causes injury to LGB people was refracted to invalidate a legal measure that pre-emptively barred LGB people from anti-discrimination protection. However, *Romer* also revealed that the judicial failure to recognise and crystallise LGBT anger towards structural and historical forms of injury narrowed recognition of class-based stigma. The lack of jurisprudential anger here made it possible for the judicial majority to decouple recognition of class-based stigma from a "heightened scrutiny" of LGB structural vulnerability that made such stigmas against LGB people (that led to Amendment 2) possible.

Animating the covering(s) of discrimination

Exclusion and discrimination have become measures of injury in law and this has precipitated angry demands from LGBT people for greater accommodation in public spaces and institutions. This part navigates two pro-LGBT cases from the US dealing with "expressive associations" to show the literal and figurative accommodation of LGBT identities and intimacies in public space. In these cases, I draw out anger to show how these cases create affective thresholds that render certain forms of discriminatory injury intolerable (and unlawful) while misrecognising the structural inequalities that cause that injury and generate anger (Ahmed 2004: 176). Pro-LGBT anti-discrimination cases enact anger in response to the injury of unjust exclusion, but following emotion shows how jurisprudential anger in these cases is limited to the recognition of LGBT identities and intimacies that do not trouble existing institutional arrangements.

80 Animating anger

Ex/inclusion of queer expressions in Hurley

Just two years before the ruling in *Romer*, the Supreme Court of the US had denied the petition of a gay and lesbian group (called GLIB) to march in Boston's St Patrick's Day and Evacuation Day Parade (an event sponsored by the City of Boston) (see *Hurley* 1995). The plaintiff was a local LGB Irish group that requested permission to march in the parade (while carrying their posters and banners about gay pride). The group was denied entry by the South Boston Allied War Veterans Council, which was responsible for organising the event. GLIB filed suit, seeking an injunction against the Council to prevent it from blocking the request. In *Hurley v Irish-American Gay, Lesbian and Bisexual Group of Boston* (1995), the Court had to consider whether a Massachusetts statute that specifically prohibited sexual orientation discrimination in public accommodations extended to requiring the Veterans Council to allow GLIB's participation in the parade.[4] The Supreme Court of the US ruled that the Veterans Council could not be compelled to change the expressive content of its parade by being required to admit GLIB; to do so would violate the Council's rights under the First Amendment to the US Constitution (*Hurley* 1996: 2348).

Cleaving public space from public expression generated judicial anger. In dissent in the Supreme Court of Massachusetts, Nolan J stated that "one must strain to recall or even to imagine such an obvious violation of the revered right to free speech" (*Hurley* 1994: 1301). Echoing Scalia J's dissent in *Romer*, Nolan J repudiated the majority's decision for imposing a "message" on the Veterans Council. Nolan J saw queer identity as a visibly "expressive" act. Even if the parade had no expressive purpose, including GLIB's message (inclusion itself was deemed to be the message) constituted the state mandating expression on the event. Nolan J considered that depriving GLIB of the possibility of speech, through the Veterans Council's refusal to accommodate the group, was an act protected under the First Amendment (*Hurley* 1994: 1304).

In taking the dissenting argument further, the Supreme Court of the US refused to "force" speech upon the Veterans Council. In a unanimous decision, the Court held that a "parade" made a collective point – it was not simply an association of people (*Hurley* 1996: 2345). By privileging "free speech" over having to associate with queer identities, the Court was able to justify the refusal to accommodate GLIB because to do so would effectively "mandate" speech in the parade and undermine the First Amendment. In the Court's own words, the decision "boil[ed] down to the choice of a speaker not to propound a particular point of view" (*Hurley* 1996: 2348). After all, the parade was deemed to be a private activity (despite being manifested in public space). The Court's concentration on individual speech (as opposed to public space) made room to dismiss the anger of LGB people and justify their exclusion from the parade. Such reasoning, however, obscured the fact that inclusion itself was the act of purported speech in this case. It did not matter what GLIB's banners may or may not have said – it was simply the public presence of participants' non-heterosexual intimacies and identities in the parade that constituted a (queer) tainting of the parade's (straight) "speech".

Anti-discrimination law may intervene to recognise minority identity and intimacy, but in the context of *Hurley* it did not have to facilitate or encourage it (Eskridge 1997: 2447). In contradistinction to *Romer*, private biases, even when given effect through exclusions in public spaces, were protected grounds of "free speech". LGB identity was recognised in the anger mobilised throughout *Romer*, but the refusal in *Hurley* to register anger at GLIB's exclusion denied a push for greater public accommodation of queer intimacies and identities. Reading anger accounts for the legal recognition of injury these cases make possible: pro-LGBT anti-discrimination cases recognise injury by striking back against the pain caused by a "bare animus" that explicitly excludes LGB people (as in *Romer*) with a desire to push forward intimacies and identities harmed by such animus. But, this anger does not extend to recognise how public institutions that take heterosexuality as a structuring social norm maintain these harms (as in *Hurley*). Making legal scholarship attentive to how anger is refracted (or not) in law helps scholars conceive of how expanding legal space for LGBT people's anger in law might energise a push to legally affirm queer intimacies and identities that are currently denied accommodation in public space.

Registering discrimination in Dale

From participating in parades to working in organisations, the "expressive association" doctrine has been used in US constitutional law to deny LGB people greater public accommodation. In 2000, the Supreme Court of the US upheld the expulsion of Scoutmaster James Dale from the Boy Scouts of America (BSA) after his sexual orientation was discovered (*Dale* 2000: 2458). This appellate decision overruled the lower court rulings that determined Dale's exclusion to be unlawful. The plaintiff, James Dale, had served for a number of years in the BSA (the defendant). Dale "had been a devoted and exemplary Boy Scout" (*Dale* 1998: 275). The Superior Court of New Jersey detailed Dale's meritorious exceptionalism. During his service, he had earned 30 merit badges and occupied the highest positions of office as a boy scout. By framing the narrative of discrimination through Dale's exceptionalism, the Court added, "stereotypical notions about homosexuals must be rejected" (*Dale* 1998: 289). Dale's merit worked to cover over any distasteful stereotypes of homosexuality as a deficiency of character – Dale was just like everybody else. Much like the situation in *Lawrence*, the idealised portrayal of Dale's historical involvement in the BSA made his expulsion more easily susceptible to judicial anger.

Much of the intermediate appellate jurisprudence used the language of invitation and intimacy to express the Court's anger over discrimination. BSA membership was not contingent on a particular sexual identification but was "available for all boys who met entrance age requirements" (*Dale* 1998: 281). The open invitation and absence of onerous eligibility requirements (aside from age and sex) distinguished it from private clubs. The Superior Court of New Jersey then moved from discussing scout participation to discussing service provision. The BSA was contracted to facilitate or organise a number of public events and was housed within public buildings (such as schools). In the New Jersey Supreme Court, Portiz CJ described this as an act of "solicitation" (*Dale* 1999: 1213). The BSA made wide-reaching invitations to the public for the purposes of both recruitment and its own accommodation. In doing so, the BSA became intimately associated both with public entities (to provide services or house its groups) and with the general public (as the source of new membership). Dale's expulsion in these circumstances was intolerable.

The New Jersey Supreme Court struck against this exclusion, as it was the "human price of bigotry" (*Dale* 1999: 1227). The Court recognised Dale's personal anger over being expelled from a club he had devoted years of service to and refracted that back against BSA to expose the injury of discriminating against a "closeted" gay man. This judicial manoeuvre relied on the fact that Dale had made no mention of his sexual orientation (and its legitimacy) or attempted to "promote" it (*Dale* 1999: 1229). He had only come to the attention of BSA bureaucracy due to a newspaper article covering his role with the Rutgers University Lesbian/Gay Alliance. Dale's apparent silence about his queer sexual intimacy and identity became pivotal. He could be accommodated within the BSA precisely because these queer elements were not expressed. Dale's presence as a meritorious leader was distinct from his presence as a homosexual.

The BSA's denial of Dale's merit and expulsion generated anger among the majority in the New Jersey Supreme Court. Even where Dale's public self-identification as gay was acknowledged, it was not made disturbing in this case because his meritorious service rendered him an asset. Visible forms of (homo)sexual intimacy and identity were foregrounded by pushing back against measures that denied gay people the ability to be either silent about their sexuality or meritorious enough to make it irrelevant. This echoed the sentimental covering of same-sex intimacy in *Lawrence* in order to invalidate the criminal penalties associated with it. Dale had to conceal the more "obtrusive" or queer parts of his sexual identity and its associated intimacy if he was to make the BSA the subject of judicial anger (Robinson 2007: 1826; Yoshino 1998: 502). The decision of the New Jersey Supreme Court majority is a reminder of anger's limited reach in this pro-LGBT anti-discrimination case: it offered injunctive relief to Dale by blocking his expulsion, but the emotional reasoning limited the accommodation of queer intimacy and identity (by refusing to strike back against BSA's demand to closet one's homosexuality in the first place).

The majority of the Supreme Court of the US dismissed this meritorious containment of gayness. While the BSA may not have had an oath that specifically condemned homosexuality, the desire to impart a particular set of values counted as an "expressive activity" (*Dale* 2000: 2452; Koppelman and Wolff 2009: 32). To require the BSA to accommodate such a person would be an act of mandated speech by the government that was prohibited by the First Amendment. Yet, the dissenters reached a different conclusion through their expression of anger over discrimination: they pushed back against a majority opinion that they viewed as threatening the very tolerance purported by the BSA. Focussing on the BSA's "public posture", the dissenters emphasised that no "expression" was burdened by the inclusion of homosexuals within the organisation. Instead, inclusion was consistent with the welcoming stance of the BSA to boys of various cultural backgrounds (*Dale* 2000: 2463). After all, the BSA's eligibility requirements seemed oriented towards open admission. In reiterating the value of anti-discrimination law, Stevens J passionately stated:

> We have squarely held that a State's anti-discrimination law does not violate a group's right to associate simply because the law conflicts with that group's exclusionary policy.
>
> (*Dale* 2000: 2467)

For Stevens J, the majority decision had failed to respect the rights of minorities to live free from discrimination. Yet, the dissenting judgment did not desire free and variable expression of queer identity and intimacy more generally. This judgment emphasised that Dale "did not carry a banner or sign" (*Dale* 2000: 2475). Arguably, if he did (as the marchers in *Hurley* desired), he would not warrant accommodation under the state's anti-discrimination law. Queer intimacy and identity was not accommodated in the case because the progressive articulation of anger made the legal striking back against discrimination possible only to those gay people who did not "flaunt" their sexual intimacy or identity and threaten institutional arrangements. Dale could serve, but he had to do so as a meritorious person who was silent about his homosexuality. The BSA's requirement to tolerate his presence was legally secured even in dissent by an affective backgrounding of his queer identity and intimacy.

Getting angry over exceptional forms of injury

The above discussion shows that pro-LGBT cases that recognise LGBT injury and respond with jurisprudential anger are not necessarily wide-reaching. *Romer* invalidated a constitutional amendment that it held, on a rational basis review, to be pre-emptively hostile. Amendment 2 could not be used to injure LGB people in every aspect, but there was no countervailing anger in the decision that insisted upon positive obligations to promote their intimacies or identities. Reading emotion shows how the Court refused to recognise the accrued anger of sexual minorities as a historically marginalised group and refracting that to offer broader accommodation of LGB people. Even the progressive dissent in *Dale* revealed that homosexuality was ordinary insofar as it remained a private feature of individual identity. In covering public expressions of queer intimacies and identities, the dissent produced discrimination against LGB people as an emotional issue precisely because homosexuals (such as Dale) chose to be ordinary, or "just like everyone else".

Emotion allows us to account for why *Romer* did not acknowledge the socially diffuse nature of LGBT discrimination: by striking back against the pain of a legal measure that irrationally excluded LGB people, *Romer* directed legal attention away from how the legal system functioned to sustain such discrimination (such as through the continuing criminalisation of same-sex intimacy). State power was simultaneously utilised, and covered over, through the invocation of what Wendy Brown refers to as a "tolerance leash" (Brown 2006: 84). Writing about the ascendancy of tolerance discourses, Brown shows how civic and political institutions pursue "social harmony" by asking people to restrain (or "leash") their aversion to offensive people and practices (Brown 2006: 16 and 25). Anger, however, breaks these restraints. In *Romer*, the Court was willing to "unleash" to invalidate the most pernicious forms of bigotry. Reading the absence and presence of anger in these cases resonates particularly with the way in which hate crime laws characterised violent homophobes as exceptions to the rule, rather than as products of an already homophobic social and economic environment. *Romer* revealed that for discrimination to warrant anger, it needed to reach a particularly high threshold by lacking any rational basis to support it.

In *Romer*, the specific naming (or isolation) of sexual minorities, coupled with a pre-emptive exclusion over any of their discrimination claims, was unlawful animus. However, had the amendment not named specific categories of people but adopted the more neutral language of "sexual orientation" (to include heterosexuals), the decision could have been very different, as there would have been no specific intentional hostility. Formal equality could render all sexual orientations fungible – all "equally" worthy of (non)protection without acknowledging the social, historical, and emotional differences between the categories (including the differences between LGB people). In *Hurley* and *Dale*, the emphasis on protecting associational expression worked to obscure the animus behind the exclusion of queer intimacies and identities from public space. In the process, the impetus towards tolerating either discriminatory speech acts or exclusions became an emotional cover that hid the more understated institutional forms of injury that could not warrant anger or be reduced to discrete forms of exclusion. The push to focus on liberty or participatory interests over substantive equality (which recognises structural injustice) transposed claims for better accommodation into the register of individual liberty (Yoshino 1998: 529–30; Yoshino 2011: 763). For LGB people to be protected (by the law), they needed to be able to show that their liberty had been both specifically and maliciously maligned by an identifiable individual or institution. *Romer* was a clear example of the "holding back" of LGB people in political life. Since Amendment 2 simply prohibited future anti-discrimination legislation in Colorado, its invalidation did not then entrench a desire in law to promote the inclusion of sexual minorities as a positive obligation. The act of striking back against an irrational, hostile amendment transformed a particular act of legislative injury into an exemplary situation – one of "bare animus". Unlawful discrimination was rendered through the recognition of homo/transphobic anger towards LGB people as both unusual and unacceptable (much like homo/transphobic hate discussed in Chapter 3) and refracting anger to invalidate prejudicial laws.

Analysing anger in the majority opinion in *Romer* alongside the dissenting opinion in *Dale* revealed that LGBT discrimination was only intolerable to the extent that the marginalisation could be compared to the position of the rest of the (heterosexual) population. Anger aimed at remedying exceptional hostility was secured by backgrounding queer intimacy and identity in both cases. Taken together, these pro-LGBT anti-discrimination cases that point back to some "ordinary" (heterosexual) population as the standard by which to recognise discrimination eclipse queer experiences of institutional and historical exclusion. As Sara Ahmed argues, scholars cannot repudiate sexual orientation as a category, but we need to recognise how it grounds social existence (Ahmed 2004: 182). Scholars, activists, lawyers, and judges also need to respond to the "assimilationist bias" of equal opportunity jurisprudence where cases are deemed to warrant remedy only when the narrative of homo/transphobic discrimination can be indexed against the position of a heterosexual/cis person (Yoshino 1998: 487). Taking this further, following the reach of anger in pro-LGBT cases shows the "affective bias" in law that persists in anti-discrimination laws. Tracking anger allows scholars to navigate how progressive legal interventions recognise the anger of LGBT people who experience injury and crystallise anger when addressing LGBT discrimination. This analytic mapping invites scholars, activists, lawyers, and judges to think about the politics of expanding the reach of jurisprudential anger to accommodate currently backgrounded queer intimacies and identities.

Queering anger

In this final section, I juxtapose the above cases with a more recent pro-LGBT anti-discrimination case – *Christian Youth Camps Ltd v Cobaw Community Health Services Ltd* (2014) – to evaluate the politics of expanding jurisprudential anger to address discrimination. Specifically, I look at how directing anger towards "bad objects" of discrimination risks producing divisions between religion and (homo)sexuality. Taking account of anger in pro-LGBT anti-discrimination cases is necessary to loosen emotional attachments that produce such divisions and this enables scholars, activists, lawyers, and judges to affectively rethink the progressive balancing of competing rights claims without pulling religion and sexuality apart (Johnson and Vanderbeck 2014: 118).

Accommodating queer identities in Cobaw

Cobaw offers a compelling example of what is gained by expanding the reach of judicial anger to strike back against the denial of public space to LGBT people. The case concerned a community organisation, Cobaw Community Health Services Ltd (Cobaw) that had sought to run a health promotion workshop for same-sex-attracted and gender-questioning young people from rural Victoria,

Australia, at a camping resort on Phillip Island. Christian Youth Camps Ltd (CYC) operated the resort. Following what was described as a "brief and polite" telephone conversation between representatives of Cobaw (Sue Hackney) and CYC (Mark Rowe) regarding the content of the proposed workshop and the attendees, the booking request was denied (*Cobaw* 2010: [126]). Cobaw then made a complaint to the Victorian Equal Opportunity and Human Rights Commission, alleging that CYC had denied the booking once it became aware of the "queer" content of the workshop and the same-sex attraction and gender nonconformity of the proposed attendees.[5] In bringing together individual and institutional accountability, *Cobaw* expanded the reach of judicial anger to account for queer identities: LGBT people were accommodated through judicial reasoning that struck back against hostile religious objections to the accommodation of LGBT people. In doing so, the jurisprudence recognised and refracted the anger experienced by those who were denied space because of their queer "lifestyles".[6]

Cobaw, however, responded to discrimination by enacting a more expansive kind of anger not seen in *Dale* or *Hurley*: the Court refused to tolerate religious objections used to shield commercial practices from the reach of anti-discrimination law by striking back against the pain of invidious LGBT exclusion. The Tribunal aimed to strike a balance between competing religious freedom and anti-discrimination human rights claims: the freedom to express one's sexual orientation and the freedom to express religion. But, the Tribunal's anger manifested here through its pushback of the idea that exclusion was an act necessary to "conform" or "avoid injury" to religious doctrines (*Cobaw* 2010: [304]–[352]). Specifically, it chastised CYC for failing to manifest its "plenary inspiration" that sex ought to occur in heterosexual conjugal contexts. CYC had refused to interrogate the sexual activity of all the people who had used its services. Instead, it had chosen to single out those who identified as same-sex attracted for exclusion and sought to use religion as a convenient cover for such discrimination. Homosexuality was not condemned by any identifiable doctrine (*Cobaw* 2010: [302]). While some religious sensitivities might have been offended by the idea of accommodating a workshop for sexual minorities, it did not amount to a collective injury against people who shared the faith (*Cobaw* 2010: 325–326). CYC's liability was assessed at $5,000 due to the hurt and injury it had inflicted on the group.

At judicial review, *Cobaw* enacted emotion in two distinctive ways: LGBT people were cradled as marginalised minorities in need of accommodation, while discriminatory groups (such as CYC) were castigated for failing to extend accommodation to them. Rights needed to be "balanced" (*Cobaw* 2014: [187]). Cobaw was not seeking to "promote homosexuality", but rather intended to provide a safe space in which to recognise and support those who identified as same-sex attracted or who questioned their gender assignment at birth. The Court sympathised with this objective when noting the difficulties faced by LGBT people who were confronted with homo/transphobia. By pursuing a secular activity (accommodation services) for the purposes of securing privilege (financial profit), CYC could not wield its religious affiliation to discriminate against Cobaw (*Cobaw* 2014: [245]). CYC had done little to make its religious values apparent (*Cobaw* 2014: [211]). Despite this omission, "expert evidence" was presented on CYC's behalf to outline the theological underpinnings of the Christian Brethren and its relationship with CYC. However, the Court decoupled such scriptural underpinning from the commercial work of CYC. Christian doctrines may have influenced CYC, but it certainly did not "control" its administration of the resort (*Cobaw* 2014: [267]). Here, Maxwell P echoed Judge Hampel's chastisement by noting that faith-based objections could not be used as wide-ranging shields to block the accommodation of LGBT people in various aspects of commercial or public life just because the entity providing that service was associated with a religious faith. Here, the Court struck back against the harms of religious objections with a push to narrow its terms in order to make the inclusion of LGBT people possible. Judicial anger was directed towards an unchallenged religious "privilege" and this made space for the Court to remedy CYC's refusal to accommodate Cobaw and confine objections to LGBT identities and intimacies in public spaces.

Enabling queer critiques of pro-LGBT anti-discrimination cases

Reading *Cobaw* in terms of anger points to why queer legal scholarship needs to engage with how law expresses emotion through jurisprudential arrangements that eliminate the injury of discrimination and further the expression of certain intimacies and identities. Critical legal scholarship on anti-discrimination law points to the problem of remedying structural injustices and benchmarking equality against existing social privileges (see Crenshaw 1988; Fredman 2016; Matsuda 1987; Robinson 2007; Spade 2011; Wolff 2012; Yoshino 2002, 2011). I am interested in how scholars, activists, lawyers, and judges can respond to this problem by reading emotion analytically to show that the increased visibility of injury is sustained by anger that backgrounds certain structural inequalities or obscures the nature of queer (religious) identities. Following the way anger arranges the terms of this legal recognition – remedying LGBT injuries by accommodating LGBT intimacies and identities – points to broader political possibilities if scholars, activists, lawyers, and judges make space for, while scrutinising, anger in progressive legal interventions.

Pro-LGBT anti-discrimination cases are circumscribed by technical rules or abstract principles that fail to consider the specific emotional enactments of their articulation. Judicial expressions of anger in *Romer* did not reach far enough to consider broader public initiatives that could have been necessary to prevent giving effect to homophobic stigma, such as anti-homophobia community programmes or services. The dissent in *Dale* generated anger that focussed so much on striking back against the pain of unjust expulsions of gay identities (like Dale's) that it did not make room to consider how non-normative expressions or queer intimacies could be accommodated within heteronormative institutions (like the BSA). In both cases, judicial crystallisations of anger framed unlawful discrimination in terms of privileged norms. Such norms governed decision-making without revealing their social or emotional location. Institutional habits that cemented the erasure of non-heterosexual intimacies (*Hurley*'s assumption that queer identity was disruptive or always already sexual), or that defined sexual identity in strictly privatised terms (*Dale*'s assumption that the visibility of sexual identity and associated intimacy could be managed), were not the subject of angry critique. These cases point to the value of recognising the anger of those invidiously discriminated against and refracting that anger as a way to register the depth of discrimination to make space to accommodate LGBT people.

Making space for anger, however, carries political risks. Individual LGBT people's anger at discrimination and a (homo/transphobic) majority's anger towards LGBT visibility maintained the conflict between parties in each case. Even when the former was recognised and refracted through law against the latter, it provided a limited remedy. The sympathetic appellate jurisprudence in *Hurley* and *Dale* had to cover over queer intimacy and identity insofar as it dared to disrupt the institutional status quo. These so-called "public accommodation" laws failed to accommodate those who were deemed too queer. Reading anger exposes how remedial action was an act of erasure, too (see Matsuda 1987). In *Cobaw*, the Court narrowed the wide-ranging objections that could be used to literally deny LGBT people space. My analytic reading of anger here is a way of legally opening up the emotion to others who would otherwise be excluded from its reach (Chakrabarti 2014: 502). Unlike the individual victim/perpetrator model discussed in the US cases, *Cobaw* broadened the ambit of reparations to account for collective historical wrongs that inhere in the present. The Court's "balancing" of freedom of religion and freedom from discrimination required a broader consideration of the specific groups involved and the social context in which those rights were articulated. Neither freedom could be discussed in abstract doctrinal terms. In subordinating discrimination to religious intolerance, *Cobaw*'s expression of anger to compel the inclusion of LGBT people in a religiously affiliated commercial venue denied the way in which the two were coextensive for queer people who identified as both LGBT and of a particular faith. Queer legal scholarship benefits from this reading by showing that claims for remedying discrimination and furthering queer intimacy and identity can be pursued through expansive expressions of anger that account for intersectionality. Reading anger makes it possible to affirm the progressive recognition to accommodate LGBT people while resisting the associated insistence to make their identities coextensive with injury.

Pushing how we understand judicial anger – maintaining the tensions between injury, intimacy, and identity – is a way of challenging the limited reach of pro-LGBT anti-discrimination cases. *Cobaw* acknowledged the historical disenfranchisement of LGBT people (rural young people specifically) and recognised the justifiable anger LGBT people had in response to this (which triggered the litigation). This individual anger was recognised and refracted by the Court in its condemnation of the privileges held by religious providers who entered into the marketplace to provide commercial services to the public. Anger enabled the Court in *Cobaw* to distinguish commercial activity from religious functioning. Rather than accept religious objections as self-evident, the Court placed a greater burden of justification on commercial institutions seeking to discriminate to explain how their religious sensibilities had been injured. Judicial expressions of anger that pushed back against the advancing boundaries of religious objections enabled the Court to accommodate more wide-ranging forms of queer identities and intimacies that, in cases like *Hurley* and *Dale* were backgrounded. Yet, it is important to note that the Court still avoided the idea that accommodation necessarily meant the "promotion" of homosexuality. Reading this anger exposes the danger of such a manoeuvre: homosexuality became an act that could be contained (you can be queer but not too queer), rather than a generous accommodation of varied queer intimacies and identities. In resisting one form of injury (LGBT exclusion), the Court created a cover that could bring about another kind of injury (through the erasure of certain forms of LGBT visibility).

Attending to individual and legal expressions of anger at discrimination in *Cobaw* allows scholars to grasp the intersectional differences that underpin queer identities. By loosening jurisprudential anger here – rendering the emotional division between sexuality and religion less secure – it is possible to acknowledge how LGBT people can be accommodated by religion, not in spite of it. If CYC had been a religious not-for-profit refuge for homeless teenagers, for example, exclusion could have been lawful. Such discrimination would have left no space for Christian sexual minorities who sought access to such accommodation. These individuals become alienated in pro-LGBT anti-discrimination cases; religious LGBT people do not register a specific mention. In accommodating secular LGBT people for secular activities, *Cobaw* failed to push for the LGBT people who may seek religious and private accommodation respectively. Such a demand may be beyond the law. It may be, to borrow Ahmed's words, asking "too much" of an anti-discrimination project that relies on maintaining a balance between competing rights claims (Ahmed 2014: 128). However, the lack of anger expressed over the self-evident divisions or hierarchies that are reproduced in statutory or regulatory schemes remains problematic. This materialisation of anger serves to entrench the idea that religion and (homo)sexuality cannot co-exist because they cannot be mutually constitutive. It is prudent, then, for scholars, activists, lawyers, and judges to confront articulations of anger that create divides between, and erasures of, queer sexuality and religion. These emotional erasures also work to entrench the idea that legal intervention or litigation is the primary means of determining a "proper" balance of the two. Yet, the affective logic of censorship and exception that defines these remedies also fails to address economic or social (in addition to existing religious and political) conditions of subordination. In order to redress broader historical circumstances that structure discrimination, a legal project of reparations must take greater account of the plural ways law politically disciplines queer identities and intimacies through the emotional arrangements that are co-constituted with them (Hunter 2015: 172). Reading emotion draws out the possibilities of using jurisprudence for such a reparative project.

Conclusion

Analysing anger in pro-LGBT cases shows how legal interventions strike back against the pain of discrimination. For LGBT people, anger over inequality shapes collective struggles to dismantle structures that injure nonconforming queer intimacies and identities. As Lorde concludes:

> Anger expressed and translated into action in the service of our vision and our future is a liberating and strengthening act of clarification, for it is in the painful process of this translation that we identify who are allies with whom we have grave differences, and who are our genuine enemies.
> (Lorde 1984: 127)

Anger, like pain, cannot be repudiated. By reading emotion in pro-LGBT anti-discrimination cases – *Romer*, *Hurley*, *Dale*, and *Cobaw* – this chapter showed how anger featured as a way to mobilise action in response to the injury of LGBT exclusion and discrimination. Following anger in these cases opened up the different possibilities of accommodating queer intimacies and identities by breaking away from institutions or individuals that sought to obstruct them. However, as my reading of *Cobaw* evinced, failing to take account of how judicial expressions of anger sustain conflict between (LGBT) individuals and (straight) institutions also runs the risk of covering over the intersections between queer identities that do not necessarily need to be in conflict (such as sexuality and religion). Pro-LGBT cases that measure LGBT experiences of injury with heteronormative ideas of inequality or by setting up oppositional binaries risk flattening out the disparate ways in which injury, intimacy, and identity disrupt public accommodations. Reading emotion, then, enables scholars, activists, lawyers, and judges to take greater account of these disruptions and push back against how progressive legal interventions emotionally foreclose the recognition of LGBT injuries, intimacies, and identities.

In the next chapter, I read how fear fights against a broader accommodation of queer injuries, intimacies, and identities through refugee law.

Notes

1 The politics of pain and the fetishisation of injury are explored further in Chapter 1. See also Brown (1995).
2 Anger can also facilitate violent acts. For a discussion of the normatively problematic use of anger as a "reasonable emotion", see Nussbaum (2016).

3 Unlike race (or even gender, which warrants intermediate scrutiny), sexual orientation was seen to lack the quality of immutability and the history of invidious discrimination that was necessary to give it more careful consideration. In the intermediate courts of Colorado, the case largely focussed on the standard of judicial review and whether Amendment 2 impacted on any constitutional protected right of "political participation" (*Romer* II 1993: 1285). The first issue for the Court to determine was the appropriate standard of judicial review. In essence, the majority observed that any law or amendment that "fence[d] out" an identifiable class of persons needed to be subject to a strict standard of review (*Romer* II 1993: 1287).
4 Under the Massachusetts statute, distinctions, discriminations, or restrictions on the basis of sexual orientation in respect of admission or treatment in a place of public accommodation, resort, or amusement were unlawful. The Massachusetts Supreme Court held that the Veterans Council had unlawfully excluded GLIB from a public venue (*Hurley* 1994: 1300).
5 When the complaint was referred to the Victorian Civil and Administrative Tribunal, Cobaw argued that CYC had breached the prohibition on sexual orientation discrimination in the *Equal Opportunity Act 1995* (Vic). CYC responded that it had not discriminated on the basis of sexual orientation because it dealt with Cobaw (an NGO) and not an identifiable group of LGBT people. CYC added that, even if it had acted in a discriminatory manner, as part of the Christian Brethren, its ability to do so was protected under the religious exceptions to the anti-discrimination law (*Cobaw* 2010: [126]).
6 The case was decided in terms of (now updated) Victorian equal opportunity legislation that provided that it was unlawful to (directly or indirectly) treat a person less favourably on the basis of their purported or actual sexual orientation. There were, however, religious exceptions within the legislation that proved to be contentious in the case (these laws have since been updated, see *The Equal Opportunity Act 2010* (Vic)). Where religious exceptions were concerned, discrimination could be lawful if the alleged discriminator could demonstrate that it was a religious body and that its act: (i) "conformed" to religious doctrines; (ii) was necessary to avoid injury to "religious susceptibilities" of people who share that faith; or (iii) was necessary to comply with "genuine" religious beliefs or principles (*The Equal Opportunity Act 1995* (Vic): ss 75, 77).

References

Ahmed, S., 2004. *The Cultural Politics of Emotion*. Oxford: Routledge.

Ahmed, S., 2014. *Willful Subjects*. Durham: Duke University Press.

Amar, A. R., 1996. Attainder and Amendment 2: *Romer*'s Rightness. *Michigan Law Review*, 95(1), 203–35.

Berlant, L., 1999. The Subject of True Feeling: Pain, Privacy and Politics. In Austin Sarat and Thomas Kearns, eds. *Cultural Pluralism, Identity Politics and the Law*. Ann Arbor: University of Michigan Press, 49–84.

Brown, W., 1995. *States of Injury: Power and Freedom in Late Modernity*. Princeton: Princeton University Press.

Brown, W., 2006. *Regulating Aversion: Tolerance in the Age of Identity and Empire*. Princeton: Princeton University Press.

Chakrabarti, S., 2014. Faith in the Public Sphere. *Journal of Law and Policy*, 22, 483–515.

Crenshaw, K. W., 1988. Race, Reform, and Retrenchment: Transformation and Legitimation in Antidiscrimination Law. *Harvard Law Review*, 101(7), 1331–87.

Crimp, D., 1992. Right On, Girlfriend. *Social Text*, 33, 2–18.
Cvetkovich, A., 2003. *An Archive of Feelings: Trauma, Sexuality, and Lesbian Public Cultures*. Durham: Duke University Press.
Dailey, J. and Farley, P., 1996. Colorado's Amendment 2: A Result in Search of Reason. *Harvard Journal of Law and Public Policy*, 20(1), 215–78.
Eskridge, W. N., 1997. A Jurisprudence of "Coming Out": Religion, Homosexuality, and Collision of Liberty and Equality in American Public Law. *Yale Law Journal*, 106(8), 2411–74.
Fredman, S., 2016. Substantive Equality Revisited. *I*CON*, 14(3), 712–38.
Hunter, S., 2015. *Power, Politics and the Emotions: Impossible Governance?* London: Routledge.
Johnson, P. and Vanderbeck, R. M., 2014. *Law, Religion and Homosexuality*. Oxford: Routledge.
Keck, T. M., 2009. Beyond Backlash: Assessing the Impact of Judicial Decisions on LGBT Rights. *Law & Society Review*, 43(1), 151–86.
Koppelman, A., 1996. *Antidiscrimination Law and Social Equality*. New Haven: Yale University Press.
Koppelman, A. and Wolff, T. B., 2009. *A Right to Discriminate? How the Case of Boy Scouts of America v. James Dale Warped the Law of Free Association*. New Haven: Yale University Press.
Lorde, A., 1984. *Sister Outsider*. Berkeley: Crossing Press.
Matsuda, M., 1987. Looking to the Bottom: Critical Legal Studies and Reparations. *Harvard Civil Rights-Civil Liberties Law Review*, 22, 323–99.
Nussbaum, M. C., 2016. *Anger and Forgiveness: Resentment, Generosity, and Justice*. New York: Oxford University Press.
Robinson, R. K., 2007. Uncovering Covering. *Northwestern University Law Review*, 101(4), 1809–49.
Rosenblum, D., 1994. Queer Intersectionality and the Failure of Recent Lesbian and Gay "Victories". *Law & Sexuality: A Review of Lesbian and Gay Legal Issues*, 4, 83–122.
Schacter, J. S., 1997. *Romer v. Evans* and Democracy's Domain. *Vanderbilt Law Review*, 50(2), 361–410.
Schiavi, M., 2011. *Celluloid Activist: The Life and Times of Vito Russell*. Madison: University of Wisconsin Press.
Spade, D., 2011. *Normal Life: Administrative Violence, Critical Trans Politics, and the Limits of Law*. New York: South End Press.
Stychin, C. F., 1998. *A Nation by Rights: National Cultures, Sexual Identity Politics, and the Discourse of Rights*. Philadelphia: Temple University Press.
Taylor, J. K., Lewis, D. C., Jacobsmeier, M. L. and DiSarro, B., 2012. Content and Complexity in Policy Reinvention and Diffusion: Gay and Transgender-Inclusive Laws against Discrimination. *State Politics & Policy Quarterly*, 12(1), 75–98.
Wolff, T. B., 2012. Civil Rights Reform and the Body. *Harvard Law and Policy Review*, 6, 201–31.
Yoshino, K., 1998. Assimilationist Bias in Equal Protection: The Visibility Presumption and the Case of "Don't Ask, Don't Tell". *Yale Law Journal*, 108(3), 485–571.
Yoshino, K., 2002. Covering. *Yale Law Journal*, 111(4), 769–939.
Yoshino, K., 2011. The New Equal Protection. *Harvard Law Review*, 124, 747–803.

Legislation

Equal Opportunity Act 1995 (Vic).
Equal Opportunity Act 2010 (Vic).
New Jersey Law Against Discrimination 1945 (NJ).
The Massachusetts Public Accommodation Law (MA).

Cases

Christian Youth Camps Ltd v Cobaw Community Health Services Ltd [2014] VSCA 75.
Cobaw Community Health Services Ltd v Christian Youth Camps Ltd [2010] VCAT 1613.
Dale v Boy Scouts of America, 706 A 2d 270 (1998).
Dale v Boy Scouts of America, 734 A 2d 1196 (1999).
Dale v Boy Scouts of America, 120 S Ct 2446 (2000).
Evans v Romer, 1993 WL 518586.
Hurley v Irish-American Gay, Lesbian, and Bisexual Group of Boston, 636 NE 2d 1293 (1994).
Hurley v Irish-American Gay, Lesbian, and Bisexual Group of Boston, 115 S Ct 2338 (1995).
Romer v Evans, 854 P 2d 1270 (1993).
Romer v Evans, 882 P 2d 1335 (1994).
Romer v Evans, 116 S Ct 1620 (1996).

Chapter 5

Fighting fear
Queer claims and asylum

Introduction

Over the last three decades, an increasing number of jurisdictions have recognised asylum claims on the basis of sexual orientation, gender identity, and intersex status. Such pro-LGBT refugee cases have been heralded for progressing LGBT rights by recognising the failure of states to protect individuals against persecution. Yet, the ways in which these pro-LGBT refugee cases have been taken up have been limited. Typically adjudicated under the rubric of a "particular social group" as a consequence of existing international refugee law, the extent to which LGBT refugees have been granted protection has been contingent on whether they subscribe to (hetero)normative ideas of injury, intimacy, and identity. Specifically, refugees must demonstrate that they have a "well-founded fear of persecution" owing to their membership in a particular social group. While the recognition (and evaluation) of an applicant's fear has been central to the grant of asylum under international law, fear has also been crystallised through adjudication of LGBT asylum claims to limit the scope of protecting queer intimacies and identities. Specifically, judicial fears of a refugee jurisprudence that is "too queer" has led scholars, judges, and states to guard against opening the proverbial "floodgates".

In this chapter, I track how fear mobilises people to flee persecution and I outline how pro-LGBT cases recognise such fear to determine an asylum claim. In doing so, I map how this recognition of individual fear crystallises legal fears in pro-LGBT refugee cases, which obstruct queer intimacies and identities that risk threatening the integrity of the refugee adjudication system. As Sara Ahmed and Gail Mason argue, fear projects us into an experience of the future, an imagining that fixates on anticipated threat or vulnerability to injury (Ahmed 2004: 69; Mason 2002: 64). Fear also functions spatially to shrink bodies: it pulls them back from their close proximity to those anticipated injuries. I take up this temporal and spatial theorisation of fear to show how fear does not only materialise through refugees' experiences but is crystallised in legal precedents that structure processes of refugee status determination. This fear is refracted in pro-LGBT cases to affirm the injuries, intimacies, and identities of some LGBT people in need of protection while obstructing the claims of those who express queer intimacies and identities (Ahmed 1995: 56; Ahmed 2004: 62–3; Ahmed 2011: 126).

I begin this chapter by outlining international refugee law and scholarship to show how progressive claims to extend asylum to those fleeing persecution on the basis of sexual orientation and gender identity have anxiously engaged with what counts as a "well-founded fear of persecution". I use this as a starting point to consider how fears over expanding the definition of persecution manifest in Australian and English cases, such as *S395/2002 and S396/2002 v Minister for Immigration and Multicultural Affairs* (2003) and *HJ (Iran) and HT (Cameroon) v Secretary of State for the Home Department* (2010), that have abandoned demands for gay and lesbian people to return to their country of origin and be "discreet" about their sexual identity and intimacy. Even when pro-LGBT refugee cases recognise the intolerable fears of gay and lesbian people forced to hide their sexual identity or intimacy, legal recognition crystallises a set of fears and anxieties that coerce LGBT people into covering queer parts of their claim that may harm their credibility. This is also apparent in cases about "proving" one's sexuality, where law anxiously maintains ethnocentric assumptions about popular culture consumption, public visibility, gender expressions, sexual practices, and social marginalisation. I conclude by looking at fear and anxiety in two recent European Court of Justice cases, *Cases X, Y, and Z* (2013) and *Cases A, B, and C* (2014), that have been heralded as progressive refugee cases for limiting assumptions about discretion and the kinds of questions or evidence that are admissible when adjudicating sexuality.

Reading fear registers how law renders the injuries, intimacies, and identities of LGBT refugees visible for protection while jurisprudential fears confine, contain, and inhibit the terms of that visibility. By reading fear analytically in pro-LGBT refugee cases, I draw out the political consequences of progressive asylum interventions. Specifically, I gesture to why scholars, activists, lawyers, and judges should resist or challenge legal enactments of fear to make more space for the recognition and protection of queer intimacies and identities.

Fear in refugee law and scholarship

Fear is central to the grant of asylum. Under international law, refugees are entitled to seek asylum if they have "a well-founded fear of persecution" owing to race, nationality, religion, political opinion, or membership of a particular social group (*Convention Relating to the Status of the Refugees 1951*: Article 1A(2)). Refugees must be outside their country of origin and unwilling or unable to seek protection from their country of residence. International law orients the analysis of a "well-founded fear" by looking to the future: it entails assessing whether there is a risk of persecution if a refugee is returned to their country of residence, irrespective of whether they have been persecuted in the past (see *Chan Yee Kin* 1989). Persecution refers to a serious injury: sustained forms of serious discrimination or physical violence that either are directly perpetrated by the state or are condoned by it (Walker 2000: 177).

LGBT people are subject to discrimination, violence, and harassment in all parts of the world. Whether in the developing or developed world, persecution remains a pernicious and pervasive problem. In a legislative context, about 70 countries criminalise consensual same-sex sexual activity and some countries have capital punishment for such "offences" (International Lesbian and Gay Association 2017: 8). Fear materialises individually for LGBT people who find themselves in spaces where they anticipate impending injuries (which may be based on ones they have already experienced), which may include state prosecution for sodomy, detention, rape, domestic abuse, public assault, or vilification (see Giametta 2017; Jordan 2011). These fears motivate some people subjected to such injuries within their home countries to flee and seek surrogate protection from other countries. Each year, thousands of LGBT asylum applications are made to the United Nations High Commissioner for Refugees (UNHCR) and individual states. While no specific gender and sexuality categories are mentioned in the Refugee Convention, a number of states accept claims from LGBT people who seek protection.[1]

Ongoing scholarly conversations about asylum processing have developed in response to the adjudicative requirement to define gay, lesbian, and bi sexuality. For the purposes of this chapter, I am interested in how scholarship that attempts to grapple with the way sexuality is not reducible to a script of genital penetration or sexual object choices crystallises fears and anxieties about accepting claims that elude proper verification. Jenni Millbank's work, in particular, is worth noting. She has mapped out two key problems facing LGB refugees when seeking protection: the notion of a "well-founded fear of persecution" is highly gendered and subscribing to stereotypes remains a key basis on which (homo)sexuality is authenticated for the purposes of being considered part of a "particular social group" (Millbank 1995, 2002, 2003, 2005, 2009a, 2009b, 2012, 2013). Scholars have also suggested that when it comes to visibility, those who do not experience discrete acts of violence are legally seen to lack a well-founded fear of persecution, while those who "attract" homophobic violence in public are considered transgressive and should be discreet (Millbank 2009b: 10; Tobin 2012: 468–72; Wessels 2013: 27). When it comes to emotion, scholars have noted that asylum seekers who are apathetic and fail to conform to sexual expectations are denied identity recognition, while those who perform sexual stereotypes too well have their intimacies considered disingenuous and insincere (Johnson 2011: 58; Middelkoop 2013: 168). Hesitancy in oral testimony undermines the credibility of the narrative, while apathetic recounting of experience may be disbelieved for an alleged lack of emotional response. Either the person fails to provide a coherent and plausible narrative because of shame or trauma, or the person responds in an unemotional manner, which makes the account of sexual persecution incredible. Critical legal scholars, motivated by a fear that LGBT people who are denied appropriate protection will face persecution, have critiqued the terms of legal recognition and offered recommendations for reform (see Chelvan 2013; Giametta 2017; Goodman 2012). Scholarly attempts to engage (and remedy) the conceptual problems in refugee law have brought to the fore an affective problem at the heart of asylum adjudication: an asylum seeker's representational fluidity (of their intimacy or identity) compromises the certainty and closure demanded of law.

Fear materialises from activists and scholars who identify how LGBT people are positioned precariously in relation to current legal categories that risk injury: LGBT people are positioned in relation to ethnocentric legal norms and scholars foreground the likelihood that such positioning will result in an impending injury (dismissal of an asylum claim and deportation to endure persecution). These fears for the welfare of LGBT people who seek asylum are also refracted in scholarship that expresses fear and anxiety over the (corroding) integrity of the refugee adjudication system. This oscillation of fear raises an important question: have pro-LGBT asylum cases overreached insofar as they have undermined the normative integrity of refugee law (Hathaway and Pobjoy 2012: 330–2)? James Hathaway and Jason Pobjoy castigate recent pro-LGBT refugee cases (discussed below) for failing to distinguish between "exogenous" and "endogenous" forms of sexual intimacy and identity in order to determine what counts as the injury of persecution (Hathaway and Pobjoy 2012: 336). Pro-LGBT refugee cases, they argue, risk injuring the foundational principles of asylum law. Hathaway and Pobjoy are not unsympathetic to LGBT asylum claims. In fact, they repudiate the idea that gay and lesbian refugees should be "discreet" as a consequence of fear and they recognise that mandated discretion might create psychological harm that can amount to persecution (Hathaway and Pobjoy 2012: 347–8). However, Hathaway and Pobjoy argue that in the pursuit to invalidate discretion, courts have given protection to "trivial" forms of expression (such as drinking "exotically coloured cocktails") (Hathaway and Pobjoy 2012: 374–5). They suggest that by lauding this jurisprudence, we have abdicated an "intellectual responsibility" to adjudicate claims within the ambit of asylum law (Hathaway and Pobjoy 2012: 387). The idea of entrenching "bad law" runs as an anxiety throughout their essay. In particular, Hathaway and Pobjoy contend that pro-LGBT refugee cases that give greater accommodation to queer intimacies and identities should be feared because they injure a system of principled adjudication. By reading (homo) sexual identity in terms of an exogenous/endogenous binary, they attempt to attend to these fears by reasserting the normative bases of international refugee law that suggest that definitions of persecution must be restrictive.

Writing more broadly about the evolution of refugee adjudication, Didier Fassin notes that the "refugee question" has been anxiously circumscribed by normative ideas of "truth" (whether an asylum claim fits within the legal framework) and "true" (the veracity of asylum experiences) (Fassin 2013: 41). What was once an issue of "humanitarian compassion" has now become a matter of "anxious control" (Fassin 2013: 46–7). By tracing a broad historical shift, Fassin also reveals an emotional shift: seeking asylum is not a right born from the recognition that everyone is entitled to seek asylum, but rather a matter of state discretion (or a "gift") conferred once claims have been thoroughly scrutinised (Fassin 2013: 55). Fassin's argument helps identify the politics of fear and anxiety that underpin adjudicating asylum claims: refugee experiences must be interrogated to avoid the presence of "bogus" claims succeeding and threatening the integrity of the adjudication system. The hypermobility of bogus refugees, as an impending threat on law's temporal radar, is met with a legal containment of them. This leads to bureaucratic processes designed to recognise and repudiate insincerity.

Reading Fassin alongside Hathaway, Pobjoy, and other scholars discussed above reveals that fears and anxieties about refugees' sincerity shape both legal interventions aimed at protecting refugees and activist-scholarly critiques of those interventions. Fear is produced through a series of legal and scholarly gestures that bring queer objects or bodies into view and, in doing so, reveal how proximity to these objects or bodies threatens the normative integrity of the refugee adjudication system itself. Claims that queer normative assumptions of injury, intimacy, and identity, rather than being accommodated, become sites of anxious disavowal. Refugee adjudication itself becomes a site of vulnerability for legal institutions: vulnerable to disingenuous claims. For states (and some scholars), such vulnerability necessitates securing borders (Ahmed 2004: 70). This vulnerability generates heightened legal scrutiny which functions as an anxious intimacy: decision-makers must attend to narrative closely in order to authenticate the sincerity (or otherwise) of a particular claim and the extent to which it falls into line with the circumscribed bases of existing refugee law. Failure to do so risks queering an "orderly" adjudication process.

The above sections draw out fear in refugee law and scholarship to highlight the analytic importance of reading pro-LGBT cases in terms of emotion. In the sections that follow, I track judicial and administrative enactments of fear to show how pro-LGBT refugee cases are shaped by temporal and spatial logics indexed to an anticipated injury to the integrity of refugee adjudication. These cases orient legal attention to the future by anticipating queer intimacies and identities that threaten the normative integrity of refugee adjudication and reveal law's proximity to these threats by identifying places where law risks making space for (to recognise) queer intimacies and identities. In asylum law, these fears manifest in attempts to secure the borders of asylum adjudication from the threats of expanding movements of people across borders in search of protection from persecution.[2] In pro-LGBT refugee cases, I map out the ways jurisprudential fears function politically to circumscribe legal recognition or protection by authenticating immutable sexual and gendered identities or intimacies and accounting for what amounts to state-based homophobic persecution (injury).

Dismantling discretion

In Chapter 4, I considered how jurisprudential anger directed at LGBT discrimination functioned to cleave apart sexual identity from religious identity and public associations. I argued that the crystallisation of anger in pro-LGBT anti-discrimination cases accommodated (homo)sexual identities insofar as they fit within existing institutional arrangements and eclipsed queer identities (such as religious LGBT people) and intimacies (such as expressive gay associations). The affective dynamic of recognition and refraction has also limited the protection afforded to sexual minorities who seek asylum. In this section, I discuss how recognising the fear of people who have to conceal their sexual identity or intimacy has prompted courts to abandon legal tests that require gay refugees to be "discreet". Specifically, I draw attention to how judicial recognition of LGBT fears of persecution has crystallised judicial fears by making visible the risks to the integrity of LGBT people who have to hide who they are. Yet, this progressive recognition is circumscribed by fears that militate against recognising queer intimacies and identities that injure the normative integrity of refugee law.

Historically, refugees who demonstrated that they were voluntarily discreet about their sexuality, or could reasonably be expected to be less visible about their sexual identity, had their claims rejected. In the Australian case of *Gui*, for example, a Chinese man had his protection claim refused because his experience of abuse from police after kissing in public was due to his "conduct in public space" rather than his sexual identity (*Gui* 1999: [28]). The approach of distinguishing sexual identity from intimacy, colloquially described as the "discretion test", formed the basis of a High Court of Australia challenge in 2003. In *S395/2002 v Minister for Immigration and Multicultural Affairs* (2003), a Bangladeshi same-sex couple, MD Jahangir Kabir (aged 28) and Syed Fazlur Rahman (aged 47), who had lived together for four years in Bangladesh, sought asylum in Australia. The couple claimed that prior to coming to Australia, they had experienced a range of violent and harassing treatment: family ostracism, a "fatwah", and physical and verbal assaults from local people in their community (*Kabir* 2001: [9]). Initially, their claims for protection were refused on the basis that the familial rejection they experienced did not amount to persecution, and they were not at risk of persecution if they were returned because they would not be "out" as a couple back in Bangladesh. Specifically, the Refugee Review Tribunal (RRT) concluded that the couple had made a "lifestyle choice" to live in a "discreet manner" (*Kabir* 2001: [14]).[3]

In responding to these decisions, the majority of the High Court of Australia overruled the administrative use of discretion (the idea of managing sexual visibility to avoid persecution) in refugee adjudication relating to sexual minorities by recognising the fear of persecution "closeted" gay people face. The majority rendered the applicants' fears about making their homosexual identity and intimacy visible by recognising how non-heterosexual people are placed in heterosocial environments and how this positioning makes LGBT people acutely aware of impending violence should their identity or intimacy be "discovered". Recognising the applicants' fears of persecution crystallised a judicial fear as the Court oriented itself towards the impending persecution that would likely occur if the applicants were returned to their country of origin and their non-heterosexuality was discovered. McHugh and Kirby JJ held:

> In such cases, the well-founded fear of persecution held by the applicant is the fear that, unless that person acts to avoid harmful conduct, he or she will suffer harm. It is the threat of serious harm with its menacing implications that constitutes the persecutory conduct.
>
> (*S395/2002* 2003: [43])

Here, the justices spatialised the risk of persecution by bringing threat of injury and legal demand for discretion into close proximity. The social compulsion to remain discreet – given the foreseeability of "serious harm with its menacing implications" – was an act of persecution itself. In orienting their remarks around the RRT's misdirection on discretion, McHugh and Kirby JJ refracted the fears of the applicants. They foregrounded the risk to the future safety of the couple given their proximity to physical abuse, employment discrimination, community expulsion, or police extortion if a legal decision were to lead to their forced removal back to Bangladesh (*S395/2002* 2003: [51]). Judicial fears over refugees facing persecution materialised as the justices foregrounded the "menacing implications" of persecution that exist in close relation to gay men who concealed their identities or intimacies.

In contrast with the majority, Heydon and Callinan JJ's dissent expressed fear of opening up the law to accommodate sexual minorities. They held:

> The appellants had in fact, and would in all likelihood continue to live, as a matter of choice, quietly without flaunting their homosexuality ... Discretion, it was put, was purely a matter of choice and not of external imposition.
>
> (*S395/2002* 2003: [106])

Fear manifested here by foregrounding the public visibility of queer identity and intimacy as an impending threat to public order and the judicial identification of this threat secured it as something for law to quickly move away from or contain (Ahmed 2004: 67). Heydon and Callinan JJ's reasoning constructed public homosexuality in a way that made it an inherently "flaunting" disruption, and discretion was invoked here as a way of militating against the public disgust towards homosexuality that generated violent rebukes in the first place. Yet, this reasoning was an expression of fear as well by rendering public same-sex relationships much more "visible", and subsequently more potentially injurious, than comparable heterosexual ones. In doing so, this judicial expression of fear functioned to shrink the space available for the protection of gay and lesbian people who sought asylum (Ahmed 2004: 69).

Judicial fears work to delimit the legal spaces available for queer intimacy and identity. Privacy, for example, has been invoked in pro-LGBT cases alongside the logic of discretion as a way to guard against public accommodation of queer intimacy and identity. In the UK, courts have adopted the language of "private life" rather than the concept of identity to dismiss refugee claims where the person was not private about their homosexuality. This subsisted in English law until the widely celebrated UK case of *HJ (Iran) and HT (Cameroon) v Secretary of State for the Home Department* (2010). The case joined together two distinct asylum claims – a gay Iranian man and a gay Cameroonian man – who at different times sought asylum in the UK. HJ was a 38-year-old man from Iran who had arrived in the UK in 2001. He claimed asylum due to a fear that if he returned he would be persecuted for his homosexuality, including his previous "discreet" relationships with men during his military service (*J* 2006: [2]). HT was a 35-year-old man from Cameroon who had arrived in the UK in 2007. He claimed asylum because he feared that his return to Cameroon would result in serious injury. He claimed that, in one instance, he was witnessed kissing his partner in public and was subsequently assaulted by a mob that attempted to castrate him (*HT* 2008: [3]). In hearing the claims together, the UK Supreme Court had to consider whether the expectation to live discreetly (or the decision to do so) amounted to an intolerable burden on fundamental human rights. Rodger LJ took up the analysis of intimate associations to consider how sexual identity was more fluid than immutable. Specifically, he held that a gay asylum seeker from Iran did not need to demonstrate that:

> ... his homosexuality plays a particularly prominent part of his life. All that matters is that he has a well-founded fear that he will be persecuted because of that particular characteristic which he either cannot change or cannot be required to change.
>
> (*HJ and HT* 2010: [61])

Rodger LJ stated that sexuality did not need to be individual, prominent, or immutable in a biological sense. By eschewing the language of whether or not an intimate expression was "fundamental", the Court did not have to make subjective assessments about the "inherent" value of particular sexual expressions and how essential they were to a particular emotional life (Goodman 2012: 438). Hathaway and Pobjoy condemn Rodger LJ's broad claim here as legally spurious because he failed to draw a distinction between "endogenous" expressions and those that are "exogenous". This enables self-expression (such as drinking cocktails or gossiping about men) to be protected regardless of how significant those expressions are to a person's sexual identity (Hathaway and Pobjoy 2012: 330–2, 374–5).

This argument exposes a fear of undermining the integrity of law: placing the expansive judicial recognition of sexual expression in close proximity to a burdened system of adjudication shows that it will compromise the future of a legal process that delineates (homo)sexual intimacy and identity. In the *HJ and HT* judgment, the particularity of persecution was evinced through the applicants' fear of not being able to live and socialise with other gay men freely without enduring violence or harassment. In rejecting the "choice" assumption that underpins discretion logic, Rodger LJ recognised that, unless HJ or HT were "minded to swell the ranks of gay martyrs", the threats of violence vitiated their choices and compelled them to act discreetly (*HJ and HT* 2010: [78]). Drawing upon McHugh and Kirby JJ's earlier judgment, Rodger LJ probed why HJ and HT were discreet in the first place. In doing so, he concluded that the reason for the applicants' discretion was a fear of physical injury – and this fear was refracted through judicial foregrounding of the threats to gay people sent back to places where they have to endure persecutory pressures to hide their sexual identities and intimacies. In *HJ and HT*, this judicial articulation of fear led to a repudiation of bureaucratic expectations ("discretion") that resulted in LGBT persecution.

According to Rodger LJ, freeing gay people from fear was key to enabling the full expression of, or lived experience of, their sexual identities and intimacies. Rather than collapse sexual identity with sexual intimacy, Rodger LJ took a more expansive view of sexuality in the context of non-sexual yet intimate associations:

> To illustrate the point with trivial stereotypical examples from British society: just as male heterosexuals are free to enjoy themselves playing rugby, drinking beer and talking about girls with their mates, so male homosexuals are free to enjoy themselves going to Kylie concerts, drinking exotically coloured cocktails and talking about boys with their straight female mates ... In other words, gay men are to be as free as their straight equivalents in the society concerned to live their lives in the way that is natural to them as gay men, without the fear of persecution.
>
> (*HJ and HT* 2010: [59])

Rodger LJ's listing of social activities here relied on, as he stated himself, stereotypes about "gay lifestyles". Despite the problematic nature of these stereotypes, they were used in a way to broadly recognise the social elements of gay life that existed and how fear of persecution militated against their expression. Rodger LJ took an expansive view of identity and intimacy to recognise the fears of "closeted" gay men: sexual minorities should be able to disclose their attraction to others, engage in conversation about their personal lives, participate in events, and consume pop culture without fear of violence.

However, this expansive recognition of LGBT fear was underpinned by a judicial articulation of fear: the judgment foregrounded the recognition of "less serious" personal injuries as a risk for the Court to contain and avoid stretching jurisprudence too far. Rodger LJ distinguished fear of persecution from other emotional pressures. In fact, Rodger LJ stated that people might choose to be discreet for reasons not related to their fear of persecution:

> For example, he might not wish to upset his parents or his straight friends ... he might worry that, if the fact that he was gay were known, he would

become isolated from his friends and relatives, be the butt of jokes ... or suffer other discrimination.

(*HJ and HT* 2010: [61])

Shame, upset, and worry were emotions distinguished from the fear of persecution. Yet, by distinguishing such feelings from persecution, Rodger LJ shrunk the scope of legal protection by obscuring ways in which gay people experienced such isolation quite distinctly from their heterosexual counterparts. Humiliation and isolation can have debilitating impacts on physical and mental health (see Jordan 2011). For the purpose of determining an asylum claim, gay men's fears needed to be isolated from other emotions when determining the nature of sexual discretion. But, by cleaving apart pressure and persecution, Rodger LJ's reasoning also crystallised a fear of moving jurisprudence too far by anticipating the risks of expanding the legal threshold of persecution and containing those risks to "less grave" emotions like upset and worry. In his judgment, fear structured the recognition of injury (such as a refugee's fear of persecution) by disconnecting it from experiences of humiliation and isolation as unexceptional and non-persecutory.

By emphasising that the Refugee Convention does not protect against "social pressures", Rodger LJ's judgment positioned some homophobic injuries outside the reach of protection obligations. It is difficult to reconcile the judgment's understanding of how refugees, on the one hand, conceal themselves due to fear and, on the other hand, conceal themselves due to pressure or worry (Wessels 2013: 73). The line where worry ends and fear begins is porous. Moreover, in the same judgment that repudiated discretion, discretion was partially revived in relation to other feelings in order to limit the "infinite" gradations of persecution definitions that may result. Hathaway and Pobjoy critique Rodger LJ's judgment as lacking necessary limits. However, the border produced between fear and other emotional pressures was the consequence of a jurisprudential fear that sought to place a limit on what counted as persecutory injury to avoid injuring norms of refugee law. In fact, I agree with Hathaway and Pobjoy's claim that the "instinct to celebrate" should be met with caution (Hathaway and Pobjoy 2012: 387). Yet, unlike them, I follow fear in Lord Rodger's judgment to show how it was an expression of fear: opening up the interrogation of discretion motivated by fear relied on containing discretion motivated by pressure. Scholars who have been critical of Pobjoy and Hathaway's argument still reiterate the need to preserve the normative dimensions of asylum law (particularly the focus on fearing serious human rights violations) (Anker and Ardalan 2012: 534). Yet, as some of the human rights concerns documented earlier show, homophobic injury need not always be motivated by fear or be exceptional. Homophobia can engender shame, worry, anxiety, humiliation, pity, and associated "pressures" that limit the expression of queer intimacy and identity. *HJ & HT* anticipated the way in which social pressures could shame and isolate sexual minorities into remaining discreet about sexual intimacy and identity, not to recognise them as injuries that sexual minorities face but to recognise them as impending injuries to the integrity of asylum law if accepted. Reading fear makes the vulnerability of legal recognition apparent by exposing the enduring fragility of a refugee system that protects against serious forms of persecution and showing how this guards against queer identities and intimacies that come close to compromising the system.

Anxious adjudication

The shift from relying on discretion logic marked a progressive turning point in refugee law by making space to protect LGBT people who sought asylum. I explore this progress further in this section through the legal scrutiny of credibility in relation to how courts and tribunals determine the veracity of an asylum seeker's sexual orientation. I track fear to show how fear of erroneous assessment and the anxiety of making the system vulnerable to "bogus" protection claims lead to heightened scrutiny of the intimate lives of LGBT people. Over the past two decades, previously discussed fears of opening up the recognition of injury has slid over into anxieties over authenticating (homo)sexual identity and intimacy or making sense of the subversive properties of queer sexualities (see Keenan 2015: 128–49; Millbank 2005). The focus has shifted from limiting what counts as a well-founded fear of persecution to limiting what counts as being a genuinely "open" (homo)sexual subject. By following anxiety, I show how pro-LGBT cases bring into judicial anticipation the dangers of ill-defined sexuality and close judicial proximity to such dangers forecloses broader recognition of queer intimacy and identity. This anxiety limits judicial review of bureaucratic interrogations (Millbank 2009b: 25).

Interrogating queer intimacy and identity

In order to tease out how anxiety militates against accommodating asylum claims, it is necessary to consider how queer intimacy and identity have been framed in decisions where the plausibility and consistency of refugee narratives have been questioned. While some decisions (see *SZMDS*) hinge on the absence of evidence for determining a particular fact, others focus on the interpretation of evidence to determine whether or not an applicant is gay and the likelihood of persecution if they are returned to their home country. In adjudicating sexuality, legal recognition evinces judicial anxieties over queer intimacies and identities that resist assimilation into specific social or legal categories.[4] In the UK, following *HJ and HT*, the Asylum and Immigration Tribunal (AIT) had to consider how broadly the obligation for protection stretched in relation to "discreet" sexual minorities.[5] This was illustrated in *SW v Secretary of State for the Home Department* (2011) where a lesbian woman from Jamaica sought protection on the basis that she would face risk of serious harm if she returned to Jamaica. Specifically, the applicant had not experienced any direct incidents of harm due to her discreet sexual relationships with women, but she now feared that given her "open" relationships with women in the UK, she was at greater risk of persecution (*SW* 2011: [27]).

Reading the decision through fear exposes how judicial anticipation of homophobic injury required a differentiation between visible/open lesbian bodies at risk of injury and those who could express their intimacy and identity without persecutory attention. Much of the judicial reasoning in *SW* focussed on the evidentiary basis of the appellant's claim about the nature of her "open lesbian lifestyle". The applicant's testimony outlined her life of fear and secrecy in Jamaica: she had an ongoing sexual relationship with a married woman and participated in an anonymous internet forum that catered for same-sex-attracted women in Jamaica. Importantly, the applicant would not "hold hands in public" with her then partner. This life of discretion because of her fears and anxieties over homophobia was then contrasted to her life upon arrival in the UK, which involved "a freer atmosphere" (*SW* 2011: Appendix A). In the UK, she had more public relationships with women, found a girlfriend, marched in a local pride parade, and signed up as a board member of a black lesbian organisation. Gleeson J observed:

> She described herself firmly as an open lesbian and was not prepared to modify her behaviour on return: The Tribunal should find that honest and credible evidence.
>
> (*SW* 2011: [80])

The Court recognised her experience of "living openly" as an affective process of moving from discretion (fearing violence) to publicity (freedom from fear of violence). Her honesty was tied to her willingness to "own" her sexuality as a public manifestation. Specifically, Gleeson J made note that the applicant was not "naturally discreet about her sexuality" (*SW* 2011: [85]). Her participation in social events, alongside having a public relationship with a woman, rendered the applicant an "open" lesbian whose earlier discretion with respect to her intimacy and identity was a feature of her fear of persecution rather than a voluntary choice. The applicant's desire to be "out and proud" constituted a marker to measure the inhibiting nature of sexual invisibility in Jamaica. Yet, by placing enormous emphasis on being "open" as the panacea to discretion, Gleeson J obscured how sexual minorities who did not express their intimacy and identity visibly were at risk of being disbelieved and, ironically, covered over. By scripting a narrative of (homo)sexual development in terms of emotional linearity – moving from secrecy and fear to openness and pride – sexual minority refugee claims were rendered more plausible (see Berg and Millbank 2009).

The associations of visibility with plausibility are structured by judicial anxieties that foreground the risks of accepting queer intimacies or identities that do not conform to norms of consumption, promiscuity, and progress. For example, in a gendered context, lesbian women can find that their sexual agency is contained through decisions that displace queer intimacy. In the case of

0802825 (2008), a female applicant from Mongolia sought asylum in Australia on the basis of her lesbianism. In addition to the public speculation she endured because of her transgressive romantic attachments, she was subject to domestic violence by her husband. While the RRT accepted the claim of domestic violence, it responded to her narrative of lesbian identity dismissively:

> I accept that the applicant has a girlfriend and that she has had a close relationship with this friend since [year] I have doubts as to whether their relationship is a lesbian relationship as the evidence as to how they first met and their lack of involvement in the lesbian community is of concern. Further the applicant gave little details of the nature of the relationship and I felt she was being evasive as to the real basis of their friendship.
>
> (*0802825* 2008: [92])

While the applicant in this case was deemed to be a refugee, the association between her claim to a lesbian identity and her lack of involvement in a purportedly public "lesbian community" became an adjudicative "concern". The adjudicative anxiety was clear in how the decision foregrounded absence to an imagined lesbian community in order to characterise the applicant as queer to "authentic" lesbianism. Anxiously rendering the applicant's queer identity risked her credibility. This "real basis" of their intimacy could then be contained in terms of friendship. Reading emotion in *080282* enables scholars to recognise how adjudicative anxieties over queer identities (not being part of the lesbian community) or intimacies (a non-lesbian friendship) in pro-LGBT refugee function to dismiss asylum claims and the crystallisation of these anxieties obstruct protection for some LGBT people who seek asylum.

Exploring the relationship between sexual identity and injury and the backgrounding of queer intimacy and identity requires a focus on how fear is manifested through the way in which the RRT understands (or fails to understand) space. Persecution is an embodied experience that cannot be reduced to singular modes of injury (Mason 2002: 59). Fear of persecution becomes embedded in a person's sense of belonging to a space and how they understand that feeling. In the case of a Lebanese man who chose not to engage in sexual activity with other men, the RRT queried the kind of persecution he risked in returning home and sought to better understand the basis of his fears:

> As to what he had feared would happen to him in Lebanon if it was known he was homosexual, he said that he had mental pressure. Also if his family knew they would have a big problem. It was a strict family. Socially he would be an outcast.
>
> (*1000152* 2010: [50])

Injury, in this testimony, was articulated through the applicant's fear of familial ostracism. The constant threat of violence undermined the ability of the applicant to make his desire visible to others: "if his family knew they would have a big problem". In order to be granted refugee status, a history of physical violence need not exist. In this case, the fear of being an "outcast" and prospective persecution was articulated through familial imaginaries. Space became crucial to the articulation of persecution: injury became a risk through residing in domestic space (including literal and symbolic isolation from the home). Understanding injury through the applicant's emotional sense of (non)belonging – the threat of being repudiated from his familial space – produced a "mental pressure" to conceal his sexual identity.

This articulation of fear as non-belonging was refracted by the RRT. The applicant's fear was dismissed by the RRT's anticipation that such harms do not belong in the space of refugee protection and, if the RRT were to make space for these harms, it would threaten narrow legal thresholds of persecution. Even where an asylum seeker's sexual identity and sense of injury were recognised, their claim for harm could be dismissed for not coming up to the level of a well-founded fear of persecution. As the majority in *HJ and HT* reminds us, such "pressure" cannot be tantamount to persecution. Like this applicant from Lebanon, LGBT people who seek asylum can find it difficult to establish a causal link to the absence of state protection when much of the "pressure" they endure occurs at home – perpetrated by their family or community. The causal link is secured by judicial fears that bring "private injuries" into view only to orient courts to a future where their creeping recognition (through refugee protection) threatens the normative basis of a refugee system concerned with public harms. This emotional delineation of public (belonging to the space of refugee protection) and private injury (not belonging to the space of refugee protection) resonates with pro-LGBT anti-discrimination cases (discussed in Chapter 4) that make space for injury and identity only where discrimination is shown to happen in public.

Queering fear

Recent pro-LGBT refugee cases from the Court of Justice of the European Union (ECJ) push back against some of the intrusive questions and stereotypes used to determine LGBT asylum claims. In limiting the scope of "anxious adjudication" described above, the ECJ has circumscribed the way in which evidence and questions can be used to assess sexual orientation. In two cases, decided one year apart, the ECJ adopted the positions in *S395/2002* and *HJ and HT* to overrule residual use of "discretion tests" and to deny using pornographic evidence to demonstrate the veracity of a person's sexual identity and intimacy. Yet, both decisions also articulate a fear of expanding the scope of asylum law too far: one rejects the idea that laws criminalising homosexuality constitute persecution per se for fear of expanding the threshold of persecution too far while the other permits the use of some stereotypes to assess the credibility of an asylum seeker's self-identification about their sexuality for fear of accepting "bogus" claims.

In this section, I show why a reading of fear is politically necessary to confront how adjudicators mobilise fear and anxiety when accommodating some LGBT refugees and identify why scholars, activists, lawyers, and judges should loosen attachments to fear that obstruct queer intimacy and identity.

Rethinking the parameters of persecution

In 2013, the Netherlands referred three asylum decisions to the ECJ to consider whether the criminalisation of homosexuality constituted persecution by itself or whether enforcement of the law needed to reach a particular level of severity (*Joined Cases X, Y, and Z* 2013). X was a national of Sierra Leone, Y was from Uganda, and Z was Senegalese. In Sierra Leone and Uganda, homosexuality was punishable by up to life imprisonment. Senegal had lower penalties: gay men could be jailed for up to five years and fined. Prior to the decision of the ECJ, the Advocate General issued an advisory opinion that circumscribed the application of EU refugee law to the facts of the case. She stated that while sexual minorities could constitute a particular social group for the purposes of claiming asylum and should not have to be discreet about their sexual identity, the question of persecution could not be addressed without careful scrutiny of their claims (*Joined Cases X, Y, and Z* I 2013: [63]). She made note that refugee status was necessarily "restrictive" – it was confined to individuals exposed to "serious denial or systemic infringement of their most fundamental rights" (*Joined Cases X, Y, and Z* I 2013: [41]). By recognising refugee fears in terms of identifiable public threats, the advisory opinion backgrounded the ways in which anti-homosexuality laws stigmatised and made sexual minorities fearful of violence by placing them in a zone of public attention with an ever-present threat of prosecution (even if the laws are not enforced). Sharpston stated:

> It is true that a person who applies for asylum on the grounds of his homosexual orientation cannot expect to be entitled to live in his country of origin in the same way as he might live in the Netherlands.
> (*Joined Cases X, Y, and Z* I 2013: [68])

By taking a progressive stance against the requirement that individual claimants exercise discretion, Sharpston's opinion recognised the fear of some gay people when condemning distinctions between "core" and "peripheral" forms of sexual orientation but also refracted fear to produce a limit to the expression of homosexuality (*Joined Cases X, Y, and Z* I 2013: [71]). Her condemnation of sexual discretion as injurious to sexual minorities opened up claims for protection. But, anticipating the threat of opening up protection to all gay and lesbian people subject to anti-homosexuality laws narrowed the reach of such condemnation.

The ECJ accepted Sharpston's conclusions and held that specific enforcement of criminal laws, not merely their general existence, must be demonstrated to satisfy the threshold of persecution. While sexual minorities required respect for their "private and family life", derogation from those rights was possible (*Joined Cases X, Y, and Z* II 2013: [51]). The ECJ also removed any lingering doubt that discretion could be expected of sexual minorities seeking to avoid persecution. Drawing from Rodger LJ's reasoning in *HJ and HT*, the Court observed that concealing sexual orientation to "exercise reserve" in its expression was not a reasonable expectation (*Joined Cases X, Y, and Z* II 2013: [76]). Here, the Court relied on defining the fear of a person fleeing persecution by enacting its own fear about opening up to all sexual minorities who seek accommodation in all areas of life. The Court was able to offer protection to those identities and intimacies that it feared would face persecution through specific enforcement of a law criminalising homosexuality. This progressive articulation of fear, however, was subtended by another fear. The Court refused to extend protection to LGBT people who experienced generalised homophobic fears because of a general law, as the Court was reticent of being in close proximity to stretching the protective criteria of refugee law too far and had to face the impending risks of undermining refugee law by shrinking the space for protection. For scholars, activists, lawyers, and judges, confronting these enactments of fear is necessary to prevent jurisprudence from containing LGBT people's fear of persecution (from the criminalisation of homosexuality) with specific enforcement of anti-LGBT (sodomy) laws.

Challenges to the adjudication of credibility

Reading emotion in asylum adjudication also invites lawyers and judges to challenge bureaucratic anxieties that underpin the containment of sexual credibility through parochial norms of intimacy and identity. This was apparent in *Joined Cases A, B, and C* where three asylum seekers were denied protection on the basis that they had not been credible. In all three cases, the applicants were either willing to submit, or had already submitted, pornographic evidence to "prove" the veracity of their sexual orientation (*Joined Cases A, B, and C* I 2014: [22]–[29]). Each claim had initially been refused by the Netherlands (the asylum state) on the basis that the narratives were "vague, perfunctory, and implausible" (*Joined Cases A, B, and C* I 2014: [26]). In determining the parameters of credibility assessment, the Court had to consider the nature of self-identification and the associated corroboration to validate a particular claim of sexual orientation. Echoing her comments in *X, Y, and Z* in relation to assessing persecution, Sharpston argued that an assessment of sexual orientation began with self-identification, which must be assessed in specific rather than general terms (*Joined Cases A, B, and C* I 2014: [43]). In condemning current methods of sexual verification, Sharpston observed that medical exams, pornographic evidence, sexual stereotypes, and prurient questioning were inconsistent with the protection of privacy and dignity in the European Charter. But, even when moving away from stereotypes or invasive sexual questioning, Sharpston reiterated the need to authenticate the veracity of a person's sexual orientation. She condemned medical testing as problematic not only because homosexuality was not a pathology, but also because sexual testing (such as determining whether or not a person is physiologically aroused by gay pornography) failed to distinguish "genuine applicants from bogus ones" (*Joined Cases A, B, and C* I 2014: [62]). Moreover, questions that relied on stereotypes were dangerous because "bogus applicants" may have "schooled themselves in preparing their application" (*Joined Cases A, B, and C* I 2014: [65]). Here, (in)sincerity was an issue for adjudicators to probe, but the current methods of credibility assessment militated against that. In fact, judicial anticipation of bogus claims worked – as a threat to the integrity of asylum processing – to rethink methods of verification. Sharpston's fear of bogus asylum claims worked to reveal the law's proximity to this threat: bogus claims were brought into circulation by stereotypes and assumptions that could be performed by anyone. Sharpston's advisory opinion revealed how fears of erroneous adjudication as a result of such misdirected interrogations in pro-LGBT refugee cases pushed away some stereotypes, while reproducing the need to heighten scrutiny of asylum claims in other ways.

In reiterating the need for credibility assessment to respect dignity and privacy, the ECJ strengthened the need for assessment to ensure the veracity of LGBT claims. Self-identification of intimacy and identity was important, but it was not determinative of an applicant's sexual orientation (*Joined Cases A, B, and C* II 2014: [52]). The Court also returned to the use of stereotypes in a partial sense: they could be a "useful element" in adjudication, but they could not be the sole basis on which an asylum claim was determined (at the exclusion of personal circumstances) (*Joined Cases A, B, and C* II 2014: [62]). The ECJ, however, repudiated the use of detailed questions about sexual experience, on the basis that it was contrary to respect for private life. In doing so, the Court suggested that even if applicants were willing to provide oral or visual evidence of their sexual activity, such evidence was to be refused on the basis that it has or had very limited probative value.[6]

However, these progressive judicial moves crystallised judicial fears: encouraging stereotypes opened up the asylum process to abuse by "bogus" claimants who threatened the integrity of adjudication. *Joined Cases A, B, and C* loosened the understanding of intimacy and expression to recognise the vulnerable position of gay and lesbian people in the status determination process. Yet, noting the performative dimensions of (homo)sexuality worked to expose the vulnerability of the adjudicative process itself. Disingenuous applicants could "game" the system by rehearsing the stereotypes used to measure (homo)sexual identity. As a consequence, the Court found that a shift from demeaning sexual questions to ones that enable personal narrative would strengthen the quality of decision-making. Adjudicators not only need to reflect on the threats facing refugees if they are returned home, they must also turn their attention to the threats of those "bogus" claimants. The act of eschewing prurient sexual questions and pornographic evidence became a means of protecting the adjudication process from the threat posed by insincerity. Fears about the fragility of sexual authenticity were crystallised in the judgment and the Court was able to pull away from the fact that sexualities are performative.

Both these decisions and critical legal scholarship discussed above have emphasised that questions should focus much less on sexual activity or testimony about "discovering" one's identity and more on uncovering personal experiences of being "different" (which do not necessarily follow a linear trajectory). LGBT refugees should be asked about what makes them different, when they realised that difference was considered socially as "wrong", how they came to experience shame because of that realisation, and finally what harms they may have experienced because of it (see Chelvan 2013). Moreover, silence must also be accommodated in the interpretation of queer asylum narratives. Adjudicators fail to grasp the emotional "tells" of oral testimony because they refuse to imagine experiences of sexuality or gender identification that contest their pervasive stereotypes of what being queer looks and/or sounds like (Johnson 2011: 70). Instead of acknowledging the reasons for silence or reflecting on its consequences, decision-makers use it as a marker to impugn a refugee's credibility. While the ECJ did not consider silence, the cases opened up progressive ways of thinking about belonging and expressed fears over LGBT people who face persecution for non-belonging. This opening up also exposed how expressing fear over homophobic violence or an LGBT person's fear to speak about sexual activity could be anxiously scrutinised to dismiss "bogus" claims. That is, the Court accepted that the absence of any scrutiny brought "illegitimate" claims into close enough proximity to injure the integrity of adjudication. Reading emotion allows scholars to track how fears manifest – through queer intimacies and identities that make proximate impending threats to the refugee adjudication system – to limit the scope of accommodating LGBT people that eschew sexual stereotypes or norms of injury. Scholars, activists, lawyers, and judges must confront these fears about persecution and credibility to make space for queer intimacies and identities currently denied recognition.

Conclusion

Queer legal scholars have offered compelling critiques of how progressive legal interventions still fail LGBT people who desperately seek safety (see Fernandez 2017; Johnson 2011; Keenan 2015; Millbank 2003, 2012; Schutzer 2012; Shakhsari 2014). In affectively tracing how recognition of sexuality-based asylum claims relied on moving away from, or containing, anticipated threats, this chapter has argued that pro-LGBT refugee cases have broadened the space for protecting LGBT people by fearfully obstructing queer intimacies and identities that risk compromising the normative integrity of adjudication. My reading of emotion has explored how the fears of LGBT people facing persecution – one that reveals proximity to injury – are crystallised and refracted through pro-LGBT refugee cases. Pro-LGBT cases like *S395/2002* and *HJ and HT* that dismantled discretion produced fears over stretching the law too far and, as a consequence, affirmed that LGBT people could be required to manage their sexual visibility in some circumstances. By reading fear analytically, this chapter showed how the scrutiny of queer intimacy and identity for credibility assessment enacted anxieties over accepting ill-defined asylum claims and, in doing so, guarded against such (potentially harmful) queer claims by authenticating identity and intimacy through parochial norms of sexual activity, pop culture, political participation, and social visibility. From identifying a well-founded fear of persecution to authenticating sexual credibility, the borders of asylum law were (re)produced by jurisprudential fears in the moments that pro-LGBT refugee cases recognised the fears of LGBT people to stretch those borders further. Making greater space for queer intimacies and identities politically requires scholars, activists, lawyers, and judges to confront such emotional attachments.

In the final case study in the book, I catalogue legal progress that expands the recognition of LGBT intimacy and identity by considering marriage equality cases from the US to show how love emerges in pro-LGBT cases that purport to secure a future where LGBT people thrive with dignity.

Notes

1 A number of common law jurisdictions, known as "refugee-receiving countries", have come to process sexual orientation and gender identity as a legally cognisable basis of persecution (see Jansen 2013). It is important to note that statutory and procedural differences exist in the application of international refugee law when compared across domestic contexts. Canada was the first Anglophone common law jurisdiction to extend protection to gay asylum seekers (see LaViolette 2009). In Australia, the protection available to sexual minorities seeking asylum has historically been defined in terms of whether a (homosexual) person "belongs to or is identified with a recognisable or cognisable group within a society that shares some interest or experience in common" (Morato 1992). In the United States (US), *Matter of Toboso-Alfonso* (1990) established the precedent that sexual orientation could constitute a valid social group. The United Kingdom (UK) had a comparatively delayed response compared to Canada, the US, and Australia when it came to recognising such claims: tangential comments in a case about gender based persecution recognised the possibility of sexual and gender minorities constituting a particular social group (see *Ex Parte Shah* 1999: 550). In 2004, the European Union issued a Qualification Directive that extended protection specifically on the basis of sexual orientation (Jansen and Spijkerboer 2011: 13).
2 The fear of enabling illegitimate claims is not unique to pro-LGBT cases but is a feature of international refugee law more broadly. See Johns (2004).
3 The RRT has since been incorporated in the Administrative Appeals Tribunal, as the Migration and Refugee Division.
4 Sarah Keenan explores the notion of queer sexualities as a form of "subversive property" at greater length in relation to lesbian asylum claims (see Keenan 2015: 128–49).
5 A comprehensive tribunal structure in England and Wales that has a specific asylum and immigration chamber in the general First-tier Tribunal and Upper Tribunal has now replaced the AIT.
6 In 2018, the ECJ built on this jurisprudence to prohibit the preparation of projective personality tests designed to authenticate an asylum seeker's sexual orientation (*Case C* 2018: [71]).

References

Ahmed, S., 1995. Deconstruction and Law's Other: Towards a Feminist Theory of Embodied Legal Rights. *Social & Legal Studies*, 4, 55–73.
Ahmed, S., 2004. *The Cultural Politics of Emotion*. Oxford: Routledge.
Ahmed, S., 2011. Problematic Proximities: Or Why Critiques of Gay Imperialism Matter. *Feminist Legal Studies*, 19, 119–32.
Anker, D. and Ardalan, S., 2012. Escalating Persecution of Gays and Refugee Protection: Comment on *Queer Cases Make Bad Law*. *NYU Journal of International Law and Politics*, 44, 529–57.
Berg, L. and Millbank, J., 2009. Constructing the Personal Narratives of Lesbian, Gay and Bisexual Asylum Claimants. *Journal of Refugee Studies*, 22(2), 195–223.
Chelvan, S., 2013. From Silence to Safety: Protecting the Gay Refugee? *Counsel*, May 2013, 26–28.
Fassin, D., 2013. The Precarious Truth of Asylum. *Public Culture*, 25(1), 39–63.
Fernandez, B., 2017. Queer Border Crossers: Pragmatic Complicities, Indiscretions and Subversions. In Dianne Otto, ed. *Queering International Law: Possibilities, Alliances, Complicities, Risks*. London: Routledge, 193–212.
Giametta, C., 2017. *The Sexual Politics of Asylum: Sexual Orientation and Gender Identity in the UK Asylum System*. New York: Routledge.
Goodman, R., 2012. Asylum and the Concealment of Sexual Orientation: Where Not to Draw the Line. *NYU Journal of International Law and Politics*, 44, 407–46.
Hathaway, J. and Pobjoy, J., 2012. Queer Cases Make Bad Law. *NYU Journal of International Law and Politics*, 44, 315–89.
International Lesbian and Gay Association. 2017. *State-Sponsored Homophobia – A World Survey of Sexual Orientation Laws: Criminalisation, Protection, and Recognition of Same-Sex Love*, https://ilga.org/downloads/2017/ILGA_State_Sponsored_Homophobia_2017_WEB.pdf (accessed 2 September 2018).
Jansen, S., 2013. Introduction: Fleeing Homophobia, Asylum Claims Related to Sexual Orientation and Gender Identity in Europe. In Thomas Spijkerboer, ed. *Fleeing Homophobia: Sexual Orientation, Gender Identity and Asylum*. Oxford: Routledge, 1–31.
Jansen, S. and Spijkerboer, T., 2011. *Fleeing Homophobia: Asylum Claims Related to Sexual Orientation and Gender Identity in Europe*, www.coc.nl/wp-content/uploads/2013/11/Fleeing-Homophobia-report-EN_tcm22-232205.pdf (accessed 5 August 2016).
Johns, F., 2004. The Madness of Migration: Disquiet in the International Law Relating to Refugees. *International Journal of Law and Psychiatry*, 27, 587–607.
Johnson, T. A. M., 2011. On Silence, Sexuality and Skeletons: Reconceptualizing Narrative in Asylum Hearings. *Social & Legal Studies*, 20(1), 57–78.
Jordan, S. R., 2011. Un/Convention(al) Refugees: Contextualizing the Accounts of Refugees Facing Homophobia or Transphobic Persecution. *Refuge*, 26, 165–82.
Keenan, S., 2015. *Subversive Property: Law and the Production of Spaces of Belonging*. London: Routledge.
LaViolette, N., 2009. Independent Human Rights Documentation and Sexual Minorities: An Ongoing Challenge for the Canadian Refugee Process. *International Journal of Human Rights*, 13(2–3), 437–76.
Mason, G., 2002. *The Spectacle of Violence: Homophobia, Gender and Knowledge*. London and New York: Routledge.

Middelkoop, L., 2013. Normativity and Credibility of Sexual Orientation in Asylum Decision Making. In Thomas Spijkerboer, ed. *Fleeing Homophobia: Sexual Orientation, Gender Identity and Asylum*. Oxford: Routledge, 154–75.
Millbank, J., 1995. Fear of Persecution or Just a Queer Feeling?: Refugee Status and Sexual Orientation in Australia. *Alternative Law Journal*, 20(6), 261–5.
Millbank, J., 2002. Imagining Otherness: Refugee Claims on the Basis of Sexuality in Canada and Australia. *Melbourne University Law Review*, 26(7), 144–77.
Millbank, J., 2003. Gender, Sex and Visibility in Refugee Claims on the Basis of Sexual Orientation. *Georgetown Immigration Law Journal*, 18, 71–110.
Millbank, J., 2005. A Preoccupation with Perversion: The British Response to Sexual Orientation Refugee Claims, 1989–2003. *Social & Legal Studies*, 14(1), 115–38.
Millbank, J., 2009a. From Discretion to Disbelief: Recent Trends in Refugee Determinations on the Basis of Sexual Orientation in Australia and the UK. *International Journal of Human Rights*, 13(2–3), 391–414.
Millbank, J., 2009b. The Ring of Truth: A Case Study of Credibility Assessment in Particular Social Group Refugee Determinations. *International Journal of Refugee Law*, 21(1), 1–33.
Millbank, J., 2012. The Right of Lesbians and Gay Men to Live Freely, Openly, and on Equal Terms Is Not Bad Law: A Reply to Hathaway and Pobjoy. *NYU Journal of International Law and Politics*, 44, 497–527.
Millbank, J., 2013. Sexual Orientation and Refugee Status Determination over the Past 20 Years: Unsteady Progress through Standard Sequences? In Thomas Spijkerboer, ed. *Fleeing Homophobia: Sexual Orientation, Gender Identity and Asylum*. Oxford: Routledge, 32–54.
Schutzer, M., 2012. Bringing the Asylum Process Out of the Closet: Promoting the Acknowledgment of LGB Refugees. *The Georgetown Journal of Gender and the Law*, 13, 669–707.
Shakhsari, S., 2014. The Queer Time of Death: Temporality, Geopolitics, and Refugee Rights. *Sexualities*, 17(8), 998–1015.
Tobin, J., 2012. Assessing GLBTI Refugee Claims: Using Human Rights Law to Shift the Narrative of Persecution within Refugee Law. *NYU Journal of International Law and Politics*, 44, 448–84.
Walker, K. L., 2000. Sexuality and Refugee Law in Australia. *International Journal of Refugee Law*, 12(2), 175–211.
Wessels, J., 2013. Discretion in Sexuality-Based Asylum Cases: An Adaptive Phenomenon. In Thomas Spijkerboer, ed. *Fleeing Homophobia: Sexual Orientation, Gender Identity and Asylum*. Oxford: Routledge, 55–81.

International Instruments

Convention Relating to the Status of Refugees (28 July 1951), www.unhcr.org/en-us/1951-refugee-convention.html (accessed 5 August 2016).
European Convention for the Protection of Human Rights and Fundamental Freedoms (4 November 1950), www.echr.coe.int/Documents/Convention_ENG.pdf (accessed 5 August 2016).

Cases

A (C-148/13), B (C-149/13), C (C-150/13) v Staatssecretaris van Veiligheid en Justitie (17 July 2014, Opinion of AG Sharpston).
A (C-148/13), B (C-149/13), C (C-150/13) v Staatssecretaris van Veiligheid en Justitie (ECJ, Grand Chamber, 2 December 2014).
Case C-473/16 v Bevándorlási és Állampolgársági Hivatal (ECJ, Third Chamber, 25 January 2018).
HJ (Iran) and HT (Cameroon) v Secretary of State for the Home Department [2009] EWCA Civ 172.
HJ (Iran) and HT (Cameroon) v Secretary of State for the Home Department [2010] UKSC 31.
HT (Cameroon) v Secretary of State for the Home Department [2008] EWCA Civ 1288.
HT (Cameroon) v Secretary of State for the Home Department [2008] EWCA Civ 1508.
Islam (AP) v Secretary of State for the Home Department; R v Immigration Appeal Tribunal; Ex Parte Shah [1999] 2 All ER 545.
J v Secretary of State for the Home Department [2006] EWCA Civ 1238.
Kabir v Minister for Immigration and Multicultural Affairs [2001] FCA 968.
Matter of Toboso-Alfonso, 20 I & N Dec 819 (BIA 1990).
Minister for Immigration and Multicultural Affairs v Gui [1999] FCA 1496.
Morato v Minister for Immigration, Local Government and Ethnic Affairs (1992) 39 FCR 401.
S395/2002 v Minister for Immigration and Multicultural Affairs (2003) 203 ALR 112.
SW (Jamaica) v Secretary of State for the Home Department (CG) [2011] UKUT 00251.
SZMDS v Minister for Immigration and Citizenship (2010) 240 CLR 611.
X (C-199/12), Y (C-200/12), Z (C-201/12) v Minister voor Immigratie en Asiel (11 July 2013, Opinion of AG Sharpston).
X (C-199/12), Y (C-200/12), Z (C-201/12) v Minister voor Immigratie en Asiel (ECJ, Fourth Chamber, 7 November 2013).

Australian Refugee Review Tribunal (RRT) Decisions
0802825 [2008] RRTA 328 (11 August 2008).
1000152 [2010] RRTA 223 (19 March 2010).
N93/00846 [1994] RRTA 347 (8 March 1994).
V97/06483 [1998] RRTA 27 (5 January 1998).

Chapter 6

Loosening love
Queer kinship and marriage equality

Introduction

I turn in this chapter to look at how love manifests to define the parameters of LGBT liberty, belonging, and social inclusion in marriage equality cases. I read love analytically to map how marriage equality jurisprudence from the United States (US) recognises the love between same-sex couples and crystallises love as a means of remedying the injury of relationship inequality. I define love as an "intensified zone of attachment" (Berlant 2012: 18) that binds our attention to individuals, objects, and institutions that promise a "good life" (Ahmed 2010: 90) and, in doing so, secures an idealised "self-evident good" of those individuals, objects, and institutions (Povinelli 2006: 17). I argue that this cultural expression of love materialises through the attachments between same-sex couples that seek marital recognition for a "good life" and this gets crystallised and refracted in pro-LGBT marriage equality cases that affectively mark out how law can protect the well-being of same-sex intimacies and identities by remedying the injury of relationship inequality. Specifically, I track how jurisprudential idealisations of the conjugal couple bind judicial attention to constitutional norms that frame liberty as the promise of monogamous intimacy, equality as a promise of a future free from discriminatory injury, and dignity as a promise to elevate homosexual identity into spaces of respectability. I undertake this analysis by showing how cases in states such as California and Massachusetts – *In Re Marriage Cases* (2008), *Perry v Brown* (2010), and *Goodrich v Department of Public Health* (2004) – recognise same-sex marriage as part of a couple's pursuit of liberty and equality based on love (of each other), hope (for future free from discrimination), and respect (for their relationships). Judicial recognition of the love between same-sex couples gets crystallised and refracted in cases that fuse liberty and equality to secure the dignity of their identities and intimacies. By turning to the recent decisions of the Supreme Court of the US in *Windsor v United States* (2013) and *Obergefell v Hodges* (2015), I examine the ways in which marriage equality purports to address the injury of inequality by idealising a dignified future for LGBT people.

Reading love analytically in pro-LGBT marriage equality cases exposes how jurisprudential articulations of love enable the legal recognition of same-sex families (intimacy) and gay and lesbian equality (identity) that conform to (hetero)normative ideas of monogamy and social productivity. This affective crystallisation obstructs the recognition of those who are in non-monogamous relationships (queer intimacy) or resist incorporation into the idealised space of couple-based equality (queer identity). Reading love becomes politically valuable for scholars, activists, lawyers, and judges who wish to confront how jurisprudential expressions of love narrowly arrange the intimacies and identities of LGBT people and loosen legal attachments that background the intimacies or identities of those who queer such emotional arrangements.

Following good feelings

Before embarking on an analysis of marriage equality, it is important to draw out the relationship between love and marriage. As Lauren Berlant writes, thinking about love involves bringing into view conventions and fantasies about idealised forms of intimacy (Berlant 2001: 440; Berlant 2012: 8). As a cultural plot, romantic and reproductive forms of love achieve their ideal expression through (heterosexual) marriage (Berlant 2001: 438). In thinking about the cultural politics of love, Sara Ahmed observes that love "becomes a way of bonding with others in relation to an ideal" – it is a desire that draws us towards others who we identify as capable of elevating us towards that ideal (Ahmed 2004: 124 and 127). Love renders "the self-evident good" of others/objects and secures the forms of intimacy they generate (Povinelli 2004: 17). I draw together these conceptualisations of love to understand love as a cultural idealisation that attaches individuals to others (partners) and institutions (marriage) capable of generating good feelings. This conceptualisation shows how love manifests through marriage (equality) narratives that not only bind individuals legally and exclusively together but also bond them exclusively to institutions and objects that promise individuals a "good life" (Ahmed 2010: 90).[1] This bonding is co-constitutive: the affective bond gives positive value to those objects and institutions, as well being formed by them (Ahmed 2004: 127).

Queer and feminist critiques of marriage equality have considered in detail the problematic way law privileges heterosexual/gendered love as the basis of relationship recognition (see Berlant 1997; Conrad 2010; Cossman 2008; Cox 2014; Fineman 2009; Franke 2015; Hull 2006; Joshi 2014; MacKinnon 1983; Polikoff 2008, Robson 1992; Warner 2000). These critiques (which I discuss further at the end of the chapter) have carefully engaged with love as an idealised object or subject of progressive legal interventions that undermine queer politics and communities. This chapter takes these critiques further by examining how love is not just an object/subject of progressive legal interventions but is also a jurisprudential means of circumscribing those interventions. By reading love analytically, I show how pro-LGBT marriage equality cases from the US affectively structure the socio-legal terms through which the injury, intimacy, and identity of same-sex couples are progressively recognised.[2]

Love of liberty

The first pro-LGBT marriage equality cases to recognise same-sex couples in the US relied on liberty and the rights to privacy recognised in *Lawrence*. These cases recognised the liberty of same-sex couples to express love and pursue a good life, and the courts were able to secure this freedom through an idealisation of constitutional liberty that bonded same-sex couples to marriage as the means of making a good life for them possible. By reading these two interrelated expressions of love together, I follow how liberty accrues value as a legal ideal capable of securing and affirming the intimacies of same-sex couples.

California provides an illuminating set of cases in this regard. California's move towards marriage equality began in 2004. San Francisco Mayor Gavin Newsom ordered that county clerks issue same-sex couples with marriage licences (see *In Re Marriage Cases* 2006). A few years earlier, the *California Family Code 1994* had been amended by a public ballot to restrict the definition of marriage to opposite-sex couples. Newsom believed, however, that such a ban was inconsistent with California's state constitution. So, he opened up the city to solemnising same-sex marriages and same-sex couples flocked from around the state (and from other parts of the country) to get married. In what was affectionately dubbed the "Winter of Love", the San Francisco City Hall was transformed from a site of gay mourning (gay activist Harvey Milk had been assassinated there three decades earlier) to a place of gay pride (same-sex couples could formalise their love and commitment). This season of love, however, had an expiration date. Within weeks, the Supreme Court of California nullified the marriages that had taken place (*Lockyer* 2004).

Bolstered by the promise of their love, the lead plaintiff couples and the City of San Francisco sought a declaration that the statutory definition of marriage breached the liberty and equality guarantees of the state's constitution (*In Re Marriage Cases* 2006: 687).[3] In delivering the majority opinion, McGuiness PJ subordinated the plaintiffs' expressions of love between them to the "public role" marriage played in "organizing fundamental aspects of our society" (*In Re Marriage Cases* 2006: 715). In the dissent, however, marriage was cast as a love of liberty (not just of a partner). Dissenting, Kline J held that pursuing marriage was a "self-defining" feature of personal integrity. Kline J refuted the majority's framing of privacy and forcefully argued for a more expansive view of privacy that encompassed the intimacy of same-sex couples. Kline J held:

> The marital relationship is within the zone of autonomy protected by the right of privacy not just because of the profound nature of the attachment and commitment that marriage represents, the material benefits it provides,

and the social ordering it furthers, but also because the decision to marry represents one of the most self-defining decisions an individual can make.
(*In Re Marriage Cases* 2006: 736)

Kline J's account recognised the "profound attachment and commitment" between those who wished to get married. Her judgment not simply oriented legal attention to marriage as a way to attach individuals together but also expressed an attachment to marriage as a "zone of autonomy" that provided the basis through which individuals could exclusively define their intimacies and identities. The dissent recognised the exclusive love between partners and refracted that through an articulation of love that idealised the exclusive personal "attachment and commitment" (love between partners) and bonding that exclusively to a zone of liberty (marriage) that represented "social ordering" of intimacies. Loving marriage as a means of ordering intimacy enabled Kline J to jurisprudentially recognise the liberty of same-sex couples to marry.

The Court of Appeal's decision was overturned on appeal to the California Supreme Court. Kline J's dissent about the connections between liberty and intimacy were more favourably received than the majority's holding about the "rational basis" of "traditional marriage". George CJ concluded:

> In view of the substance and significance of the fundamental constitutional right to form a family relationship, the California Constitution properly must be interpreted to guarantee this basic civil right to all Californians, whether gay or heterosexual, and to same-sex couples as well as opposite-sex couples.
> (*In Re Marriage Cases* 2008: 782)

In the California Supreme Court, liberty was tied to intimacy: a right to formulate relationships. Echoing the holding in *Lawrence*, the Court refused to distinguish privacy and kinship (*In Re Marriage Cases* 2008: 814). The autonomy to form a family was blocked by the state's refusal to grant a marriage licence. Marriage was not a privilege granted by the government but a civil right mandated by the Constitution. Yet, the continued invocation of family was also used to sustain an idealised intimacy between liberty and a "good life". In particular, marriage was not simply a subpart of the right to intimate association. Rather, it remained an opportunity to be recognised "with a loved one" that was of the "deepest and utmost importance" to the individual or couple (*In Re Marriage Cases* 2008: 818).

Loving liberty secured loving same-sex intimacies. In bringing together liberty and intimacy, George CJ held that marriage afforded the plaintiffs an "opportunity to live a happy, meaningful, and satisfying life as a full member of society" (*In Re Marriage Cases* 2008: 820). By recognising the marital love between partners in terms of well-being and satisfaction, George CJ articulated marital liberty as a fantasy capable of "simplifying living" (Berlant 2012: 89).

Marriage, as a constitutional right, accrued affective value by the Court investing in the public recognition of same-sex couple intimacies (Ahmed 2004: 127). While the majority opinion in the case eschewed the contention that marriage could be restricted to a "responsible" reproductive purpose, a judicial articulation of love crystallised in this case by idealising marital love and attaching value to it through the emphasis on relationship stability (*In Re Marriage Cases* 2008: 826).

Following the decision of the California Supreme Court, a number of groups petitioned the state to give the public a say on same-sex marriage by subjecting it to a popular vote. Dubbed Proposition 8, an amendment was put at the 2008 election to constitutionally define marriage as the union between a man and a woman (see *Perry* 2010).[4] The amendment created a precarious legal environment for same-sex couples in the state. This led to a challenge on federal constitutional grounds, *Perry v Schwarzenegger* (2010). The courts had to resolve whether the bar on same-sex marriage violated the Due Process Clause of the Fourteenth Amendment of the US Constitution. At trial, the plaintiffs testified about what marriage meant to them as a matter of love. Lead plaintiff Sandy Stier distinguished between domestic partnerships and marriage:

> There is certainly nothing about domestic partnership as an institution – not even as an institution, but as a legal agreement that indicates the love and commitment that are inherent in marriage and [domestic partnership] doesn't have anything to do for us with the nature of our relationship and the type of enduring relationship we want it to be.
>
> (*Perry* 2010: 939)

Stier's plea for recognition concentrated on the liberty to define the relationship in the terms that she (and her partner) deemed appropriate. The term "domestic partnership" may have offered equivalent legal benefits, but it was not imbued with the love and commitment that were promised by marriage. This was the primary reason why the plaintiffs sought (and were granted) injunctive relief from the Court against Proposition 8: they wanted liberty to proclaim their love.

In recognising Stier and her partner's desire for law to recognise their love, the Court attached same-sex couples wanting to marry to constitutional liberty through an idealisation of marital liberty capable of securing the intimacy between same-sex couples. Walker CJ held that same-sex couples were "identical" to their opposite-sex counterparts when it came to forming "deep emotional bonds and strong commitments" (*Perry* 2010: 967). The Court recognised the plaintiff's personal desires to love freely by refracting them through a legal institution capable of elevating those desires. Marriage provided the "weight" and "shine" for existing same-sex family commitments (Mohr 2005: 66). Same-sex couples were not seeking to acquire a "new right"; they were merely asserting their existing right to marry a partner of their choice. By making this claim, Walker CJ expressed an attachment to marriage in a way that divested it of gendered meaning but idealised the dyadic and monogamous terms through which recognition could be conferred. This account of love, expressed through judicial reasoning that bonded same-sex couples to institutions that elevated their intimacies, secured the worthiness of marriage while affirming the intimacies and identities of (LGBT) people included within it.[5]

Hope for equality

In pro-LGBT marriage equality cases, liberty has been mobilised alongside an "equal protection" doctrine (see Chapter 4) that scrutinises invidious discrimination perpetrated against LGBT people. This section looks at how hope animates equality, alongside claims of love, in pro-LGBT marriage equality cases from Massachusetts and California. Judicial recognition expresses hopes for a future free from injury when same-sex couples are able to marry.

Massachusetts

In 2003, Massachusetts became the first US state to legalise (and keep) marriage equality. Fourteen plaintiffs – same-sex couples who resided in Massachusetts – came together to challenge the failure of the Department of Public Health to issue them with marriage licences (*Goodrich* 2003). The plaintiffs were committed, loving, and "active in church, community, and social groups" (*Goodrich* 2003: 314). The only obstacle they faced to the full realisation of this expression of productivity was not a personal trait but an institutional blockage that denied them the rights and protections of marriage. For Marshall CJ, an analysis of relationship recognition began with history:

> History must yield to a more fully developed understanding of the invidious quality of the discrimination.
>
> (*Goodrich* 2003: 328)

In focussing on discrimination, the Court held that exclusion from marriage was not about preserving "traditions" or maintaining responsible reproduction. Rather, the legal denial was based upon a "destructive stereotype" that same-sex relationships were inherently more unstable than heterosexual ones (*Goodrich* 2003: 333). In response, the Court pulled towards evidence that same-sex couples made "excellent parents" (*Goodrich* 2003: 334). Marshall CJ held that discrimination against same-sex family forms did not strengthen the traditions of heterosexual parenting, but merely denied security to existing gay and lesbian couples who were raising children. This holding not simply relied on expressing an attachment to marriage as a means of affirming the intimacy between same-sex couples but also functioned as a way to bond those couples to a family form that facilitated positive rearing of children and used that legal bond to alleviate the denial of parental security caused by exclusion.

By foregrounding judicial emotion towards the litigants, scholars can note how this case expressed hopes for equality by first recognising the lack of legal protections for same-sex couples (injury) and then remedying this lack by formally recognising same-sex relationships (intimacy) as marriages. For Greaney J, inclusion was not about a "grudging acknowledgment" of same-sex couples but rather involved a "hope ... more liberating" that the community as a whole would become more welcoming (*Goodrich* 2003: 349). Here, sexual well-being was derived from judicial hope of community hospitality. This was expressed by idealising marriage as a fantasy that promised the integration of gay and lesbian people in the community. Hope underscored this fantasy by orienting legal attention to the future (Berlant 2012: 43). In other words, elevating same-sex couples to legal terms equivalent to opposite sex couples promised freedom from discrimination and social belonging – for both same-sex and opposite-sex couples. *Goodrich* not just presented equality as a remedy for the injury of sexuality marginalisation, but also bound the opportunities to expand the horizon of social inclusion to the legal equality made hopeful by marriage.

California

Kline J's dissent in the *In Re Marriage Cases* (2006) stated the problem of framing "alternative forms of recognition" as equality. At the time of the decision, California had one of the most comprehensive forms of domestic partnership legislation, conferring on same-sex couples most rights and responsibilities afforded to married couples. However, this "opportunity" was limited because it did not "eradicate the stain of their exclusion from the institution of civil marriage" (*In Re Marriage Cases* 2006: 759). In a similar vein to Kline J's analysis, on appeal in the *In Re Marriage Cases* (2008), George CJ held that formal equality was the only way couples could be granted durable and portable recognition (*In Re Marriage Cases* 2008: 806). Marriage was relationship currency – the way in which couples could purchase recognition at the federal level, in other states, and in other parts of the world. Marriage accrued affective value in this decision as a means of regulating dyadic relationships, and this had to include same-sex couples. This attachment to marriage and equality was sustained through the refusal of other intimate relationships – that is, the Court expressly precluded polygamous relationships from its constitutional consideration of equal protection (*In Re Marriage Cases* 2008: 829). This inclusion was not about aligning to new modes of queer intimacy, or even about expanding same-sex relationships more broadly in the public sphere; rather, the litigants' and judicial formulation of love narrowed the terms of protection by bonding sexual minorities to an ideal of equal intimacy (i.e. monogamous love).

Following Proposition 8, *Perry* (2010) put facts relating to equality and equal treatment for same-sex couples under critical scrutiny. The trial brought to the fore hopes that equality would not only deliver substantive rights to same-sex couples and their families, but also provide LGBT communities with a greater sense of belonging (Yoshino 2015: 11). In distinguishing domestic partnerships from marriage, plaintiff Jeffrey Zarrillo testified that "it would just be easier to describe the situation" (*Perry* 2010: 933). Equality promised to be a descriptive currency – one that would make it easier for Zarrillo and his partner to participate in society (in this instance, by opening a shared bank account). The Court idealised marriage in terms of its promise to ease the burden of everyday activities and attaching value to that promise (rather than romanticised in terms of the broad claims made about love and commitment raised by the other plaintiffs throughout the litigation). Marriage equality promised to alleviate a range of injuries – everything from awkward administrative inconveniences (such as filling out forms) to intense practical burdens (such as moving interstate) – through judicial decisions that exclusively bonded same-sex relationships to the widely idealised form of (opposite-sex) marriage.

The Ninth Circuit's decision narrowed but affirmed the association between hope and equality when cultivating the appropriate remedy for the injury of marital exclusion (*Perry* 2012: 1075). Reinhardt J observed that Proposition 8 served "no purpose" other than to "officially classify [same-sex couple] relationships and families as inferior to those of opposite-sex couples" (*Perry* 2012: 1063). Proposition 8 subordinated an entire class of relationships (*Perry* 2012: 1085). In discussing couples' desires to participate in marriage, Reinhardt J observed:

> That designation is important because "marriage" is the name that society gives to the relationship that matters most between two adults. A rose by any other name may smell as sweet, but to the couple desiring to enter into a committed lifelong relationship, a marriage by name of "registered partnership" does not.
>
> (*Perry* 2012: 1078)

Love made recognition of equality possible. Although same-sex couples could still access all the same legal rights and obligations, the change in nomenclature amounted to a tangible harm. For same-sex couples, the denial had an injurious impact on everything from the legitimacy afforded to their children through to how their relationships were socially (mis)perceived (Cruz 2014: 445). Moreover, an individual's desires for equality could not be satisfied by access to substantively similar rights alone – they could only be satisfied by identical treatment under the same institutional framework. By bonding to marriage as an institution that delivered legitimacy and reputability to existing forms of impaired kinship, the Court idealised the terms of repair (to the injury of same-sex couples unable to get married) through the guarantee of "sweet smelling" equal legal recognition.[6]

Respecting dignity

The cases discussed above made constitutional liberty and equality for same-sex couples possible by idealising marriage the means of securing same-sex intimacy and bonding the identities of same-sex couples to the institution. Walker CJ held in *Perry* that the bar on marriage obstructed gay men and lesbian women from realising "happy, satisfying" commitments (*Perry* 2008: 970). Marriage was the "principal manner" in which the state attached "respect and dignity to the highest form of a committed relationship and to the individuals who entered into it" (*Perry* 2012: 1079). Overturning the bans on marriage promised hopes of a life free from the injury of discrimination and social exclusion. *Goodrich* used emotional language of deprivation to highlight that barring same-sex couples from marrying demeaned the dignity of those who desired "membership in one of our community's most rewarding and cherished institutions" (*Goodrich* 2003: 313). I now turn to read the emotional tether between liberty and equality to show how pro-LGBT marriage equality cases cultivate a mode of legal recognition that elevates the dignity of (homo)sexual identity (see Wolfe 2013). Dignified forms of legal visibility are not simply social goods; they are legal expressions of "good feeling" that cultivate respect through social acceptance and denial of bigotry (Ahmed 2010: 5; Waldman 2013: 757–8).

Windsor v United States

Windsor v United States (2013) was the first decision of the Supreme Court of the US that coupled respect with marriage equality, and humiliation with marital exclusion (see *Windsor* 2013). *Windsor* was the culmination of two decades of strategy and litigation to overturn the *Defense of Marriage Act* (DOMA) (1 USC § 7 and 28 USC § 1738C).[7] Edith Windsor, an 83-year-old widow, came forward to lead a test case to invalidate the legislation (Archibald 2014: 701). Windsor and her recently deceased partner, Thea Spyer, were prominent gay rights advocates who had been together for over 40 years. In 1993, both were registered as domestic partners under New York City's laws. By 2007, Spyer's multiple sclerosis had begun to rapidly deteriorate. The couple flew to Canada and were legally married later that year. Spyer died in 2009 and bequeathed all her assets to Windsor. At the time, New York did not have marriage equality, but it did recognise marriages that were validly contracted in other jurisdictions. However, DOMA denied Windsor federal relationship recognition and she was required to pay $363,053 in federal estate tax (*Windsor* 2012: 397). DOMA treated Windsor and Spyer as legal strangers, not spouses.

As a result, the courts had to resolve whether § 3 of DOMA constituted a violation of the Equal Protection Clause of the Fifth Amendment of the US Constitution.[8] At the initial trial, Judge Jones observed that it was illogical to assume that extending federal benefits to same-sex couples took away the "incentive" for opposite-sex couples to procreate (*Windsor* 2012: 404). DOMA served to indirectly target or injure same-sex families by denying them recognition on the perception of "family", rather than the reality of family (which came in multiple forms). The Second Circuit built on the trial court's DOMA analysis (to one of heightened scrutiny) by pointing to the history of discrimination faced by same-sex couples and the hostilities affecting their public participation (*Windsor* II 2012: 184).

The Supreme Court of the US affirmed the earlier decisions, noting that DOMA constituted a violation of the Fifth Amendment, but moved the discussion of federalism into an emotional terrain of dignity. Kennedy J's opinion brought the injury of exclusion to the fore: "DOMA seeks to injure the very class New York seeks to protect" (*Windsor* 2013: 2695). New York had sought to provide protections for same-sex couples through their recognition under the law. In contrast, the federal government had impermissibly tried to curb that recognition by refusing to recognise their lawful status. The Court knotted together liberty and equality by idealising its attachment to marriage as a means of securing intimacy from the injury of a federal law that resulted in non-recognition of state same-sex marriages (making individuals "legal strangers") and elevating that intimacy into a zone of equal protection shielded from demeaning state interference.

Kennedy J's judgment held that DOMA "wrote inequality into the entire US Code" (*Windsor* 2013: 2694). Entrenching inequality and limiting liberty meant that same-sex couples were also injured by the imposition of stigma:

> The avowed purpose and practical effect of the law here in question are to impose a disadvantage, a separate status, and so a stigma upon all who enter into same-sex marriages made lawful by the unquestioned authority of the States.
>
> (*Windsor* 2013: 2696)

First, the law curbed the expression of intimacy by imposing a "disadvantage" that burdened married same-sex couples, as they could not access the rights and protections granted to opposite-sex ones. Second, this burden subordinated same-sex relationships, enforcing an inequality by relegating their relationships to a "separate status". By pulling towards marriage as an institution that nurtured intimacies, the Court was able to render the burden of legal inequality as imposing a stigma on same-sex intimacies and couples that prevented their flourishing. DOMA targeted and humiliated a class of relationships that had been lawfully sanctioned in their respective states. *Romer* was also cited to illustrate that this inequality (and the associated denial of dignity) was motivated by a "bare desire to harm", rather than any legitimate state interest (*Windsor* 2013: 2694).

Kennedy J expanded on the statutory stigma by affectively drawing attention to the injurious impact that DOMA had on children. He held:

> The law in question makes it even more difficult for the children to understand the integrity and closeness of their own family and its concord with other families in their community and in their daily lives.
>
> (*Windsor* 2013: 2698)

DOMA fractured the integrity of same-sex families. By blocking marriage recognition, it isolated children raised in same-sex families and denied them protections given to "other families" who were similarly situated. This was not simply a question of rights, but one of respect too – the integrity of same-sex families and their capacity for intimacy had been foreclosed by DOMA's blanket refusal to treat them as a family in the first place. DOMA injured children as well as couples (Widiss 2015: 551). This "anti-humiliation" rhetoric arose in response to the Court's consideration of the injurious consequences of social exclusion and marginalisation (Yoshino 2014: 3085). By taking family as his primary object of concern, Kennedy J was able to secure the dignity of same-sex families by bonding them to marriage: respectful recognition of kinship was possible by idealising promises of "understanding" and cultivating those idealisations through marriage as a way to achieve the social acceptance of same-sex families.

Obergefell v Hodges

Windsor did not consider the constitutionality of same-sex marriage per se and the ruling did not affect the existing state bans on same-sex marriage. However, advancing upon the emotional footsteps taken in *Lawrence*, *Windsor* created a path for the "enduring bonds" of same-sex intimacies by bonding those intimacies to a constitutional liberty to marry (see *Lawrence* 2003: 578; Ho 2014). Following *Windsor*, numerous federal district courts began to strike down the remaining state bans on same-sex marriage (see *Bourke* 2014; *Lee* 2014; *Bostic* 2014; *Brenner* 2014; *Baskin* 2014).

Obergefell v Hodges (2015) was the culmination of two decades of jurisprudence on the topic of same-sex marriage (see Tribe 2015). The decision joined together cases involving 14 same-sex couples (including two gay men whose partners were deceased) who had sought to challenge remaining state bans on same-sex marriage in Michigan, Kentucky, Tennessee, and Ohio. Much like the plaintiffs in the *Perry* and *Windsor* cases, all had been in "loving, committed relationships" at the time of the litigation (*Obergefell* 2013: 976). A majority of justices on the Supreme Court of the US quashed the bans on same-sex marriage holding that the denial of marriage equality infringed on the Equal Protection and Due Process guarantees of the Fourteenth Amendment.

In writing for the majority of the Court, Kennedy J held that marriage was "essential to our most profound hopes and aspirations" (*Obergefell* 2015: 4). The Court was drawn towards the ability of marriage to elevate sexual relationships and, in doing so, idealised a future for enduring same-sex intimacy. This loving recognition was made possible because Obergefell and the other couples were not seeking to "devalue" the promise of marriage, but sought inclusion because they, too, respected the good life it had to offer their loving relationships (*Obergefell* 2015: 5). By recognising the ideal love between same-sex couples seeking to marry and refracting these idealisations, the Court made possible what the plaintiffs' "hearts" left "unspoken" – it respected their dignity by articulating romanticised narratives of marriage that attached the respectability of gay and lesbian people to it.

Respectability crystallised better futures for same-sex couples, free from the injury of inequality, in the sphere of marital intimacy. Kennedy J cultivated equality rights through a hopeful aspiration for couples wanting to quell the fear of loneliness. The liberty to achieve this aspiration was conditional on being able to get married. Moreover, referring back to *Lawrence*, the Court observed that while moving from "outlaw to outcast" may be a "step forward", it did not achieve the "full promise of liberty" (*Obergefell* 2015: 14). The prohibition on marriage merely carved out same-sex families and placed them in a space where they would "suffer the stigma of knowing that their families are somehow lesser" (*Obergefell* 2015: 15). This injury was made apparent by the fact that such relationship forms have been the subject of a "long history of disapproval" and the denial of marriage worked as a "grave and continuing harm" (*Obergefell* 2015: 22). The Court referred to *Bowers* and the persisting indignities inflicted on same-sex couples that had to hide their relationships to avoid criminal penalty or social stigma. Such "dignitary wounds cannot always be healed with the stroke of a pen", but the Court continued to cultivate its attachment to, and idealisation of, marriage as a way of attempting this repair (*Obergefell* 2015: 25).

Kennedy J concluded his judgment with a poetic piece of constitutional jurisprudence. He brought same-sex couple's fights for dignity through liberty and equality to a dramatic close:

> No union is more profound than marriage, for it embodies the highest ideals of love, fidelity, devotion, sacrifice, and family. In forming a marital union, two people become something greater than once they were. As some of the petitioners in these cases demonstrate, marriage embodies a love that may endure even past death. It would misunderstand these men and women to say they disrespect the idea of marriage. Their plea is that they do respect it, respect it so deeply that they seek to find its fulfillment for themselves. Their hope is not to be condemned to live in loneliness, excluded from one of civilization's oldest institutions. They ask for equal dignity in the eyes of the law. The Constitution grants them that right.
> (*Obergefell* 2015: 25)

Marriage delivered emotional recognition: the Constitution affirmed same-sex love, fidelity, devotion, sacrifice, and kinship. For same-sex couples seeking to realise the "highest ideals" of their love, the Court crystallised that love by elevating and bonding to marriage as the (constitutional) right means of conferring these couples with the liberty to find that "fulfilment" in "something greater". Hope for inclusion was also expressed through a judicial call for dignity that oriented towards marriage as a way to deliver gay and lesbian people a future free from injury: same-sex couples did not seek to "disrespect" the institution but humbly sought its embrace in order to be free from a "condemned" life of "loneliness". The Court idealised marriage equality as the way to legally repair this injury of exclusion and isolation by offering up "good feelings" (Ahmed 2010: 6–7).

Queering love, hope, and respect(ability)

By tracking emotion, scholars can make sense of the relationship between the love that underscores liberty and the hope that animates equality and how these judicial expressions of emotion narrow the legal scope of respecting the intimacies and identities of LGBT people (Berlant 2012: 110). In the above section, I used love as an analytic register to draw out how pro-LGBT marriage equality cases recognised the love between same-sex couples and showed how jurisprudence crystallised love by cultivating idealised attachments to marriage and the "good feelings" marriage generates to secure the liberty of same-sex intimacy and equality of gay identities. I concluded my emotional reading with *Obergefell*'s poetic exclamation that love had triumphed over a humiliating legal exclusion. In this final section, I move to a political terrain to consider how reading love allows scholars to queer idealising enactments in jurisprudence. While marriage exclusion has been emotionally conceived in progressive jurisprudence as an attempt to "lock out" LGBT people from social belonging, the loving push for marital inclusion has worked to "lock in" (hetero)normative fantasies of injury, intimacy, and identity. Queering this love requires scholars, activists, lawyers, and judges to make sense of the affective consequences of exclusive forms of love in law and consider alienating such emotion or loosening its exclusive bonds when progressing the rights of LGBT people (Ahmed 2010: 87).

Problematising liberal love

Marriage equality is a powerful love story – one that accrues legal significance through cases that cultivate loving narratives through attachments to order, maturity, and commitment. Marriage equality also measures political progress (see Kimport 2014; Mohr 2005; Vaid 1995; Warner 2000). Berlant refers to this social form of measuring in terms of a "love plot" where marriage becomes a social descriptor of intimacy through which individuals are able to measure the affirmation of love (Berlant 2000: 440). While numerous queer scholars have pointed out how this narrative limits the nature of relationship recognition, reading love in pro-LGBT marriage equality cases gives scholars an understanding of how these limits are affectively produced in jurisprudence that cultivates idealised attachments to forms of liberty that obstruct queer intimacies and identities. In *Goodrich*, the Court "cherished" the way in which marriage could be expanded to eschew sexual stereotypes by attaching to the desires of same-sex couples to live a life just like their opposite-sex counterparts and cultivating these desires through access to marriage (*Goodrich* 2003: 314). Much like the sentimental covering of sodomy in *Lawrence*, the decisions in *Windsor* and *Obergefell* were able to idealise same-sex forms of intimacy – exclusively attaching same-sex relationships to conjugal intimacy – in a way that covered over disgusting or disruptive queer intimacy (like the polyamorous or promiscuous kind). In doing so, the jurisprudence produced fantasies of intimacy that emotionally mimicked the "revered" and "respected" institution of marriage and secured this intimacy by idealising their content (*Windsor* 2013: 2700; *Obergefell* 2015: 28). As Walker CJ held in *Perry*, marriage provided a social order through which same-sex couples could find love from "deep emotional bonds" and "strong commitments" (*Perry* 2010: 967). The jurisprudential expression of love, by recognising and refracting the enduring, exclusive conception of commitment expressed by same-sex couples, only made way here for couples who mimicked heterosexual couples in all respects bar the gender constitution of the couple.

Queer activism has maintained a critical relationship with institutions that define love in privatising or exclusive terms (Berlant 1997: 11; Duggan 2003: 50). Queer politics relies on challenging reproductive sexual assimilation (Charles 2012: 154). Mutually supportive communities and associations are encouraged (in varied erotic, intergenerational, caring, platonic forms) over recognition that privileges "the couple" as the primary vehicle for recognising intimacy. Foregrounding judicial expressions of love in progressive jurisprudence – by directing attention to the terms of their emotional enactment – is necessary if scholars, activists, lawyers, and judges seek to unsettle how these exclusive idealisations of the couple occlude liberty claims for queer intimacies and equality claims for queer identities. This does not require abandoning the pursuit of marriage equality but draws focus to how we might render the idealised attachments that these cases generate less secure to make space for queer intimacies and identities. For example, in *Perry*, Sandy Stier invoked love as the means by which to claim the right to "self-define" her relationship with her partner, Kristin Perry (*Perry* 2010: 939). By unsettling the Court's love of liberty – as an expression that aligns intimacy to marriage – lawyers and judges can make space for queer paths of liberty that let people "grow" and determine their own "endings" (Mohr 2005: 71). In doing so, lawyers and judges can recognise that what limits "self-defining" intimacies is not a technical legal doctrine but is a parochial emotional expression produced by bonding liberty to elevated ideals like monogamy and fidelity.

Judicial recognition of marriage equality is not just a formal pairing of two people who exclusively commit by forsaking all others, but it also involves a judicial pairing of idealised intimacies with marriage in a way that excludes the liberty of queer (non)sexual intimacies. In a queerly insightful dissent, Roberts CJ argued in *Obergefell* that the majority's emphasis on love as the basis for marriage could logically extend to polyamorous couples (*Obergefell* 2015: 20). Despite cases such as *Perry* and *Obergefell* explicitly noting shifting definitions and eliminating the gendered criteria of marriage, the identification with marginalised gay and lesbian individuals (identity) who were aligned to conjugal same-sex relationships (intimacy) precluded support for other consensual relationships. The holdings in *Perry* and *Obergefell* cultivated the terms of liberty by idealising intimacy in a way that excluded others from relationship recognition. By distinguishing polyamory (and polygamy) from marriage equality, these cases closed off the purported "slippery slope" invoked by opponents (Gher 2008: 600;

Cahill 2007: 780). In these pro-LGBT cases, love did not liberate intimacy – it solidified it into a conjugal pair. Reading emotion shows how love mobilises choice for some LGBT people, while relating other relationships to a site of social disapproval or abjection. Reading emotion makes room for scholars, activists, lawyers, and judges to pursue queer intimacies that disturb, disgust, or threaten the romanticisation of marriage (such as polyamory) by registering, and rendering less secure, legal idealisations of liberty that only enable recognition of monogamous same-sex couples.

Confronting equality

Reading emotion in the above cases exposes how expressions of hope, along with love, insidiously cover over the continuing injuries faced by queer individuals who are unwilling or unable to get married. In *Goodrich*, the aspiration for inclusion was not exceptional – it reflected a desire of couples wishing to be equally productive. The Court recognised this hope and refracted it by investing marriage with rights and obligations to idealise, among other things, the welfare of children and the rights of spouses to access their (employed) partner's health insurance made possible by marriage. The decision generated hope by recognising the value of same-sex couples that cared for children or looked after partners. Marshall CJ cultivated an attachment to equality by tethering same-sex intimacy to marriage in order to deliver a future that guaranteed the welfare of children (*Goodrich* 2003: 314). In *Perry*, relationship equality was idealised by foregrounding the way in which marriage worked as a currency of recognition in everyday life – it made accessing sick partners, seeking custody, and even opening up joint bank accounts easier (*Perry* 2010: 933). While it is important to acknowledge how attachments to equality extended these rights to a number of same-sex couples, it is necessary to read emotion to register the limits of this recognition in order to challenge them within their judicial enunciation. In pro-LGBT marriage equality cases, idealisations of sexual intimacy and kinship through marriage remained unquestioned in pursuing legal hopes for equality. Judgments such as *Goodrich* and the *In Re Marriage Cases* held that families come in diverse forms. But, the failure to register the idealisations of same-sex families living free from discrimination, cultivated through attachments to equality, meant current definitions of marriage (even if extended to same-sex couples) precluded recognition of some families (such as those living in polyamorous arrangements, extended families, and domestic care relationships). In *Windsor*, children raised in families excluded from recognition were considered to suffer not only legal precarity but also social humiliation, because their families were stigmatised by the state.

Scholars, activists, lawyers, and judges who account for these positive emotions can challenge the ways pro-LGBT cases secure gay and lesbian identity by parsing how these decisions cultivate legal equality in hopeful terms that obstruct queer individuals who live in non-nuclear, non-dyadic families that are denied basic state benefits. In my discussion above, equality animated the future by relishing the comforting emotional familiarity of the status quo. Even in those cases that explored the evolving couple definition of marriage to demonstrate its changes over time, inclusion of same-sex couples only served to idealise the couple in a way that strengthened, rather than troubled, the "vibrant" and "revered" value of the institution (*Goodrich* 2003: 340). Judicial elevation of same-sex couples through marriage equality represented freedom from discrimination by compelling same-sex couples to participate in its hopeful terms or risk losing state support. Marriage was a hopeful demand – one that pro-LGBT cases entrenched for couples who desired equality.

Following the hopeful expectations of same-sex couples and how the courts recognise and refract these hopes also reveals why pro-LGBT marriage equality cases legitimise legal structures that subordinate queer life and render some LGBT people to perpetual precarity. *Obergefell* envisioned a future where no gay or lesbian person would suffer the injuries of loneliness with the promise of (a right to) marriage. In referencing both *Lawrence* and *Romer*, the Court observed that the path to equality had been an ongoing and challenging one. The Court's hope of bringing an end to this was expressed through the possibility of marriage conferring social acceptance. Yet, this judicial expression of hope was conditional: it was available only to those who were eligible for (homo)sexual belonging. That is, belonging alleviated injustice where couples were willing to inhabit the sanctity of marriage. This judicial attachment covered over persisting forms of state violence: undocumented LGBT people deported through administrative discretion (see Lewis 2014), LGBT people criminalised and incarcerated (see Stanley 2010), trans and gender nonconforming people denied legal documentation that affirmed their (non)gender (see Spade 2011), LGBT people unable to access basic healthcare or accommodation (see Kaufman and Miles 2010), and individuals summarily fired from work and denied social services for their sexual orientation or gender identity (see Reed 2014). Hopeful recognition of equality, as expressed through pro-LGBT marriage equality cases, obscured ongoing economic and social marginalisation.

Rethinking respect(ability)

The pro-LGBT marriage equality cases discussed in this chapter combine a love of (marital) liberty and hope for (legal) equality to bond LGBT well-being to marriage. *Windsor* and *Obergefell* oriented towards marriage as a means of eliminating the injury faced by same-sex couples, such as stigma and negativity, and also securing the respect of their identity by extending marriage to them. *Windsor* redeemed same-sex couples and their children from the injury of exclusion by eliminating the stigma that came from the denial of a legal status. Refusing to allow the federal government to "single out" same-sex relationships for the purposes of denying benefits meant that the Court could respect intimacies that had been dignified by the state. *Obergefell* expanded the push for dignity by locating the desire for relationship recognition within the respectable history of marriage (see Franke 2015). This dignity was expressed by orienting to the plight of same-sex couples denied lifelong companionship, enabling the hope of social acceptance that secured the integrity of children, and foreclosing the precarity that came with isolation and vulnerability.

This judicially generated respectability of same-sex couples, however, turned LGBT well-being into a question of reputation. Writing on *Obergefell*, Nan Hunter observes that dignity is the judgment's "centre of gravity" – same-sex couples are thereby pulled within marriage's orbit of respectability (Hunter 2015: 109). While rethinking the norms about heterosexual procreation helped dislodge the insistence on "traditional marriage", the respect shown to why same-sex couples "revere" the "tradition" of marriage narrowed legal recognition of relationships to same-sex couples that exhibited respect for marriage. Many queer intimacies disturb or disgust (such as those discussed in Chapter 2). For sadomasochists or leather queens, the desire to engage in rough, uncompromising, and non-procreative forms of sexuality are neither worthy nor wanting of respect or recognition but endure criminalisation (see Bersani 1987). Taking account of how jurisprudential respectability frames the terms of dignity draws attention to why queer intimacies are cast out of the frame of recognition because they do not seek respect or redemption.

Loosening judicial enactments of respect is necessary to make space for queer intimacies and identities that "undignify" the institution of marriage. Rather than seek to heal injury and secure intimacy and identity through the expulsion of sexual shame, reading emotion identifies how scholars, activists, lawyers, and judges might unsettle some of the ways legal recognition reproduces state legitimacy and respectability by confronting jurisprudential idealisations of (homo)sexual intimacies and identities without having to abandon jurisprudence for marriage equality. This affective analysis makes space in progressive legal interventions for queers (and others) who continue to live unrespectable lives that involve transient attachments, disturbing sexual practices, and offensive identities (Sedgwick 2009: 61). In other words, registering how pro-LGBT marriage equality cases dignify sexual intimacy and identity through expressions of respect – by showing how they emotionally elevate marriage as the primary means of securing relationship justice – draws attention to how scholars and lawyers might unsettle forms of respectability that eclipse the recognition of queer intimacies and identities.

Troubling emotional politics of visibility

Reading love, hope, and respect enables scholars to grasp the ways in which "good feelings", as Ahmed writes, work to obstruct and cover over the troubling aspects of queerness. In the pro-LGBT marriage equality cases, sexual minorities were recognised as loving, committed, and productive subjects. Love, hope, and respect made them palatable for inclusion within marriage, and judicial crystallisation of these positive feelings conditioned their visibility. Yet, the emotional underpinnings and the injurious capacity of marriage remain covered. For same-sex couples, the urgency of relationship recognition in situations of domestic violence was covered over (see Samons 2013; Greenberg 2012). For children being raised by three or four parents, a dyadic model of parentage compromised their rights and protections in situations where a parent was sick or killed (see Polikoff 2008: 123–45). Instead of liberating queer kinship, emotional notions of liberty and equality expressed in jurisprudence helped secure oppressive socio-economic arrangements (see Vaid 1995: 179).

This is not to suggest that emotional visibility (through marriage) is unimportant. The fact that same-sex relationships are now included as marriages means that they are covered in relevant state criminal laws dealing with domestic violence or movements for more functional forms of family law (see Pfeifer 2005). But, by affirming attachments that idealise marriage as a means of eliminating inequality and furthering social acceptance, progressive jurisprudence risks minimising the messy, difficult, troublesome, and even violent dimensions of the institution. Legal interventions may "deinstitutionalise" some definitional features of marriage (such as its presumed link to procreation), but continuing to cultivate it through emotions (such as love, hope, and respect) that maintain fidelity, futurity, and dignity does nothing to contest its self-evident, "fundamental" positive value. While selective approaches to using judicial review to vindicate constitutional rights are part of "strategic choices" – scholars, activists, and lawyers need to account for how this legal progress compels "assimilation" (at least partially) within the specific emotional terms of law. Reading emotion is vital if scholars, activists, lawyers, and judges are to navigate the consequences of LGBT visibility derived from the cultivation of love, hope, and respect that leaves marginalised LGBT people without institutional support to thrive (see Berlant 2011).

The queer scholarship discussed earlier attests to the politics of affirming kinship networks that contest what Judith Butler has termed the "psychic investment" in the couple:

> It is crucial ... that we maintain a critical and transformative relation to the norms that govern what will not count as intelligible and recognizable alliance and kinship.
>
> (Butler 2004: 117)

Butler attempts to negotiate the complex terrain of queerness and normativity. On the one hand, LGBT people must be made visible in order to engage in political activism and be afforded rights within a state discourse. Simultaneously, on the other hand, there is a need to transform the prevailing heteronormative rhetoric of romantic love in order to prevent pathologising identities or rendering certain forms of intimacy as aberrant or deviant because they do not conform to our perception of what we understand to be normal or morally desirable. Katherine Franke, for example, suggests that a queer alternative of "friendship" – based on supporting networks of care and dependency – is a recognition that does not seek to circumscribe the form (sexual and non-sexual) that intimacy takes (Franke 2006: 2702). This would strengthen activist and scholarly attempts to broaden the horizon for social and legal pursuits to support ethical kinds of kinship.[9]

When it comes to the role of jurisprudence in sustaining these investments, reading emotion allows scholars to map the space available in law for queer intimacies and identities and invites activists and lawyers to loosen the emotional bind that a judicial fixation on "the (monogamous) couple" produces. Interestingly, it was not Kennedy J in *Obergefell* but rather Roberts CJ (in dissent) who opened the space for such an affective queer critique. After all, if love could be articulated beyond gender, why could it also not be shared between more than two people? If marriage is a pursuit of love, one secured through a "fundamental right" of liberty and equality, then rendering that love visible is necessary to challenge the "positive" terms that exclude non-dyadic loving couples and make room for queer intimacies and identities in progressive jurisprudence.

Conclusion

Marriage equality has been framed as a happy ending in the struggle for LGBT people seeking dignity from injury, liberty for intimacy, and equality of identity. Some same-sex families now enjoy durable legal protections. For others, however, marriage equality jurisprudence offers little in their struggle to eliminate injury or enable intimacy and identity that do not adhere to loving heteronormativity. Loosening (hetero)normative expressions of love in jurisprudence and unsettling expectations that LGBT people subscribe to idealised attachments is necessary to avoid marginalising queer intimacies and identities in law.[10] Reading emotion makes room for scholars, activists, lawyers, and judges to do this work by analysing pro-LGBT marriage equality cases through the recognition jurisprudential emotions like love, hope, and respect make possible. Reading emotion is not about condemning those who gleefully washed their Facebook profile photos in rainbows when *Obergefell* was decided. Rather, it is an analytic strategy that can politically affirm the partial utility of such decisions while making legal room to support queer intimacies and identities.

Notes

1 Like Sara Ahmed, I am interested in thinking about love as a performative cultural phenomenon rather than defining the relations between romantic, filial, platonic, love, etc. (see Ahmed 2004: 124). For a detailed discussion of different theorisations and expressions of love, see hooks (2000) and Secomb (2007).
2 The US provides a useful case study to examine the legal paths towards marriage equality because marriage has been extensively litigated and contested in constitutional, statutory, and judicial contexts. Rights to same-sex marriage in the US have

been granted, circumscribed, and withdrawn in the last few decades (see Pierceson 2013). Alternative forms of recognition, such as civil unions and domestic partnerships, have also varied considerably between states. In 1971, a gay couple from Minnesota sought a marriage licence. They were denied. The couple's subsequent state appeals were quashed and ultimately the Supreme Court of the US dismissed their application with a single sentence: "The appeal is dismissed for want of a substantial federal question" (*Baker* 1972). This one line became binding precedent to dismiss a range of applications from same-sex couples seeking marriage licences. Marriage equality was effectively laughed out of court (Yoshino 2015: 36–7). Surprising cracks in the legal terrain as it was in the mid-1990s invigorated the push for marriage equality. In *Baehr v Lewin* (1993), the Hawaii Supreme Court held that denying someone the ability to marry a partner of the same sex constituted sex discrimination (see Gushiken 2000). The Vermont Supreme Court introduced the first comprehensive guarantee of equality by requiring Vermont to give same-sex couples all the rights and responsibilities afforded to married couples, though the legislature was free to determine whether this would be done through marriage or an equivalent scheme (*Baker* 1999). These moves prompted a number of other states and the federal government to pass statutory and constitutional changes to prohibit same-sex marriages (see Pierceson 2013). Referred to as a "backlash", marriage equality also led to the homophobic policing of gay and lesbian relationships (see Keck 2009). This fight for marriage recognition between courts, legislatures, and the people continued in the following decades until its national realisation in June 2015 in the Supreme Court of the US case of *Obergefell v Hodges*.

3   The *In Re Marriage Cases* consolidated six appeals from various couples across the state. At the California Court of Appeal, the claims were dismissed on the basis that the gender-specific marriage laws were "rationally" enacted and there was no "fundamental right" to a same-sex marriage.

4   Both sides, in a vicious public campaign, spent millions of dollars to sway Californian voters. Proposition 8 passed narrowly, with 52 per cent of the public vote. Proponents of the measure were successful largely by framing the issue in terms of (threats to) children: "we should not accept a court decision that may result in public schools teaching our own kids that gay marriage is ok" (*Perry* 2010: 930).

5   The Ninth Circuit narrowed the trial court's reasoning. Proposition 8 was unconstitutional for taking away a right that had previously been granted, rather than the broader liberty reasoning advanced by Walker CJ. While I discuss the equality and dignity reasoning more closely in the following sections, it is important to note here how, even in the narrower frame, the judgment reaffirmed the "unique recognition that society gives to harmonious, loyal, enduring, and intimate relationships" (*Perry* 2012: 1078). In dismissing the subsequent appeal on justiciability grounds, the Supreme Court of the US vacated the Ninth Circuit judgment and affirmed Walker CJ's ruling (see *Perry* 2013).

6   While the Supreme Court of the US vacated the Ninth Circuit decision and dismissed the appeal, it did so on the basis that the proponents of Proposition 8 had not suffered an injury that would grant them standing to appeal Walker CJ's trial ruling (*Perry* 2013: 2668). By implication, the Ninth Circuit rejected the argument that same-sex marriages impaired opposite-sex marriages (at least in a materially significant way). Those who claimed that marriage equality denigrated their marriages had only a "generalized grievance" for which they were unable to seek judicial relief.

7   In 1996, in response to *Baehr* – the decision that opened up marriage to same-sex couples in Hawaii – the US Congress passed legislation to define marriage as the union between a man and a woman for the purpose of recognising marriages for federal benefits. DOMA amended over 300 statutes. It also allowed states to refuse to

recognise same-sex marriages that had been validly solemnised in other states (which subsequently created legal difficulties when it came to dissolving marriages performed in other states) (see Hameroff 2012; Manasfi 2014). During its operation, same-sex couples lawfully married in states such as Massachusetts and Iowa were denied the approximately 1,200 federal benefits granted to their opposite-sex counterparts (Herzig 2011: 623).
8 *Windsor* raised a number of procedural issues relating to standing and states' rights. Interestingly, at the time of Windsor's suit, the federal government conceded that DOMA was likely unconstitutional. When it refused to defend the legislation in court, the Bipartisan Legal Advisory Group of the US House of Representatives intervened (see *Windsor* 2012).
9 This is not to suggest that queer intimacies are more ethical or less abusive.
10 It is also important to note that other scholars have devoted significant attention to the possibilities of using love as a means of justice and community building (see Liao 2015; Raghavan 2017: 157–190). Love has also been central to activist mobilisations (see, for example, Amnesty International's "Love is a Human Right" campaign).

References

Ahmed, S., 2010. *The Promise of Happiness*. Durham: Duke University Press.
Archibald, C. J., 2014. Is Full Marriage Equality for Same-Sex Couples Next? The Immediate and Future Impact of the Supreme Court's Decision in *United States v. Windsor*. *Valparaiso University Law Review*, 48, 695–713.
Berlant, L., 1997. *The Queen of America Goes to Washington City: Essays on Sex and Citizenship*. Durham: Duke University Press.
Berlant, L., 2000. Love, a Queer Feeling. In Tim Dean and Christopher J. Lane, eds. *Psychoanalysis and Homosexuality*. Chicago: Chicago University Press, 432–52.
Berlant, L., 2011. *Cruel Optimism*. Durham: Duke University Press.
Berlant, L., 2012. *Desire/Love*. Brooklyn: Punctum Books.
Bersani, L., 1987. Is the Rectum a Grave? *AIDS: Cultural Analysis/Cultural Activism*, 43, 197–222.
Butler, J., 2004. *Undoing Gender*. New York: Routledge.
Cahill, C. M., 2007. "If Sex Offenders Can Marry, Then Why Not Gays and Lesbians?": An Essay on the Progressive Comparative Argument. *Buffalo Law Review*, 55, 777–814.
Charles, C., 2012. *Critical Queer Studies: Law, Film, and Fiction in Contemporary American Culture*. Surrey: Ashgate.
Conrad, R., 2010. Against Equality, in Maine and Everywhere. In Ryan Conrad, ed. *Against Equality: Queer Critiques of Gay Marriage*. Chico: AK Press, 43–50.
Cossman, B., 2008. Betwixt and between Recognition: Migrating Same-Sex Marriages and the Turn toward the Private. *Law and Contemporary Problems*, 71, 153–68.
Cox, B. J., 2014. Marriage Equality Is Both Feminist and Progressive. *Richmond Journal of Law and the Public Interest*, 17, 707–38.
Cruz, D. B., 2014. "Amorphous Federalism" and the Supreme Court's Marriage Cases. *Loyola of Los Angeles Law Review*, 47, 393–450.
Duggan, L., 2003. *The Twilight of Equality: Neoliberalism, Cultural Politics and the Attack on Democracy*. Boston: Beacon Press.
Feinberg, J. R., 2013. Avoiding Marriage Tunnel Vision. *Tulane Law Review*, 88, 257–315.

Fineman, M. A., 2009. The Sexual Family. In Martha A. Fineman, Jack E. Jackson, and Adam P. Romero, eds. *Feminist and Queer Legal Theory: Intimate Encounters, Uncomfortable Conversations*. London: Ashgate, 45–64.

Franke, K. M., 2006. The Politics of Same-Sex Marriage. *Columbia Journal of Gender and Law*, 15(1), 236–48.

Franke, K. M., 2015. *Wedlocked: The Perils of Marriage Equality*. New York: NYU Press.

Gher, J. M., 2008. Polygamy and Same-Sex Marriage – Allies or Adversaries within the Same-Sex Marriage Movement. *William and Mary Journal of Women and the Law*, 14, 559–603.

Greenberg, K., 2012. Still Hidden in the Closet: Trans Women and Domestic Violence. *Berkeley Journal of Gender, Law & Justice*, 27, 198–251.

Hameroff, R., 2012. I Do. Is That Okay with You?: A Look at How Most States Are Circumventing the Full Faith and Credit Clause and Equal Protection Clause to Not Recognize Legal Same-Sex Marriages from Other States and Its Effect on Society. *Florida A & M University Law Review*, 8, 133–55.

Herzig, D. J., 2011. DOMA and Diffusion Theory: Ending Animus Legislation through a Rational Basis Approach. *Akron Law Review*, 44, 621–78.

Ho, J., 2014. Weather Permitting: Incrementalism, Animus, and the Art of Forecasting Marriage Equality after *U.S. v. Windsor*. *Cleveland State Law Review*, 62, 1–74.

hooks, b., 2000. *All About Love: New Visions*. New York: Harper.

Hull, K. E., 2006. *Same-Sex Marriage: The Cultural Politics of Love and Law*. New York: Cambridge University Press.

Hunter, N. D., 2015. Interpreting Liberty and Equality through the Lens of Marriage. *California Law Review*, 6, 107–16.

Joshi, Y., 2014. The Trouble with Inclusion. *Virginia Journal of Social Policy and the Law*, 21, 207–65.

Joshi, Y., 2015. The Respectable Dignity of *Obergefell v. Hodges*. *California Law Review*, 6, 117–25.

Kaufman, M. J. and Miles, K., 2010. Queer Kids of Queer Parents against Gay Marriage. In Ryan Conrad, ed. *Against Equality: Queer Critiques of Gay Marriage*. Chico: AK Press, 59–70.

Keck, T. M., 2009. Beyond Backlash: Assessing the Impact of Judicial Decisions on LGBT Rights. *Law & Society Review*, 43(1), 151–86.

Kimport, K., 2014. *Queering Marriage: Challenging Family Formation in the United States*. New Brunswick: Rutgers University Press.

Lewis, R. A., 2014. "Gay? Prove It": The Politics of Queer Anti-Deportation Activism. *Sexualities*, 17(8), 958–75.

Liao, S. M., 2015. *The Right to be Loved*. London: Oxford University Press.

MacKinnon, C., 1983. Feminism, Marxism, Method and the State: Toward Feminist Jurisprudence. *Signs: Journal of Women in Culture and Society*, 8(4), 635–58.

Manasfi, J. A. D., 2014. Joint Federal Income Tax Returns: DOMA's Dead – If You Are Married, You Are Married, But What If You Are Married-Like? *Journal of Law, Business, & Ethics*, 20, 43–76.

Mohr, R. D., 2005. *The Long Arc of Justice: Lesbian and Gay Marriage, Equality, and Rights*. New York: Columbia University Press.

Pfeifer, T., 2005. Out of the Shadows: The Positive Impact of *Lawrence v. Texas* on Victims of Same-Sex Domestic Violence. *Penn State Law Review*, 109, 1251–77.

Pierceson, J., 2013. *Same-Sex Marriage in the United States: The Road to the Supreme Court.* Lanham: Rowman & Littlefield.

Polikoff, N. D., 2008. *Beyond (Straight and Gay) Marriage: Valuing All Families under the Law.* Boston: Beacon Press.

Povinelli, E., 2006. *The Empire of Love: Toward a Theory of Intimacy, Genealogy, and Carnality.* Durham: Duke University Press.

Raghavan, A., 2017. *Towards Corporeal Cosmopolitanism: Performing Decolonial Solidarities.* London and New York: Rowman & Littlefield.

Reed, A., 2014. Abandoning ENDA. *Harvard Journal on Legislation*, 51, 277–314.

Robson, R., 1992. *Lesbian (Out)Law: Survival under the Rule of Law.* New York: Firebrand Books.

Samons, C., 2013. Same-Sex Domestic Violence: The Need for Affirmative Legal Protections at All Levels of Government. *California Review of Law and Social Justice*, 22, 417.

Sedgwick, E. K., Shame, Theatricality, and Queer Performativity: Henry James's *The Art of the Novel*. In David Halperin and Valerie Traub, eds. *Gay Shame*. Chicago: University of Chicago Press, 49–62.

Spade, D., 2011. *Normal Life: Administrative Violence, Critical Trans Politics, and the Limits of Law.* New York: South End Press.

Stanley, E., 2010. Marriage Is Murder: On the Discursive Limits of Matrimony. In Ryan Conrad, ed. *Against Equality: Queer Critiques of Gay Marriage*. Chico: AK Press, 15–8.

Tribe, L. H., 2015. Equal Dignity: Speaking Its Name. *Harvard Law Review Forum*, 129, 16–32.

Vaid, U., 1995. *Virtual Equality: The Mainstreaming of Gay and Lesbian Liberation.* New York: Anchor Books.

Waldman, A. E., 2013. Marriage Rights and the Good Life: A Sociological Theory of Marriage and Constitutional Law. *Hastings Law Journal*, 64, 739–79.

Warner, M., 1999. *The Trouble with Normal: Sex, Politics, and the Ethics of Queer Life.* Cambridge: Harvard University Press.

Widiss, D. A., 2015. Non-Marital Families and (or after?) Marriage Equality. *Florida State University Law Review*, 42, 547–72.

Wolfe, Z., 2013. Gay Marriage: Accommodationist Demands Expand the Conception of Human Dignity. *National Law Guild Review*, 70, 88–96.

Wollstonecraft, M., 1792. *A Vindication of the Rights of Women.* London: T Fisher Unwin.

Yoshino, K., 2014. The Anti-Humiliation Principle and Same-Sex Marriage. *Yale Law Review*, 123, 3076–103.

Yoshino, K., 2015. *Speak Now: Marriage Equality on Trial – The Story of Hollingsworth v. Perry.* New York: Crown Publishers.

Ziegler, M., 2012. The Terms of the Debate: Litigation, Argumentative Strategies, and Coalitions in the Same-Sex Marriage Struggle. *Florida State University Law Review*, 39, 467–510.

Legislation

Defense of Marriage Act 1996 (US).

Cases

Baehr v Lewin, 74 Haw 530 (1993).
Baehr v Miike, 1996 WL 694325.
Baker v Nelson, 409 US 810 (1972).
Baker v State, 744 A 2d 864 (1999).
Baskin v Bogan, 766 F 3d 648 (2014).
Bostic v Rainey, 970 F Supp 2d 456 (2014).
Bourke v Beshear, 996 F Supp 2d 542 (2014).
Brenner v Scott, 999 F Supp 2d 1278 (2014).
DeBoer v Snyder, 772 F 3d 388 (2014).
DeBoer v Snyder, 973 F Supp 2d 757 (2014).
Goodrich v Department of Public Health, 440 Mass 309 (2003).
Henry v Himes, 14 F Supp 3d 1036 (2014).
Hollingsworth v Perry, 133 S Ct 2652 (2013).
Lee v Orr, 2014 WL 683680.
Lockyer v City and County of San Francisco, 33 Cal 4th 1055 (2004).
Marriage Cases, In Re, 49 Cal Rptr 3d 675 (2006).
Marriage Cases, In Re, 43 Cal 4th 757 (2008).
Obergefell v Hodges, 576 US ___ (2015).
Obergefell v Wymyslo, 962 F Supp 2d 968 (2013).
Perry v Brown, 671 F 3d 1052 (2012).
Perry v Schwarzenegger, 704 F Supp 2d 921 (2010).
Perry v Schwarzenegger, 790 F Supp 2d 1119 (2011).
Strauss v Horton, 46 Cal 4th 364 (2009).
Windsor v United States, 833 F Supp 2d 394 (2012).
Windsor v United States, 699 F 3d 169 (2012).
Windsor v United States, 113 S Ct 2675 (2013).

Conclusion
Towards queer reparative futures

Justice Kennedy from the Supreme Court of the United States (US) observes, "our society has come to the recognition that gay persons and gay couples cannot be treated as social outcasts or as inferior in dignity and worth" (*Masterpiece Cakeshop* 2018: 9). In *Masterpiece Cakeshop* (2018), the judicial majority upheld an appeal by a baker who refused to bake a wedding cake for a same-sex couple citing religious reasons and was initially found to have breached Colorado law that prevented discrimination on the basis of sexual orientation in "public accommodations". The Court held that the commission tasked with adjudicating breaches of Colorado's anti-discrimination law had expressed hostility towards the baker's religious convictions when dealing with the initial complaint made by the same-sex couple who were denied a wedding cake (*Masterpiece Cakeshop* 2018: 12). While the outcome of the case hinged on a procedural constitutional matter, Justice Kennedy noted that the substantive issues raised in the case (such as the conflict between religious freedom and freedom from discrimination) must "await further elaboration…without undue disrespect to sincere religious beliefs, and without subjecting gay persons to indignities when they seek goods and services in an open market" (*Masterpiece Cakeshop* 2018: 18). By identifying the substantive constitutional rights at stake, the majority judgment briefly mapped the violations of gay persons' dignities through references to respect, hostility, and humiliation. This recent decision is a powerful reminder of how LGBT people's emotional responses to injury shape the precarious terrain of judicial recognition: judicial crystallisation of emotion makes visible certain types of injury, intimacy, and identity for recognition while inhibiting forms that queer normative institutional arrangements. The ambivalent obiter in *Masterpiece Cakeshop* illustrated that legal repudiation of a commercial service provider's hostility towards LGBT people and reparation for the indignity LGBT people suffer as a result (such as the discrimination same-sex couples face when purchasing baked wedding goods) was affectively possible to the extent that legal repudiation/reparation did not disrespect genuine religious beliefs.

Feeling Queer Jurisprudence invites us to rethink how to feel about legal progress that seeks to secure the futures of LGBT people. As an activist-scholar, my emotional responses to LGBT struggles for social justice, and the ambivalence that arises when using jurisprudence to repair injury (as gestured to in *Masterpiece Cakeshop*), provided the impetus for writing this book.[1] Existing queer legal scholarship has extensively parsed the effectiveness of pro-LGBT law reform proposals that affirm the lives of LGBT people and condemned the extent to which these progressive reforms further harm marginalised (LGBT) populations (see Adler 2018; Bassichis and Spade 2014; Leckey 2015; Moran 1996; Spade 2011; Stychin 1995; Stychin and Herman 2000; Zylan 2011). This book has used emotion to further the analytic and political dimensions of this scholarship by drawing out the affective costs of legal interventions and providing a framework for scholars, lawyers, activists, and judges to emotionally grasp the terms of those progressive interventions. Reading emotion recasts how pro-LGBT cases assume significance through the emotions they generate and shows how giving a critical account of emotions allows scholars to register both possibilities and limits of making space within pro-LGBT cases to affirm queer intimacies and identities. This allows scholars, activists, lawyers, and judges to confront how jurisprudential enunciations of emotions problematically circumscribe the terms of legal progress, without having to abandon legal pursuits.

In order to pursue a jurisprudential analysis that foregrounds queer relationships between injury, intimacy, and identity, it is necessary to deviate from the methodological constraints required of "traditional" doctrinal scholarship. Using emotion analytically lets legal scholars theorise what emotions do across disparate sub-disciplines of law when jurisprudence intervenes to address the emotions of LGBT people who are seeking recognition of their injuries, intimacies, and identities (see Ahmed 2004; Butler 1994). This queer legal undertaking is not about diagnosing emotion in pro-LGBT cases in a way that is exhaustive for scholars interested in evaluating the individual emotions of parties or the cultural variations of emotions between jurisdictions or the doctrinal value of emotions as precedents. Instead, a queer socio-legal analysis of emotion in pro-LGBT cases is politically important because it draws attention to how specific claims of legal progress are emotionally structured in ways that make visible certain forms of homo/transphobic violence and marginalised sexual lives while covering over troubling forms of them. As my use of the case studies in each chapter shows, emotions cannot simply be categorised in pro-LGBT cases as simply "good" or "bad". By reading pro-LGBT cases in terms of the emotional enactments they generate, scholars can move closer to exposing the affective ways in which law makes progress possible. Whether it is using anger to address harm, disgust to contain relationships, or love to affirm sexuality, I have sought to expose how jurisprudential interventions that are celebrated in the name of legal progress have paradoxically made visible and covered over systemic inequalities that LGBT people face.

This book's queer critical engagement with emotion is not just of theoretical interest to scholars, but it is also politically relevant for activists, lawyers, and judges who are engaged in creating, pursuing, and/or critiquing those affective tethers between pro-LGBT forms of visibility and covering or containment of queerness. Reading emotion can make space for queer intimacies and identities by identifying ways to loosen some of the problematic affective attachments in law that block their recognition while making space to pursue progressive claims of legal recognition to repair LGBT injury, intimacy, and identity.

In Chapter 1, I outlined how "queer affect theory" offers queer legal scholars a rich set of analytic tools to explore the interaction of emotion and law reform designed to progress the rights of LGBT people by remedying their injuries and affirming their intimacies and identities. I brought together Eve Sedgwick's conceptualisation of "reparative reading" with Sara Ahmed's "cultural politics of emotion" to draw out the queer analytic and political possibilities of reading emotion in case law that seeks to address the emotions of LGBT people who refuse to adhere to norms of social reproduction, sexual fidelity, nuclear kinship, and monogamous domesticity. I used Sedgwick's and Ahmed's work as a departure point to navigate the challenges that face queer legal scholars interested in critiquing how the jurisprudential terms of progressing LGBT people from positions of injury can marginalise queer intimacies and identities.

Queer affect theory draws attention to how emotions crystallise in jurisprudential texts that recognise and refract the emotions of LGBT people who face pain and trauma. These emotions function to fetishise LGBT identities that seek reparation for harm into what Wendy Brown describes as "wounded attachments". Fetishised attachments to injury and the reparative promises of law reform cover over how law continues to inhibit the expression of queer intimacy and identity. Queer affect theory allows scholars to register the heteronormative political consequences of such "feeling politics", as Lauren Berlant articulates, in legal interventions that background various homo/transphobic injuries and block the expression of queer intimacies and identities. By bringing Sedgwick's, Ahmed's, Brown's, and Berlant's work on emotion and politics into conversation with queer legal scholarship, I sought to outline how judicial expressions of emotion in pro-LGBT cases arrange LGBT injury, intimacy, and identity for the purposes of recognition. This was necessary to contextualise how emotions make possible, while also circumscribing, the reach of LGBT progress. Scholars, activists, lawyers, and judges who follow feelings to understand the arrangement of LGBT injury, intimacy, and identity in jurisprudence can work to address varied emotional attachments in pro-LGBT cases and make space for queer intimacies and identities that threaten to unsettle the socio-legal terms of such LGBT progress.

In Chapter 2, I used disgust to situate how case law crystallised and refracted individual people's disgust towards homosexuality to render queer intimacy and identity visible through judicial expressions of revulsion and recoil. I specifically followed jurisprudential containments of this disgust to demonstrate the ways in which law has affectively produced a public/private divide to protect conjugal (homo)sexual intimacies in the bedroom from the injury of sodomy criminalisation while dismissing "evil" sadomasochist ones. By juxtaposing the recoil and revulsion expressed towards homosexual sodomy in *Bowers v Hardwick* (1986) with the sentimental covering offered in *Lawrence v Texas* (2003), I was able to expose the affective distinctions pro-LGBT cases draw between abject and sentimental forms of homosexual intimacy and identity in order to repel the former and contain the latter. Analysing emotion to identify how "bad" feelings of disgust function alongside "good" feelings of sentimentality is politically useful to confront the legal embrace of privacy as a progressive shield against sexual policing. For activists and lawyers, this means confronting delineations of sexual conduct through censures made of disgust and ensuring that litigation for sexual freedom is not contingent on reproducing stereotypes of gay social palatability (such as domesticity, reproduction, and monogamy). For judges, making space to decriminalise varied consensual sexual expressions requires making space for disgust and loosening the binds created by sexual sentimentalities that contain judicial disgust over queer sex. This was clear through my reading of *R v Brown* (1994), where judicial recoil at sadomasochist sex functioned to criminalise consensual but un(re)productive queer intimacy in private space, while doctrinally similar (though not abjected) cases like *R v Wilson* (1997) involving marital intimacy at home remained free from judicial stigma.

I then shifted from reading jurisprudential containments of disgust to navigate progressive judicial articulations of disgust used to condemn homophobia. This analysis helped draw out how disgust at a homophobic killer obscured persisting and pervasive forms of homophobia. Reading emotion in *R v Green* (1997) showed that analysing progressive redirections of disgust allows scholars to register how the relationship between sentimentality, (hetero)masculinity, and privacy in law exclude queer intimacies. This analysis is important for lawyers and judges because emotion sets out how forms of (homo)sexual touching and sensibility are sentimentalised for protection or abjected for repudiation, and this account shows how legal recognition relies on containing abject forms of queer intimacy and identity that threaten sentimental emotional attachments. A critical account of disgust allows judges and lawyers, for example, to pursue the sexual intimacy that comes with no longer being abjected by legislative criminalisation (gay sex in *Lawrence*) while also confronting the jurisprudential disgust directed at "public" expressions of queer intimacy (same-sex flirtations in *Green*). Reading emotion also makes space for lawyers and judges to rethink or refuse progressive moves to attach disgust to violent homophobes, as queer identities to an otherwise non-homophobic social order. Progressive uses of disgust risk covering over institutional homophobias and further obstructing queer intimacies and identities.

Criminal law does not just abject homosexuality. As evident in cases decriminalising homosexuality or rejecting homophobic defences, it emotionally moves from being an instrument that polices LGBT people to one that embraces them to remedy the violence and injury that they have experienced. In Chapter 3, I looked at the affective relationship between punishing individual homo/transphobes and recognising institutional conditions that make homo/transphobia possible by drawing on the *Hate Crimes Prevention Act of 2009* and cases dealing with the murders of Gwen Araujo and Brandon Teena in the US. Here, I considered the emotional effects of hate that stem from pro-LGBT cases that recognised the hatred of homo/transphobes who perpetrated violence and judicially refracted that hostility to punish them. Reading emotion in these cases demonstrated how judicial expressions of hate – expressed through enhanced responsibility and punishment – worked to render homo/transphobic violence an individual and exceptional problem to be expelled, rather than one that was institutionally ingrained. Making Teena's killers the objects of judicial loathing, for example, meant they became "bad objects" to be expelled from an otherwise inclusive or tolerant public space.

The reading of emotion offered in Chapter 3 is important because it maps out how jurisprudential enactments of hate can eclipse institutional complicity in legal interventions designed to address homo/transphobic violence. Like disgust, hate works in these cases to cover the pervasive forms of criminalisation and the disproportionate impact of policing by invoking law as a symbol of inclusion. In other words, reading emotion in pro-LGBT hate crime cases and legislation reveals how hate organises the terms of recognition through individualised accountability for exceptional forms of homo/transphobic injury while reducing LGBT intimacy and identity to their proximity to those sensationalised injuries. Taking account of the emotional parameters of legal recognition set by these cases is important for activists who wish to loosen the way pro-LGBT cases cultivate hateful attachments in law that punish homo/transphobes while obscuring institutional accountability. This is also important for prosecutors who bring such claims in order to hold people accountable for bigoted violence, as emotionally exceptionalising the "hateful homophobe" fails to draw attention to how such hate-motivating violence is socially maintained. By contesting what jurisprudential expressions of hate cover over, lawyers can pursue legal claims that foreground to judges a broader context of accountability (like in the Teena civil litigation). The loosening of hate when pursuing pro-LGBT hate crime cases becomes politically necessary if lawyers and judges are to address socially sanctioned forms of injury LGBT people face in everyday life that block queer associations and visibility without reducing injury to an exceptional cause.

Registering emotion in the first two case studies showed how progressive criminal laws limit protection for LGBT people by affectively delineating between palatable/unpalatable and ordinary/exceptional injuries, intimacies, and identities. By shifting the discussion from criminal law to public law, I was able to explore how non-punitive forms of pro-LGBT legal reform sought to accommodate injury, intimacy, and identity more broadly in the public sphere. In Chapter 4, I was able to show that governments did not just have negative obligations to allow LGBT people to live free from government intervention; they were passionately called upon to create broader remedies to accommodate LGBT people who experienced inequality, harassment, and discrimination in public. Here, I identified the anger of LGBT people who faced discrimination and read emotion to follow the way in which pro-LGBT cases crystallised this anger when refracting the hurt LGBT people faced and striking back against the injury of discrimination. Judicial expressions of anger were a way to distinguish between forms of lawful and unlawful discrimination. Overlapping pro-LGBT cases, such as *Romer v Evans* (1996), *Hurley v Irish-American Gay, Lesbian and Bisexual Group of Boston* (1995), and *Dale v Boy Scouts of America* (2000) with *Christian Youth Camps Ltd v Cobaw Community Health Services Ltd* (2014) exposed how animus (as opposed to constructions of "good faith" or "conscientious objection") circumscribed the justiciability of injury.

By reading pro-LGBT anti-discrimination cases through anger, I was able to unpack divergent ways in which jurisprudential anger worked to mask how law demands LGBT people conceal queer aspects of their identities and intimacies to be publicly accommodated. Moreover, I could follow how this anger cleaved apart (homo)sexuality from religion in pro-LGBT anti-discrimination cases to obscure how the two were imbricated in ways that unsettle current anti-discrimination norms. Following emotion, then, allows scholars and activists to account for how refracting anger in law frames LGBT injury, intimacy, and identity in ways that reproduce hierarchies (between religion and sexuality) or power structures (between heterosexuality and homosexuality) that make LGBT accommodation conditional on their acceptability to a (hetero)sexual status quo. In doing so, my analysis highlights why activists and lawyers need to make space for LGBT people's anger when facing discrimination to accommodate their identities and intimacies. Anger foregrounds the pain of injury by drawing attention to how specific institutions injure LGBT people through the energising "striking back" such injury prompts from LGBT people.

However, in doing so, activists and lawyers must be cognisant of how progressive enactments of jurisprudential anger can obscure queer intimacies and identities that threaten (hetero)normative terms of legal inclusion. For example, reading judicial anger in the majority judgment in *Romer* and dissenting judgment in *Dale* – directed at institutional exclusions – revealed how striking back against discrimination failed to accommodate queer identities that "flaunted" their non-heterosexuality (by simply refusing to remain silent about it) to interrupt the privileged position of heterosexuality. Activism and litigation that seeks to progress LGBT inclusion needs to expand the reach of judicial anger by identifying how these insidious forms of closeting identity or intimacy emerge in progressive jurisprudence. In expanding the reach of anger, however, lawyers and judges must guard against reproducing divisions between marginalised social differences, as *Cobaw* evidenced. Lawyers and judges must loosen the tense binds that foreclose space to queer identities – such as identities formed through the imbrication of religion and (homo)sexuality – to better accommodate LGBT people.

In Chapter 5, I looked at pro-LGBT refugee cases as another area of law that has sought to accommodate LGBT people fleeing persecution. I used fear as an analytic lens to show that the (threats of) injuries recognised in pro-LGBT refugee cases were not isolated to individuals who feared for their personal liberty or safety if returned to their country of origin. I tracked the jurisprudential articulation of fear by registering how queer refugee claims brought the refugee status determination process into close proximity of an impending threat. That is, pro-LGBT cases expressed fears over queer asylum claims that risked "opening the floodgates" to disingenuous applicants or less serious claims of persecution. This prompted anxious forms of administrative and judicial scrutiny with respect to authenticating the relationship between (homo)sexual injury, intimacy, and identity. Pro-LGBT refugee cases such as *S395/2002 v Minister for Immigration and Multicultural Affairs* (2003) and *HJ (Iran) and HT (Cameroon) v Secretary of State for the Home Department* (2010) negated the requirement of "discretion" only to the extent that such concealment was attributable to specific, causal narratives of state-sanctioned homophobic harm. *SW (Jamaica) v Secretary of State for the Home Department* (2011) made protection available to the extent that a claimant could meet ethnocentric assumptions about lesbian relationships, visibility, and community while relieving administrative anxieties about insincerity.

Following these legal expressions of fear allows scholars and activists to confront how administrative and judicial adjudication of refugee claims rely on the spectre of insincerity as a foreboding threat. Adjudication is structured by fears that foreground an approaching horizon of "bogus" claims from people who fabricate sexual intimacy or identity (as in *SW*) and over-expansive legal inclusions that risk compromising the normative integrity of the current refugee protection system (as in *S395/2002* and *HJ & HT*). Navigating emotion becomes politically useful for lawyers and judges who wish to expand legal terms of visibility used to recognise the "well founded fear" of LGBT people who seek asylum. In order to achieve this, they need to critically engage with how legal fears and anxieties foreclose recognition of queer intimacies and identities. Fighting these insidious emotional enactments would have been useful in *Joined Cases X, Y, and Z* (2013) and *Joined Cases A, B, and C* (2014) to render a more inclusive "particular social group" and elaborate more capacious criteria to determine a "well-founded fear of persecution". By critically accounting for emotion, bureaucrats and judges can navigate LGBT refugees' fears or anxieties, and resist crystallising emotional attachments that seek to limit the complex emotional narratives of LGBT people who seek asylum. This is crucial to avoid dismissing the protection claims of those who require it.

I brought my reading of pro-LGBT cases to a close in the final chapter by navigating how monogamous love secured the achievement of marriage equality. In Chapter 6, I tracked how the exclusive (romantic) love between same-sex partners was recognised and refracted in marriage equality jurisprudence from the US that "equalised love" by legally elevating same-sex relationships and faithfully binding them to a single ideal of marriage. For LGBT people seeking greater freedom for their intimacy and equality for their identity – evidenced in cases like *Goodrich v Massachusetts* (2003), *Perry v Schwarzenegger* (2010),

Windsor v United States (2013), and *Obergefell v Hodges* (2015) – orienting towards an object of love (marriage) rather than fear (persecution) provided a promise of personal affirmation and public respect. On an individual level, "feeling good" was possible for same-sex couples in these cases because marriage was jurisprudentially inscribed as a sentimental love story that promised greater liberty, equality, and dignity.

Reading love analytically was necessary to show how pro-LGBT marriage equality cases from the US affirmed same-sex couples' desires for marital recognition in terms of ideas about liberty, equality, and dignity – ideas made possible by jurisprudential enactments of love, hope, and respect. Love indexed liberty to (hetero)normative ideas of fidelity, monogamy, reproduction, and family in *Perry*. Hope promised equality by covering over the injuries sustained by LGBT people who lived on the economic, social, and racial peripheries in *Goodrich*. Respect solidified sexual identity in ways that made marriage the primary means by which to achieve dignity or respectability in *Windsor* and *Obergefell*. Giving a jurisprudential account of love, hope, and respect in pro-LGBT marriage equality cases shows analytically how judicial expressions of love promise social elevation, but these emotional enactments also inhibit individuals who seek out different horizons for their queer intimacies and identities. Accounting for love is important for scholars to draw out the affective arrangement through which pro-LGBT cases make visible harms of relationship exclusion, conjugal intimacies, and marital identities for public accommodation while backgrounding queer intimacies and identities that contest heteronormativity.

Reading love is politically important, too, if activists and lawyers are to affirm the possibilities of legal claims of relationship recognition while making room in litigation to challenge the heteronormative consequences of romantic love that manifest through their judicial enunciation. For example, confronting and loosening the binds created by judicial expressions of conjugal love in US constitutional jurisprudence would make room for activists and lawyers to pursue kinship liberties that are transient, non-monogamous, and eschew romantic love. Additionally, judicial hesitation about sentimentalising intimacy would also make room to legally affirm emotionally different, non-romantic, or non-sexual forms of queer kinship by broadening the reach of relationship liberty. Registering emotion, then, is crucial if scholars, activists, lawyers, and judges are to loosen the (hetero)normative attachments to sexual intimacy and identity "good feelings" progress in law.

Queering the emotional terms of progressive law reforms that engage scholars, activists, lawyers, and judges is not a call for abandoning either law or emotion for a future that supports LGBT (and queer) people. Drawing inspiration from the work of José Munoz, this book has been animated by the possibility of using law for a queer reparative future – one where understanding law by taking account of emotion not only lets queer scholars and activists expose law's capacity to remedy injuries but also allows them to challenge the ways law compounds injuries to affirm queer intimacies and identities (Munoz 2009: 1). This would encourage lawyers and judges to rethink the emotional dimensions of progressive legal interventions and make room to recognise the intimacy and identity of LGBT people. This approach is not unique to sexual or gender minorities either. The reading advanced in this book could be extended to other marginalised social groups that are beyond my current scope of discussion. With that in mind, I am not in a position to "conclude" the emotions that continue to be contested in scholarly, activist, and legal communities, as this would foreclose conversations that I have complicated through this book. I offer this book, then, as a departure point for emotional exegeses on the interactions of law and justice more broadly conceived that hopefully speaks to the concerns of critical scholars, activists, lawyers, and judges interested in social justice.

I began this book with an emotional anecdote about what my queer feelings about marriage equality in Australia indicated about the progressive possibilities and limits of law reform. Disgust, anger, hope, frustration, and worry (to name just a few emotions) characterised my encounter with that single area of progressive reform in Australia. *Feeling Queer Jurisprudence* has taken these ambivalent emotional encounters with legal progress seriously to show that reading emotion in pro-LGBT cases can expose both the limits and possibilities of progressive legal interventions that deal with the injury, intimacy, and identity of LGBT people. Existing queer and critical legal scholarship points to the problems of pursuing progress through law and identifies possibilities for social transformation. Reading emotion allows scholars to analytically track the parameters of progressive legal recognition in terms of their emotional enactments in order to recognise how LGBT injuries, intimacies, and identities are affectively arranged for legal recognition. This mapping exposes how such injuries, intimacies, and identities are emotionally recognised by covering or obscuring queer intimacies and identities.

Feeling Queer Jurisprudence opens up a queer politics of law reform. This book is an illustration of why reading emotion analytically is a politically important queer strategy because it allows us (as queer scholars, activists, lawyers, and judges) to maintain a critical and capacious stance towards law as we pursue progressive legal claims for LGBT people. This strategy is not necessarily an invitation for lawyers and judges to redeem or reject emotions as part of ongoing pursuits of legal recognition nor is the strategy about scholars and activists abandoning claims of legal recognition altogether for alternative political or social projects (though, these are also important pursuits). By drawing attention to the emotions pro-LGBT cases generate to repair injury, intimacy, and identity, this book has aimed to equip scholars, activists, lawyers, and judges with an affective framework to confront, evaluate, and loosen emotional arrangements that cover over or contain queer intimacies and identities in law. The specific forms that this confrontation and loosening will take in future legal, activist, and judicial work will vary between jurisdictions and areas of law.

In concluding this book, I want to emphasise that following emotion is a starting point, not a point of conclusion, for those of us interested in queer(ing) social justice. Feeling jurisprudence is an opportunity for us to critically account for the emotional terms of legal progress if we are to pursue jurisprudential interventions for marginalised LGBT people. This task will have scholarly, activist, lawyerly, and judicial implications. For scholars, reading emotion is necessary to better understand the emotional terms through which pro-LGBT cases make the legal recognition of injury, intimacy, and identity possible. For activists, this work is important in order to find opportunities to repair the injuries faced by LGBT people whose intimacies and identities remain emotionally obscured or marginalised by law. For lawyers, reflecting on emotion is useful to think about how best to pursue litigation that confronts emotional attachments in law to advocate more expansive accommodation of queer intimacies and identities. For judges, unpacking the emotional binds of progressive precedents and doctrines is valuable in order to avoid reproducing narrow forms of progress that further entrench existing homo/transphobic biases. This multilayered socio-legal work will be difficult and cannot be resolved by making prescriptions about reform in advance. By feeling queer jurisprudence, then, we can contribute towards a reparative future that allows all queer people to flourish.

Note

1 I have written in more detail about some of my ambivalent emotional engagements with "LGBT progress" across different jurisdictions (Australia, the United Kingdom, India, and the US) and areas of law reform (refugee, criminal, and constitutional) elsewhere. This has been published for non-academic audiences online (see Raj 2014, 2017, 2018, 2019).

References

Ahmed, S., 2004. *The Cultural Politics of Emotion*. Oxford: Routledge.
Adler, L., 2018. *Gay Priori: A Queer Critical Legal Studies Approach to Law Reform*. Durham: Duke University Press.
Bassichis, M. and Spade, D., 2014. Queer Politics and Anti-Blackness. In Jin Haritaworn, Adi Kuntsman, and Sylvia Posocco, eds. *Queer Necropolitics*. London: Routledge, 191–210.
Butler, J., 1994. Against Proper Objects. *Differences: A Journal of Feminist Cultural Studies*, 6(2–3), 1–26.
Leckey, R., 2015. Introduction. In Robert Leckey, ed. *After Legal Equality: Family, Sex, Kinship*. London: Routledge, 1–22.
Moran, L., 1996. *The Homosexual(ity) of Law*. London and New York: Routledge.
Munoz, J. E., 2009. *Cruising Utopia: The Then and There of Queer Futurity*. New York: New York University Press.
Raj, S., 2014. 'Come Out' to Immigration Officials or be Deported? Gay Asylum Seekers will Suffer under Morrison's New Regime. *The Guardian* (26 September 2014), www.theguardian.com/commentisfree/2014/sep/26/come-out-to-immigration-officials-or-be-deported-gay-asylum-seekers-will-suffer-under-morrisons-new-regime (accessed 31 August 2019).

Raj, S., 2017. On Sexuality, the Law Still Caters to the Norms of Public Disgust. *Slate* (28 July 2017), https://slate.com/human-interest/2017/07/on-sexuality-the-law-still-takes-public-disgust-into-account.html (accessed 31 August 2019).

Raj, S., 2018. How Indian Judges Wrote Love into Law as They Decriminalised Gay Sex. *The Conversation* (10 September 2018), https://theconversation.com/how-indian-judges-wrote-love-into-law-as-they-decriminalised-gay-sex-102810 (accessed 31 August 2019).

Raj, S., 2019. Stonewall Riots: Global Legacy Shows There's No Simple Story of Progress for Gay Rights. *The Conversation* (28 June 2019), https://theconversation.com/stonewall-riots-global-legacy-shows-theres-no-simple-story-of-progress-for-gay-rights-119257 (accessed 31 August 2019).

Spade, D., 2011. *Normal Life: Administrative Violence, Critical Trans Politics, and the Limits of Law*. Brooklyn: South End Press.

Stychin, C., 1995. *Law's Desire: Sexuality and the Limits of Justice*. London: Routledge.

Stychin, C. and Herman, D., 2000. Introduction. In Carl Stychin and Didi Herman, eds. *Sexuality in the Legal Arena*. London: Athlone Books, vii–ix.

Zylan, Y., 2011. *States of Passion: Law, Identity and the Social Construction of Desire*. Oxford: Oxford University Press.

Legislation

Hate Crimes Prevention Act of 2009 (US).

Cases

A (C-148/13), B (C-149/13), C (C-150/13) v Staatssecretaris van Veiligheid en Justitie (ECJ, Grand Chamber, 2 December 2014).
Bowers v Hardwick, 478 US 186 (1986).
Christian Youth Camps Ltd v Cobaw Community Health Services Ltd [2014] VSCA 75.
Dale v Boy Scouts of America, 120 S Ct 2446 (2000).
Goodrich v Department of Public Health, 440 Mass 309 (2003).
HJ (Iran) and HT (Cameroon) v Secretary of State for the Home Department [2010] UKSC 31.
Lawrence v Texas, 539 US 558 (2003).
Masterpiece Cakeshop, Ltd. v Colorado Civil Rights Commission, 584 US ___ (2018).
Obergefell v Hodges, 576 US ___ (2015).
Perry v Schwarzenegger, 704 F Supp 2d 921 (2010).
R v Brown [1994] 1 AC 212.
R v Green (1997) 191 CLR 334.
R v Wilson [1997] QB 47.
Romer v Evans, 116 S Ct 1620 (1996).
S395/2002 v Minister for Immigration and Multicultural Affairs (2003) 203 ALR 112.
SW (Jamaica) v Secretary of State for the Home Department (CG) [2011] UKUT 00251.
Windsor v United States, 113 S Ct 2675 (2013).
X (C-199/12), Y (C-200/12), Z (C-201/12) v Minister voor Immigratie en Asiel (ECJ, Fourth Chamber, 7 November 2013).

Index

Note: Page numbers followed by "n" denote endnotes.

activist-scholar-advocate 4
adjudicative anxiety 106
Adler, Libby 5
administrative violence 3
affect 8, 9
affect alien 44
affective bias 85
affective turn 8
aggression 37, 38
Aharonson, E. 52, 64
Ahmed, S. 7, 9, 11, 14, 44, 85, 89, 117, 132, 142
Amendment 2, Colorado Constitution 76–8, 84
anal sex 25
anger: animating 73–91; injury, exceptional forms of 83–5; materialisation of 89; queering 85–90
Anglophone common law jurisdiction 112n1
animus: pro-LGBT case of *Romer* 76–9
anti-discrimination law 17, 78, 81, 83, 140
anti-gay hostility 43
anti-gay violence 57
anti-LGBT hostility 58
anxious adjudication 104–7; queer intimacy and identity, interrogating 104–7
Ashford, Chris 4
assimilationist bias 85
asylum 94–112
Asylum and Immigration Tribunal (AIT) 104
Australian Bureau of Statistics 1

Baehr v Lewin (1993), 135n2
bare animus 81
Bennett v Texas (1992) 55
Berlant, Lauren 13, 14, 26, 74, 117, 142
bigotry, human price 82
Blackstone, William 24
bogus claimants 110
bogus refugees, hypermobility 98
Bower, Lisa 4, 5
Bowers cases 26–9, 41, 127
Bowers v Hardwick (1986) 143
Bowles v Florida (1998) 67
Brandon, Jo-Ann 61
Brandon cases 63, 65, 67
Brandon v County of Richardson (2000) 61, 70n9
Brandon v Lotter (1998) 69n8
Brennan CJ 36–8, 42
Brown, Wendy 13, 14, 84
Brown case 31
Butler, Judith 6, 133

California Family Code 1994 118
Callinan J 100
case law 5, 6, 10, 11
Cases A, B, and C (2014) 95, 108–11, 146
Cases X, Y, and Z (2013) 95, 108–11, 146
Christian Youth Camps Ltd v Cobaw Community Health Services Ltd (2014) 74, 85–7
citizenship 52
Cobaw case 88, 89, 145
Colorado Supreme Court 77
common humanity 58

compassionate dissent 39–41
consensual homosexual acts 25
counterpublics 18n1
Crimes Act 1900 46n6
cruel optimism 14
Cvetkovich, Ann 43, 45

Dale v Boy Scouts of America (2000) 74, 81–3, 145
decriminalisation: and privacy 25–6
Defense of Marriage Act (DOMA) 124–6
destructive stereotype 121
deviate sex 27
dignity, respecting 123–7; *Obergefell v Hodges* (2015) 126–7; *Windsor v United States* (2013) 124–6
disciplinary logics 12
discretion: dismantling 98–104; tests 99, 107
discrimination law: LGBT anger and 74–6
disgust 16, 46n7; castigating majority 36–9; compassionate dissent 39–41; criminalising buggery 24–5; departures of, *Green* 35–6; directing 23–46; gay intimacy 33; gay male sex and 26; homosexuality to homophobia 33–41; LGBT people 50; in private 24–9; queering 41–5; reading 42, 44, 50; revulsion and 26; *R v Wilson* (1997) 33; violence in sex 30
dispassionate doctrines 6
disturbing privacy 26–9
domestic partnership 120
Dressler, Joshua 35
Duggan, Lisa 5

emotions 8–12, 34, 35, 45, 51, 59, 63, 68, 73, 90, 103, 106; in case law 11; criminal judgments 60; distress 69n7; emotional thinking 58; "gut" reactions 9; injuries 3; jurisprudence 1–19; scholarship 8; space 2; stereotypes 42
Equal Opportunity Act 1995 91n5
"excessive" violence 55

Fader, Michael 74, 75
Fassin, Didier 97–8
fear 17; anxious adjudication 104–7; discretion, dismantling 98–104; fighting 94–112; queering 107–11; in refugee law and scholarship 95–8
federal hate crime statute 57
feelings 9, 12–18

femaleness 55, 60
Franke, Katherine 27, 134

Garner, Tyrone 27
gay and lesbian group (GLIB) 80, 81
gay asylum seekers 112n1
gay intimacy 33
gay lifestyles 102
gay male sex 23, 25
gay panic defence 34–5
Gay Pride parade 17
gay sadomasochism 16, 29–33
gay sexual freedom 29
gender affirming healthcare 3
gender identity 60–2
gender nonconforming identities 59
gender nonconformity 69n6
genital torture 31
George CJ 119, 122
Gleeson J 105
Goodrich case 121–2, 124, 128, 130
gross indecency 24
group sadomasochism 31
Gwen Araujo Justice for Victims Act (2006) 56

Halley, Janet 42
Hardwick, Michael 26, 27
hate: defined 53; queering 63–70
hate, healing 50–70; case(s) of Brandon Teena 59–63; individual responsibility and 59–61; institutional accountability 61–3; Lotter and Nissen, punishment of 59–61; state compensations, negligence 61–3
hate crime: jurisprudence, United States 55–6; laws 54, 56–8; legislation 51; paradigm 44; responses, affective architecture 52–3
Hate Crimes Prevention Act of 2009 16, 50, 53–6, 58, 65, 66, 144
Hate Crimes Statistics Act of 1990 53
hate-cultivating process 65
hateful homophobe 44
hateful intent, identifying 56–8
hateful "wilfulness" 57
Hawaii Supreme Court 135n2
healing, hate *see* hate, healing
heteromasculine anxieties 55
heteronormativity 75
heterosexual masculinity 36
Heydon J 100
High Court of Australia 34, 36, 99

HJ (Iran) and HT (Cameroon) v Secretary of State for the Home Department (2010) 101–4
homophobes 16
homophobia 33–41, 44, 45, 54, 55; articulation 43; discrimination 77; disgust 36, 44; exceptionalising 39–41; prejudice 68; violence 34, 35, 39, 66, 96
homosexual advance defence (HAD) 16, 34–43
homosexual advances 34, 36
homosexual intimacy 15, 26
homosexuality 24, 26, 28, 33–41, 64, 78, 86, 100; decriminalisation of 23; in English criminal law 25; as mental illness 34
homosexual sadomasochism 32
homosexual sodomy 27
homo/transphobes 14; discrimination 85; hate 51–2, 62, 66; violence 63–5, 68
hope 128–34; confronting equality 130–1
hope, for equality 121–3; California 122–3; Massachusetts 121–2
Howe, Adrian 34
Hurley v Irish-American Gay, Lesbian and Bisexual Group of Boston (1995) 74, 80–1

identity knowledges 12
indulgence 30
In Re Marriage Cases (2006) 118–20, 122, 130, 135n3
intellectual responsibility 97

Jacobs, James 57
Jauncey, Lord 31–2, 42
Johns, Fleur 7
Jones, Aphrodite 59
judicial reasoning 36
judicial revulsion 32

Kahan, Dan 44, 55
Keenan, Sarah 112n4
Kennedy J 28, 30, 78, 125–7, 140
Kirby J 39, 40, 42, 44, 45, 54, 55, 58, 60, 100, 102
Kline J 118, 119, 122

Lamble, Sarah 63
Laux, Sheriff Charles 61–3
Lawrence, John 27

Lawrence v Texas (2003) 26–29, 32, 41, 118, 119, 127, 131, 143
Lee, Cynthia 42–3
legal emotions 4
legal scholarship 29
legal tests 62
lesbian, gay, bisexual, and transgender (LGBT) people 1–4, 6, 10–18, 88, 90, 95, 97, 99, 109, 111, 112, 121, 128; activism 29; anti-violence 67; asylum 94, 96, 97, 107; discrimination 73; equality discourse 5; intimacies 58; law reform movements 14; law reform projects 4; pro-LGBT cases, emotion 3; "pro-LGBT cases," categorising 6–8; refugees 95, 108, 111; sexual freedom for 24; well-being of 18
lesbian identity 106
lethal violence 56
Lorde, Audre 75, 90
love 18; dignity, respecting 123–7; emotional politics, visibility 132–4; good feelings 117–27; hope, for equality 121–3; of liberty 118–21; loosening 116–36; problematising liberal love 128–30; same-sex couples 116; self-evident good 117

MacDougall, Bruce 64
male homosexuality 24
marital sex, non-reproductive forms 25
marriage, zone of autonomy 119
marriage equality 1, 116–36; judicial recognition of 129; problematising liberal love 128–30
marriage equality reform 2
Marriage Law Postal Survey 1
marriage licence 119
Marshall CJ 121, 130
masculine identity 60
Mason, Gail 51, 52, 58, 94, 106
Masterpiece Cakeshop (2018) 140
matrimonial coupling 3
Matter of Toboso-Alfonso (1990) 112n1
Maxwell P 87
McHugh J 37, 38, 42, 99, 102
Mison, Robert 34
moral sentiments 9
Moran, Leslie 25, 31, 32, 54, 58, 66
Munoz, José 147

Nebraska v Lotter (1998) 60–1
negative emotions 42

Index

Newsom, Gavin 118
New South Wales Court of Criminal Appeal 35
New York v DeLee (2013) 63–4
Nolan J 80
non-heterosexual intimacies 88
non-normative sexuality 26
Nussbaum, Martha 28, 31, 44, 75, 90n2

Obama, Barack 54, 58, 66
Obergefell v Hodges (2015) 116, 126–9, 131, 132, 134, 135n2
Object Lessons 12
Offences Against the Person Act 1861 29
offensiveness 40
"On Writing Dangerously" 7
"Operation Spanner" 29

pain 13–14
passions 9
Perkiss, David 43
Perry v Schwarzenegger (2010) 120, 122–4, 129, 130
political affirmation 3
Portiz CJ 82
Potter, Kimberley 57
privacy: and decriminalisation 25–6; disturbing 26–9; logic 26
private "indulgences" 28
professional anxieties 5
pro-hate 55
pro-LGBT 55–6; anti-discrimination 82, 87–90; criminalisation jurisprudence 50; hate crime 51, 63, 67; law reform 14; marriage equality 117; refugee 94; sodomy decriminalisation 15
pro-minority criminalisation 52
Proposition 8, California Constitution 12–13, 135n4, 135n6
provocation 34–5
psychic investment 133
public accommodation 74, 88, 91n4
public interest 29

queer advances: exceptionalising 36–9
queer affect theory 9, 142
queer claims: and asylum 94–112
queer discrimination: and accommodation 73–91; covering(s) of, animating 79–85; queer expressions, ex/inclusion 80–1; registering, Dale 81–3
queering anger 85–90; queer critiques, pro-LGBT anti-discrimination cases 87–90; queer identities, *Cobaw* 85–7

queering fear 107–11; credibility adjudication, challenges 109–11; persecution parameters, rethinking 108–9
queering hate 63–70; accountability, addressing 65–8; homo/transphobic violence 63–5; queer intimacies and identities, space 65–8
queer legal scholarship 68, 88; mapping 4–6
queerness: activism 129; analysis 3; commitment 18n4; criminalising buggery 24–5; criminality and 23–46; critical legal studies 5; critiques, pro-LGBT anti-discrimination cases 87–90; disgust 41–5; friendship 39; identity 104–7; intimacies 29, 36, 40, 74, 83, 85, 90, 104–7; kinship 39, 116–36; love 128–34; in private 24–9; project 1–4; in public 29–33; reparative future 140–9; sadomasochism 29–33; scholarship 1–19; sexual acts 32; spaces 18n1
queer theory 2, 3; of legal emotions 8
queer violence: and punishment 50–70

refugee adjudication 98, 99
refugee-receiving countries 112n1
Refugee Review Tribunal (RRT) 99, 106, 107, 112n3
Reinhardt J 123
reproductive sexual assimilation 129
reproductive sexuality 3
respect(ability) 128–34; rethinking 131–2
Rodger LJ 101–3, 109
Romer v Evans (1996) 73, 76–9, 87, 131, 145
R v Brown (1994) 23, 29–33, 143
R v Green (1997) 23, 33–41, 143
R v Konzani 46n5
R v Meachen 46n5
R v Wilson (1997) 32–3, 143

S395/2002 v Minister for Immigration and Multicultural Affairs (2003) 99–100
sadomasochism 29–33, 35, 42, 45, 74; "barbarous" qualities 31; violence and 30
sadomasochist promiscuity 32
same-sex advances 34, 37, 40
same-sex couples 1, 2, 18, 44, 50, 116, 118, 127
same-sex intimacies 34, 116, 126

same-sex marriage 1, 2, 120
Scalia J 28, 78, 80
Sedgwick, Eve 10, 142
self-defence 34
self-reflexive discursive engagement 43
sentimentality 27–9, 41
sexual advance 37
sexual assault 60, 61
sexual excitement 32
sexual identity 82, 88, 107, 147
sexual intimacy 33, 97, 102
sexual justice 5
sexual minorities 11, 45, 57, 78, 84, 99, 100, 104, 108
Sexual Offences Act 1967 46n4
sexual orientation 84, 91n3
sexual violence 51, 61
Sharpston 108–10
Smart J 35–6
social injury 31
social intelligibility 8
social intolerance 57
social justice 13, 148
social norms 2, 11
social stigma 2
socio-legal norms 8
socio-sexual "deviance" 30
sodomy 35, 42, 45, 74; zoning 28
solicitation 82
Spade, Dean 3
special sensitivity 38
Spinoza, Baruch 8
Stevens J 83
Stonewall Riots 74–5
strong physical retaliation 36
Stychin, Carl 5

Superior Court of New Jersey 82
SW v Secretary of State for the Home Department (2011) 104–5

Templeman, Lord 30–1, 38
textual community 9
tolerance leash 84
Tomsen, Stephen 38–9, 51–2, 66
"traditional" doctrinal scholarship 141
tranquillity 54
trans identity 60
transphobia 50, 55, 59, 61

United Nations High Commissioner for Refugees (UNHCR) 96
"unpredictable" violence 31
"unusual" homosexuality 40
US Sixth Circuit Court of Appeals 57

Valverde, Mariana 4
Vermont Supreme Court 135n2

Walker CJ 120, 123, 129, 135n5, 135n6
well-founded fear 95
White, James Boyd 9
Wiegman, Robyn 12
Wilde, Oscar 23–5
Wills J 24, 25
Windsor v United States (2013) 116, 124–6, 136n8
Wolfenden Report 23, 25–6, 28, 41, 46n4
working-class masculinity 64

Yoshino, Kenji 11, 84–5, 123, 126

Zanghellini, Aleardo 3
Zylan, Yvonne 4, 53, 66

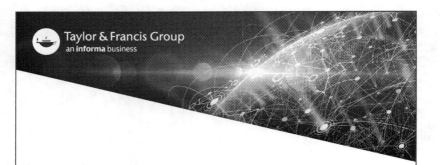

Printed in the United States
by Baker & Taylor Publisher Services